I0212957

FROM
FRONTIERS
TO THE
HEARTLAND

'In *From Frontiers to the Heartland*, Rouhin Deb and Nabaarun Barooah bring to light the Sangh Parivar's decades-long involvement in India's Northeast. From relief efforts to healthcare and education, and helping to formalize indigenous religious traditions instead of imposing on them, it gradually became a part and parcel of the Northeast's socio-cultural fabric and political evolution. This important new book is a must-read.'

Baijayant 'Jay' Panda,
Member of Parliament, Lok Sabha

'India's Northeast is both geographically and culturally a complex place. The last 100 years have dramatically transformed the demographics of the region. This was not merely the colonial experience but also the post-Independence continuation of external influences that fed insurgency, migration and mass conversion. This book is a remarkable first attempt to document from primary eye-witness accounts the relentless efforts by the Sangh Parivar to help traditional, indigenous communities push back against these threats.'

Sanjeev Sanyal,
Bestselling Author and Economist

'A brilliant, bold and insightful study, *From Frontiers to the Heartland* provides unparalleled scholarship into the Sangh Parivar's evolution in one of India's most ethnically diverse regions. Rouhin Deb and Nabaarun Barooah not only provide a fresh understanding of the RSS's role in shaping the Northeast but also challenge prevailing academic biases, positioning itself as a critical work in Indian political scholarship, redefining the discourse for years to come.'

Anand Ranganathan,
Author and Scientist

FROM **FRONTIERS** TO THE **HEARTLAND**

A CENTURY OF **SANGH PARIVAR** *IN THE* **NORTHEAST**

ROUHIN DEB
NABAARUN BAROOAH

RUPA

Published by
Rupa Publications India Pvt. Ltd 2025
7/16, Ansari Road, Daryaganj
New Delhi 110002

Sales centres:
Bengaluru Chennai
Hyderabad Jaipur Kathmandu
Kolkata Mumbai Prayagraj

P-ISBN: 978-93-7003-495-2
E-ISBN: 978-93-7003-804-2

First impression 2025

10 9 8 7 6 5 4 3 2 1

Printed in India

To
the valiant karyakartas
who sacrificed their lives
fighting for a united Bhārata

Contents

Foreword

I am pleased to extend my heartfelt congratulations to Rouhin Deb and Nabaarun Barooah on their book *From Frontiers to the Heartland*. This seminal work stands as a testament to their intellectual rigour, historical acumen and an insightful exploration of the Sangh Parivar's evolution in one of India's most culturally diverse regions—the Northeast.

The Northeast of India is a dynamic and historically rich heartland, where a confluence of diverse traditions, linguistic heritage and indigenous identities intertwines with the shifting currents of modernity, shaping the region's socio-political consciousness. Through meticulous research and incisive scholarship, the authors have highlighted the multifaceted role of the Sangh Parivar—its humanitarian endeavours, fostering of cultural consciousness, and its sustained engagement in education and social welfare.

As someone deeply rooted in this land, I have always held that the Northeast is a pulsating core of India's civilizational ethos—a land where resilience, cultural vitality and historical depth define its spirit. Works such as this play an instrumental role in ensuring that our narratives are told with authenticity, depth and a commitment to intellectual honesty. I am confident that *From Frontiers to the Heartland* will serve as a cornerstone for scholars, policymakers and citizens who seek a deeper and more comprehensive understanding of the region's evolving political and cultural landscape.

I extend my warmest wishes to Rouhin Deb and Nabaarun Barooah for this remarkable scholarly contribution. May this book inspire further inquiry, enrich contemporary discourse and deepen our collective understanding of the intricate socio-political fabric that defines our great nation.

(Dr. Himanta Biswa Sarma)

7 February 2025

Abbreviations

AASAA	All Adivasi Students' Association of Assam
AASU	All Assam Students' Union
AATSA	All Assam Tea Students' Association
ABPS	Akhil Bharatiya Pratinidhi Sabha
ABSU	All Bodo Students' Union
ABVP	Akhil Bharatiya Vidyarthi Parishad
AGP	Asom Gana Parishad
ATASU	All Tai Ahom Students' Union
ATTF	All Tripura Tribal Force
BJP	Bharatiya Janata Party
BJS	Bharatiya Jana Sangh
BLTF	Bodoland Liberation Tigers Force
BPF	Bodoland People's Front
BSF	Border Security Force
BTC	Bodoland Territorial Council
CPI	Communist Party of India
CPI(M)	Communist Party of India (Marxist)
CRPF	Central Reserve Police Force
HJM	Hindu Jagran Manch
HNLC	Hynniewtrep National Liberation Council
HSPDP	Hill State People's Democratic Party
HYCP	Hindu Yuba Chattra Parishad
ILP	Inner Line Permit
INC	Indian National Congress
INC(O)	Indian National Congress (Organization)
INC(R)	Indian National Congress (Requisitionists)

JDSSM	Janajati Dharma Sanskriti Suraksha Manch
KCP	Kangleipak Communist Party
KMSS	Krishak Mukti Sangram Samiti
MNF	Mizo National Front
MNFF	Mizo National Famine Front
NDA	National Democratic Alliance
NDFB	National Democratic Front of Bodoland
NEDA	North East Democratic Alliance
NLFT	National Liberation Front of Tripura
NNC	Naga National Council
NSCN	National Socialist Council of Nagaland
PLA-M	People's Liberation Army of Manipur
PREPAK	People's Revolutionary Party of Kangleipak
	Rashtra Sevika Samiti
RSS	Rashtriya Swayamsevak Sangh
SCM	Seemanta Chetana Mancha
SSP	Sanskriti Suraksha Parishad
SSV/OTC	Sangh Siksha Varg/Officers Training Camp
TTAADC	Tripura Tribal Areas Autonomous District Council
UDP	United Democratic Party
ULFA	United Liberation Front of Assam
UNLF	United National Liberation Front
VHP	Vishwa Hindu Parishad
VKA	Vanavasi Kalyan Ashram
VKIC	Vivekananda Kendra Institute of Culture
VKV	Vivekananda Kendra Vidyalaya

Prologue

It was 21:35 on 11 December 2019. The *karyakartas* (organizers) staying at the *karyalaya* (office) of the Rashtriya Swayamsevak Sangh (RSS) in Dibrugarh had just had their dinner and were going to sleep. They had to wake up by 05:00 to embark on a busy day tomorrow. Suddenly, noises were heard in the distance. Tossing in bed with their eyes wide open, the karyakartas slowly realized that the noise was getting closer. As footsteps approached the office building, the slogans became distinct—*'Joi Aai Oxom'*, victory to Mother Assam. They could finally sense the hell that was about to unfold upon them. The mob outside consisted of youth activists belonging to the All Assam Students Union (AASU), Bir Lachit Sena and Krishak Mukti Sangram Samiti (KMSS).[1] While the angry slogans continued to echo, some protestors poured kerosene inside the office and lit the building to flames. The four motorcycles parked outside the office were also torched.

The karyakartas somehow managed to escape this near-death situation by taking the rear exit of the office. They immediately phoned for help. The local police arrived by 21:45 and helped disperse the miscreants. By 22:00, fire trucks arrived to douse the flames. The police and the fire department had a long night ahead. Over the next hour, Chabua railway station and Panitola railway station were also set on fire. An ASTC bus parked at Chowkidinghee stand was damaged and set on fire. The private

[1]Interview with Dipen Phukan (name changed).

residences of Chief Minister Sarbananda Sonowal and MLA Prasanta Phookan were pelted with stones.[2] Meanwhile, the private residences of MP Rameshwar Teli and MLA Binod Hazarika were partially set on fire. Several RSS *pracharak*s (promoters) and karyakartas were threatened. Many of their houses were torched, family members attacked, and they themselves were beaten up.[3] This was the toughest time for the Sangh and its affiliates in the north-eastern region.

On 9 December 2019, the Citizenship (Amendment) Bill was introduced in the Lok Sabha by the Union Home Minister Amit Shah.[4] It immediately sparked protests in two prominent university campuses in Guwahati—Cotton University and Gauhati University. The Bill was passed by the Lok Sabha on the next day and the Rajya Sabha on 11 December 2019.[5] By then, the protests had spread to all of Upper Assam, particularly Dibrugarh and Tezpur.[6] Agitated students led by the AASU and KMSS took to the streets and staged torch marches throughout the major cities as elders were reminded of the Assam Agitation of the 1980s.

The main targets of protestors—anything and anyone associated as a symbol of power. Protestors marched on to the

---

[2]Ibid.

[3]Ibid.

[4]PTI, 'Amit Shah introduces Citizenship Amendment Bill in Lok Sabha', *India Today*, 09 December 2019, https://tinyurl.com/24u4xnmc. Accessed on 05 May 2025.

[5]PTI, 'Rajya Sabha passes Citizenship Amendment Bill', *Times of India*, 11 December 2019, https://tinyurl.com/znts8bac. Accessed on 05 May 2025.

[6]Chakraborty, Avik, and Sanjoy Hazarika, 'Thousands flock to protest in Upper Assam', *Telegraph India*, 24 December 2019, https://tinyurl.com/yaw2uaca. Accessed on 12 February 2025.

Assam Secretariat building in Dispur.[7] Guwahati became the epicentre of discontent as state-owned vehicles were targeted, and the police had to resort to lathi-charges and blank firing to disperse protesters.[8] In Tezpur, the office of the Bharatiya Janata Party (BJP) was torched.[9] Also targeted by the angry students were workers of the RSS and its affiliate organizations such as Akhil Bharatiya Vidyarthi Parishad (ABVP), Vishwa Hindu Parishad (VHP) and others.[10] Repression is nothing new for the Sangh, it had been targeted twice before—first, post the assassination of Mahatma Gandhi in 1948, and second, during the Emergency, from 1975 to 1977. But this was the first time that the Sangh and its sister organizations were directly attacked by the people—the same people it had earlier supported during the Agitation of the 1980s and the days of rampant insurgency.

Fast-forward five months to May 2020—the whole world was gripped by the COVID-19 pandemic. India was in complete lockdown. The day-to-day life of common people was disrupted and many could not afford the bare minimum necessities such as food grains. Worse, many were affected by the virus and were hospitalized. During these trying times, the first people to come out to serve the society were the pracharaks and karyakartas of the RSS. They came out in huge numbers to conduct relief work and health camps. The same workers—broken, battered and scarred five months back—came out with full enthusiasm to serve and help the people who had tortured and attacked them. Many workers took up the mission of providing free ration

---

[7]CNN-News18, 'Locals Stage Anti-Govt Demonstration Over CAB Approval Outside Assam Secretariat', *YouTube,* 09 December 2019, https://tinyurl.com/3xsw2jkh. Accessed on 17 February 2025.

[8]TNN, 'Violence Rages in Assam over CAB, net suspended in Tripura', *Times of India,* 11 December 2019, https://tinyurl.com/3uz7f2n5. Accessed on 12 February 2025.

[9]Interview with Bijoy (name changed).

[10]Interview with Bijoy (name changed).

daily to people below poverty line. From village to village, when people were restricted to the four walls of their houses, Sangh workers distributed food grains—rice, flour, lentils, millets, et cetera—door to door. This distribution work was carried on for every single day of the lockdown.

Others affiliated with Seva Bharati conducted free medical camps, which not only helped save lives through early detection of the virus but also eased the mounting pressure on the state administration. For instance, Seva Bharati organized Dhanvantari Seva Yatra where several doctors, medical students and Aarogya Mitra pass-outs put up free medical camps in remote areas.[11] They conducted COVID tests, cooperated with authorities in isolating positive patients, and distributed free medicines.[12] Many RSS workers working with Seva Bharati and other organizations contracted the virus, and some even passed away in the course of their selfless service to society.

What is this inherent quality that drives the pracharaks and karyakartas of the Sangh Parivar to continue on their path to *seva* despite such challenges? What motivates them to remain undeterred on their journey even in the face of threats? What drives them to fight even death for the act of social service and the propagation of their ideology? More importantly, what is the motivating factor for Sangh workers in the absence of clear tangible benefits, such as wealth, luxury and status? This book will attempt to answer all these questions through a study of how the Rashtriya Swayamsevak Sangh and its sister organizations worked, struggled, built a base and rose to power in the Northeast. By sister organizations of the Sangh Parivar, we include the various branches, ideological wings and affiliate organizations, such as Rashtra Sevika Samiti, Vishwa Hindu Parishad, Vanavasi Kalyan Ashram, Seva Bharati, Siksha Bharati, Vidya Bharati,

---

[11]Interview with Surendra Talkhedkar.

[12]Ibid.

Akhil Bharatiya Vidyarthi Parishad, Ekal Vidyalaya, Bajrang Dal, Seemanta Chetana Manch, Janajati Dharma Sanskriti Suraksha Manch, other organizations such as Seng Khasi or Khasi Sangh, Zeliangrong Heraka Association, Vivekananda Kendra, and various associated tribal and animist groups. It is crucial to note that in several states, it has been these organizations that have made their mark instead of the RSS, which, for the longest time, was viewed with suspicion.

The Northeast is a challenging landscape, not just for the RSS but also for any other nationalistic organization, including national political parties. The extreme diversity and heterogeneity along with strong ethnic consciousness among the communities have always eluded nationalist and integrationist parties such as the Bharatiya Janata Party (BJP). The Northeast has an unlikely demography for the rise of a family of organizations often associated with a socio-cultural and political idea such as Hindutva. When Prime Minister Narendra Modi came to power in 2014, he was successful in convincing the people of the Northeast in favour of his *Sabka Saath, Sabka Vikas* agenda. Following that, the Northeast has seen BJP-led governments in Assam, Arunachal Pradesh, Manipur and Tripura, with its regional allies forming governments in Meghalaya, Nagaland and Mizoram under the aegis of the North East Democratic Alliance (NEDA). How, then, did the BJP come to power in a region as demographically challenging as the Northeast?

Among the north-eastern states, only Assam, Manipur and Tripura have significant Hindu populations, while Arunachal Pradesh is home to a huge number of animist people. The remaining states—Nagaland, Mizoram and Meghalaya—have a Christian-majority owing to a strong influence of the Church. The region also faces the problem of illegal influx of Bengali Muslim immigrants from Bangladesh in states such as Assam, Meghalaya and Tripura, along with the immigration of ethnic

Burmese people in the states of Arunachal Pradesh, Nagaland, Manipur and Mizoram. In addition to this, the Northeast has also witnessed several ethnic movements such as those led by the National Socialist Council of Nagaland (NSCN), United Liberation Front of Assam (ULFA), National Liberation Front of Tripura (NLFT), and National Democratic Front of Bodoland (NDFB), among others. Despite these threefold challenges, the Sangh Parivar has made a significant mark in the region socially, culturally and politically over time.

These factors make the Northeast an interesting case study for political scientists. Winning over Northeast isn't as simple as winning over Uttar Pradesh or Maharashtra, where the political climate favours nationalist sentiments built around Hindu religion. While Uttar Pradesh is the birthplace of many mythological heroes such as Lord Rama and Lord Krishna, Maharashtra has been the cradle of *Hindavi Swarajya*, propounded by Chhatrapati Shivaji Maharaj. However, in the case of the Northeast, there is an absence of such a political climate dominated by nationalist and religious rhetoric.

The Overton window, or the window of discourse, is judged and situated on the regional, linguistic and tribal axis in almost all states. Hence, the Sangh Parivar had to first embrace and assimilate these regional, linguistic and tribal identities, and then build sentiments along nationalistic lines. In a sense, they constructed narratives from scratch and won over the people using a plethora of different measures, ranging from defence of indigenous faiths to social service.

Despite the intricate complexities, the Sangh Parivar has etched a remarkable presence within the region, gently extending its outreach and resonating with the hearts and minds of the people. This is why the study of Rashtriya Swayamsevak Sangh and its sister organizations in building a cohesive socio-political coalition in the Northeast is a unique phenomenon that needs to be studied by social scientists around the world. This book seeks to fill the lacuna in available literature on the Sangh, particularly on its role in frontier provinces such as the Northeast. We will look at how various organizations of the Sangh Parivar have built their base in different north-eastern states throughout history and continued their work despite the manifold challenges, eventually paving the way for the Bharatiya Janata Party to win power in all the seven states.

Another reason why this book is particularly interesting is that it challenges dominant academic narratives on the Sangh Parivar, its endeavours and efforts. Mainstream academic narratives, usually dominated by one particular worldview, often cast aspersions of secrecy and prejudice upon the Sangh's endeavours. There are several major prejudices and misconceptions regarding the RSS. First, that it seeks to impose a uniform standardized vision of Hinduism, centred around vegetarianism, Hindi dominance, and predominantly the worship of Lord Rama. This is far from the truth.

Almost all the top office bearers and pracharaks that we interviewed spoke in Assamese, not Hindi. In fact, when we talked to Sunita Haldekar, Akhil Bharatiya Sampark Pramukh of the Rashtra Sevika Samiti, she said, 'Language is only a fictitious division. We can easily learn each other's language when we shift to different regions and promote the practice of embracing each other's culture. Politics of hate based on linguistic lines has destroyed the unity of Hindu society.'[13] The other fact is that many Sangh pracharaks and karyakartas—who came from Brahmin families with vegetarian dietary backgrounds—have, in the course of their *sampark*, consumed non-vegetarian culinary delicacies in the Northeast. When Shashikant Chauthaiwale first came to the Northeast, M.S. Golwalkar, the then *sarsanghchalak*, asked him, 'Have you started eating fish?' When Chauthaiwale

[13]Interview with Sunita Haldekhar.

responded in the negative, Guruji explained, 'In Maharashtra, if we eat fish, it would be considered a big sin. In Assam, if you do not eat fish, you will become weak and fall sick.'[14]

In another example, we find Guruji Golwalkar convincing the *mathadheesh* of Pejawara Matha of Udupi, when he refused to attend a tribal conclave at Jorhat due to them being beef consumers, 'Yes, they do eat beef. But they do it out of compulsion as no alternative is available. And when is the last time we have approached them? We were busy all the time in performing rituals, sitting in a glass house.'[15] The other myth that the Sangh only promotes Vishnu-*bhakti* or worship of Lord Rama was also busted during the course of our research, as we unravelled the work of the Vanavasi Kalyan Ashram in the Northeast. This organization solely aims at preserving and protecting the indigenous faiths of the Northeast and has contributed significantly towards the revival of Donyi-Polo and Rangfrah faiths in Arunachal Pradesh, Sanamahism in Manipur, the Zeliangrong Heraka movement in Nagaland, and the Seng Khasi movement in Meghalaya. When we asked Kalyan Ashram's Akhil Bharatiya Sah Sangathan Mantri, Sandeep Kavishwar, about how he convinces tribal people of the organization's work in the midst of rumours surrounding Hindu proselytization, he replied, 'We tell them: your form of worship is our faith. We won't impose our Hinduism on you, but embrace your faith.'[16]

Another prejudice against the Sangh is that it is a cult of uneducated and illiterate foot soldiers of an ideology. When talking to a prominent columnist in Assam, he said, 'RSS is like a drug that brainwashes illiterate subalterns.'[17] This comes at a

---

[14]Chauthaiwale, Shashikant, *Mor Pracharak Jatra,* Tirthankar Das (trans.), Prachi Prakashan, Guwahati, 2023.

[15]Interview with Shankar Das.

[16]Interview with Sandip Kavishwar.

[17]Interview with Sunita Haldekar.

time when mainstream academic and media narratives paint the organization and its supporters with slurs such as 'Sanghi', 'Chaddi', or as people graduating from 'WhatsApp University'. This is also far from the truth. The first batch of pracharaks that we interviewed showcased a tremendous amount of academic backing, qualification and intellectual rigour. Thakur Ram Singh, the *prant pracharak* of the Assam *prant*, was a gold medallist in the 1942 MA (History) batch from FC College of Lahore.[18] The batch of karyakartas that worked under him were all highly qualified.

For example, Gurupada Bhowmick, whom we interviewed, did his graduation in chemistry and then pursued a stellar career in law.[19] Dr Vishwamitra is a respected doctor who dedicated his life to running a free-of-cost clinic in Meghalaya.[20] Dr Sunil Mohanty holds a PhD in political science from Jawaharlal Nehru University (JNU), Delhi.[21] The Sangh is a culmination of such academically gifted and tremendously talented people that dedicated their lives to the service of the nation, instead of seeking to become wine-sipping elites of Lutyens Delhi. As such, our book attempts not only to bridge the void in existing literature but also to challenge such prevailing biases. It seeks to present the Sangh Parivar's efforts as a testament to inclusivity and resilience, countering misperceptions rooted in centralizing Hindu proselytism.

However, writing this book wasn't an easy task. The biggest hurdle that we encountered was the obvious lacuna in available literature on the Sangh and the Northeast. There is also a lack of primary data, documents and archives within the RSS itself on the inception of its operations in the Northeast.

---

[18]Interview with Gurupada Bhowmick.

[19]Interview with Guru Bhowmick.

[20]Interview with Dr Vishwamitra.

[21]Interview with Sunil Mohanty.

There is also a dearth of secondary material, newspaper clippings and documented evidence of the work conducted by RSS in the Northeast before the twenty-first century. When we started this book, we were uncertain about how to begin and whether we would be able to write this at all. Then we decided to talk to pracharaks and karyakartas from the Sangh Parivar who served in the region at different time periods. Many of whom we met are septuagenarians, octogenarians and nonagenarians, and do not remember dates and events that transpired in the early decades of Independence accurately. We had to talk to many people and collate the information, match the dates with the events, and then construct their story in our words. A significant chunk of this book is based on such face-to-face interviews with Sangh Parivar associates and the memoirs, diaries and articles that a few of them left behind.

Another noteworthy feature is the history of collective trauma that members of the organization talk about. The soil of Northeast bears witness to the violence against those affiliated with the Rashtriya Swayamsevak Sangh. There were echoes of anguish as many of our interviewees narrated heart-wrenching stories where insurgent outfits ruthlessly kidnapped, tortured and silenced the voices of dedication and service.

In 2005 in Nalbari, for example, RSS Vibhag Karyavah Sukleswar Medhi was shot dead by ULFA outside Balitara High School, where he taught.[22] Four years before this incident in 2001, Kshetra Karyavah Shyamal Sengupta and three pracharaks—Dinendranath De, Sudhamoy Dutta and Shubhankar Chakraborty—were killed by the NLFT in Tripura after two years of their abduction and repeated tortures.[23] Despite the spectre of fear that looms large, defiant flames of courage and

---

[22]Kavishwar, Sandip, *Mrityunjay Veer*, Rouhin Deb and Nabaarun Barooah (trans.), Prachi Prakashan, Guwahati, 2022.

[23]Ibid.

commitment flicker within the souls of many, igniting a steadfast determination to continue their noble work, undeterred by the looming shadows of threats and violence. These are but five among many whose names are whispered with reverence, their sacrifices serving as a poignant reminder of the indomitable spirit that continues to fuel the RSS's mission in the face of adversity.

Built on riveting accounts and interviews of pracharaks, karyakartas and affiliates of various organizations associated with the RSS, this book will provide a personalized insider account of how the Sangh operated in the Northeast from Independence to the present day. The book travels through time to look at how the various organizations toggled through the first party system, the wars of 1962, 1965 and 1971, the various linguistic riots, the Emergency, the days of rampant regionalist movements and insurgencies in Assam, Nagaland, Manipur and Tripura, the challenges posed by the Church in Arunachal Pradesh, Meghalaya and Nagaland, and various other challenges, to build a formidable social base and unlikely consensus that helped the BJP storm to power post-2014. It is a story of the trials and tribulations, struggles and sacrifices, and commitment and determination that pracharaks and members displayed through monumental events in history.

Within these pages lie the chronicles of those whose steadfast dedication has shaped the Sangh's narrative and whose collective endeavours stand as a testament to the enduring influence and resonance of the Sangh Parivar within the verdant landscapes of the Northeast.

1

From the Dark Days of the Raj

They are not Indians in any sense of the word, neither in origin, nor in language, nor in appearance, nor in habit, nor outlook and it is by historical accident that they have been tacked on to an Indian Province.

—Sir Robert Niel Reid[24]
(Governor of Assam, 1937–42)

To understand why the Northeast has been a challenging frontier for the Rashtriya Swayamsevak Sangh and its affiliate organizations that align themselves on nationalism, we must first look at the history of the region pre-1947 and assess the impact of colonial rule and how these colonial tropes were passed on to the first generation of leaders of independent India.

The region of the Northeast has been subjected to a sense of 'othering' by the rest of India.[25] Eminent scholar Sanjib Baruah

---

[24]Kapesa, Pfokrelo, 'The Politics of Reorganization: The Case of Jammu & Kashmir and Nagaland', *Rising Asia Journal,* Vol. 4, No. 2, 2024, pp. 360–384, https://tinyurl.com/pawh6kvv. Accessed on 17 February 2025.

[25]Originally attributed to feminist philosopher and theorist Simone de Beauvoir, othering is defined by Lajos Brons as 'the construction and identification of the self or in-group and the other or out-group in mutual, unequal opposition by attributing relative inferiority and/or radical alienness to the other/out-group';

argues that the very term 'Northeast' is not just a product of geographical othering but also expresses a certain hierarchy and relation of power to the mainland which has racial connotations. Due to the presence of Mongoloid features, the people of the Northeast do not fit into the predefined framework and imagination of the 'Indian face' and are treated as lesser Indians.[26] This—combined with their knowledge of English, due to the advent of Christian missionaries—has 'de-Indianized' the people of the Northeast in the eyes of 'mainland India'. Being a Northeasterner is having a lived experience of racial gaze, racial taunts, and racial discrimination.

The racial othering of the Northeastern region is best exemplified by the Hindi term *pardes*—a place of danger located outside the effective boundaries of the nation or *des*.[27] This was a prominent view held by colonialists who considered the regions inhabited by tribal groups under 'excluded areas' reduced to the frontiers of the nation. Prasenjit Duara, an eminent scholar from the Northeast, presents the duality of an adaptive and relatively modern and urban sector, integrated—under however unequal terms—with metropolitan society, and the contradictory hinterland where historical forms of social life, economic organization and exploitation continue to exist, but hardly as pristine 'tradition'.[28] This dichotomy is described as 'articulation of modes of production', where capitalist production is achieved through non-capitalist and traditionalist modes of production and exploitation.[29]

Brons, Lajos, 'Othering, an Analysis', *Transcience*, Vol. 6, No. 1, 2015, pp. 69–90.

[26]Baruah, Sanjib, *In the Name of the Nation: India and its Northeast, South Asia in Motion* Series, Standford University Press. California, 2020.

[27]Yadav, Anil, *Is That Even a Country, Sir! Journeys in Northeast India by Train, Bus and Tractor,* Speaking Tiger, India, 2017.

[28]Duara, Prasenjit, 'Introduction', *Decolonization: Perspectives from Now and Then,* Prasenjit Duara (ed.), Routledge, India, 2003.

[29]Marxist philosophy in which separate modes of production are seen as coexisting within the same single social formation.

In the Northeast, the people got disengaged from their nature-dependent livelihoods when the colonialists used these areas as capitalist resource frontiers, which were exploited for natural resources such as coal and oil. Another example is the creation of a plantation economy in the state of Assam, where *adivasi*s were employed in the tea gardens in service of the modern capitalist sector of the metropolitan economy but received few, if any, of its benefits. Duara argues that this gap isn't merely a difference between tradition and modernity, but of variations in incorporation or assimilation into the capitalist system of colonial rule.[30] The colonial administration in India did not extend its institutions in the Northeast but ruled these areas 'indirectly' under customary law. This took shape in the form of the Crown Colony Plan as proposed by Sir Robert N. Reid, who was the governor of Assam from 1937 to 1942.[31] The Crown Colony Plan was devised to include the so-called excluded areas located in the middle of Assam and Burma within the colonial state of Assam when Burma was given independence.[32] This zone would give the British direct access to the resources of the hills with no responsibility over its development. Although the Plan never materialized, the same modus operandi continued under the garb of the Inner Line Permit.

Inner Line Permit

The origins of the Inner Line Permit (ILP) system trace back to the colonial era, particularly from 1826 to 1878, when British

---

[30]Duara, Prasenjit, 'Introduction', *Decolonization: Perspectives from Now and Then*, Prasenjit Duara (ed.), Routledge, India, 2003.

[31]Syiemlieh, David R., 'THE CROWN COLONY PLANTS: The British And The Hill Areas Of North-East India, 1945-46', *Proceedings of the Indian History Congress*, Vol. 59, 1998, pp. 691–98, https://tinyurl.com/yzkjyabf. Accessed on 14 February 2025.

[32]Ibid.

expansion into Northeast India for commercial ventures, notably tea cultivation, sparked tensions among indigenous tribes.[33] These tribes, accustomed to using raids as a means of defence and sustenance, viewed the influx of outsiders with apprehension and responded with raids to assert control over their land and deter further encroachment.[34] This resistance, along with broader discontent towards colonial rule, prompted widespread protests and criticism in public discourse and media outlets. In response, the British administration implemented the Bengal Eastern Frontier Regulation of 1873, introducing the Inner Line Permit system.[35] This regulation required non-tribal individuals to obtain permits from district authorities to enter tribal areas, aiming to maintain order and protect tribal interests while regulating external access to these regions.

Under this system, outsiders and tea planters were prohibited from acquiring land within the inner line territory, with the primary objective of regulating entry, appeasing tribal communities, and preventing raids.[36] This regulation specifically applied to areas with sovereign tribal governance, such as the Naga and Lushai Hills, while regions like the Khasi Hills, under direct British administration, were initially excluded from its scope. However, as British jurisdiction extended to these areas later, the effectiveness of this system waned, though it persisted in a relaxed manner. Initially driven by commercial interests, and to safeguard plains people from tribal incursions, the ILP's objectives eventually shifted towards preserving tribal rights and culture. Despite changes in interpretation,

---

[33]Mahanta, Ratul, 'Inner Line Permit as an Instrument of Protecting Identity: Benefits, Costs and its Effectiveness', *Identity Aspirations, Developmental Backlogs and Governance Issues in Northeast India*, M.P. Bezbaruah (ed.), Maliyata Offset Press, Mirza, 2016, pp. 55–65.

[34]Ibid.

[35]Ibid.

[36]Ibid.

the ILP endured as a mechanism for managing access to tribal territories.

Moreover, the implementation of the Inner Line Permit was primarily driven by a subset of colonial administrators in Northeast India, serving the interests of British rule aimed at safeguarding colonial business ventures and maintaining dominance over potential rivals.[37] This policy, enacted in the Crown's interest, focused on expanding and securing trade in commodities like tea, oil and elephants, while preventing others from entering these lucrative markets. Essentially, the Inner Line served to protect the interests of non-tribal individuals and restrict the movement of both hill tribes and non-tribal British subjects.[38] Under this regulation, the Lieutenant Governor possessed the authority to exempt certain categories of foreigners from obtaining permits. Furthermore, the ILP included provisions for elephant conservation and granted the government the power to establish regulations for their capture in the Naga and Lushai Hills regions.[39]

The primary concern of colonialists was to gain acceptance and affection from indigenous tribes by fundamentally reshaping their beliefs, eliminating perceived uncivilized practices, and instilling Christian moral principles as swiftly as possible. This also enabled missionaries to actively evangelize and bring non-believers into the Christian faith and teachings.[40] Hence, it became the duty of the white colonizers, as expressed by Kipling in 1899, to compel tribal communities to adopt Christianity. These tribes were not afforded the freedom to select from the various religions present in British India, particularly Hinduism, which was the predominant religion among the Indian population. The Inner Line regulation

[37]Ibid.

[38]Ibid.

[39]Ibid.

[40]Ibid.

aimed to isolate tribal communities from outside religious influences by denying entry to European speculators, Hindu and Muslim traders from regions like Assam and East Bengal. This decision stemmed from two primary reasons: first, the duty-bound British administration sought to prevent tribal communities from drawing unfavourable comparisons with profit-driven European speculators; secondly, they aimed to prevent non-Christian influences from reaching the tribes through contact with local Indian traders. Additionally, the success of evangelical efforts in the Khasi Hills, then a part of Assam, spurred further missionary endeavours among tribal populations across various hills. These efforts targeted animist tribes—characterized by mystical beliefs and superstitions—as they were considered receptive to conversion due to their vulnerable socio-economic status.

The exclusion of tribal communities from interactions with plains people was possibly driven by a concern that such interactions could foster political awareness among the tribes.[41] Moreover, the hills remained untouched by Mahatma Gandhi's largely non-violent freedom movement, which had posed a significant challenge to the British Empire and its authorities. As the administrators and the Church faced mounting pressure and uncertainty, they found little resistance to the idea of maintaining the Inner Line regulation, recognizing it as a necessary measure to preserve the status quo and prevent potential upheaval.[42] This resulted in rampant proselytization and an almost total conversion of the populations to Christianity in areas that later became the states of Nagaland, Mizoram and Meghalaya.

---

[41]Thangtungnung, H., 'Extension of Inner Line Regulation and Excluded Areas in the Lushai Hills', *E-PAO*, 6 June 2013. https://tinyurl.com/358b93cd. Accessed on 06 May 2025.
[42]Ibid.

Converting the Northeast—Christian Proselytization in the Region

Since its inception, the East India Company had dispatched chaplains to India with the mission to spread the gospel among the Indian population.[43] However, as the Company established itself as a formidable political power towards the end of the eighteenth century, authorities in England recognized the importance of maintaining religious neutrality to consolidate their influence. Consequently, the Company adopted a policy of 'non-interference' in the religious affairs of its Indian subjects. This stance persisted until the enactment of the Charter Act of 1813, which authorized the granting of residence licenses to individuals seeking to promote religious and moral improvement among the Indian people.

By the 1820s, a gradual rise in evangelical influence among the younger generation of civil and military officers in India led to a shift in attitudes towards missionaries. Company officials began to view missionaries with sympathy rather than derision or alarm, marking a significant departure from previous perceptions. Despite initial resistance and hindrances, missionary activities gained traction across India, including in the Northeast.

Assam emerged as a significant venue for missionary endeavours, with the involvement of notable figures such as William Carey and Krishna Pal. Carey, who established the Serampur Mission in 1800, dispatched his earliest convert, Krishna Pal, to Northeast India to propagate the gospel.[44] Although Krishna Pal purportedly baptized individuals from the Khasi and Assamese communities, these early efforts did

---

[43]Ghosh, Anupama, 'CONVERSIONS, EDUCATION AND LINGUISTIC IDENTITY IN ASSAM THE AMERICAN BAPTISTS MISSIONARIES, 1830S-1890', *Proceedings of the Indian History Congress,* Vol. 72, 2011, pp. 863–74, https://tinyurl.com/2dcpst9j. Accessed on 14 February 2025.

[44]Ibid.

not sustain, and subsequent updates on these converts were scarce. The transformative impact of the Charter Act extended to the north-eastern frontier of India, facilitated by the efforts of Company officials like David Scott and Captain Jenkins. At the instigation of David Scott, a centre of the Baptist Missionary Society was established in Guwahati in 1829, under the charge of James Rae. By 1836, six individuals had been baptized under Rae's guidance, and a church comprising 12 members was organized.[45]

However, none of the Indian members of this early church in the Brahmaputra Valley remained steadfast in their faith, highlighting the challenges and complexities inherent in missionary work. The real initiative for evangelism in Assam gained momentum with the arrival of American Baptist missionaries. Their presence marked a significant turning point, injecting renewed vigour and purpose into missionary endeavours in the region. Despite initial setbacks and the transient nature of early converts, the arrival of American Baptist missionaries heralded a new chapter in the propagation of Christianity in Assam, in both the plains and the hills (which were then a part of the state).

The role of American Baptist missionaries in shaping the history of Assam during the nineteenth century was profound and multifaceted. From the 1830s to the 1890s, these missionaries coincided with significant developments in education, the press, and the emergence of a distinct linguistic identity for Assam.[46] One notable aspect of the missionary impact in Assam was the significant presence of tea garden labourers within the membership of churches in the Brahmaputra Valley. This demographic shift underlined the missionaries' success in reaching out to diverse segments of Assamese society, including

---

[45]Ibid.

[46]Ibid.

marginalized labour communities. The conversion of tea garden labourers not only expanded the reach of Christianity but also provided these communities with access to education and social upliftment, furthering the missionaries' broader agenda of societal transformation.

Educational initiatives spearheaded by American Baptist missionaries played a crucial role in uplifting the socio-cultural landscape of Assam. Through the establishment of schools and educational institutions, missionaries sought to impart Western knowledge and values while simultaneously promoting Christian teachings. These efforts contributed to the spread of literacy and modernization in Assam, empowering individuals and communities with the tools for social and economic advancement.

Additionally, the missionaries' advocacy for the press played a crucial role in disseminating information and shaping public discourse in Assam. The establishment of printing presses and the publication of newspapers and religious literature facilitated the exchange of ideas and information, fostering intellectual engagement and cultural exchange. The press became a powerful tool for spreading the Christian message and promoting missionary endeavours, while also serving as a platform for indigenous voices and expressions. Furthermore, the missionaries' engagement with the language agitation in Assam highlighted their commitment to the welfare of the masses.

As Assam grappled with questions of linguistic identity and cultural autonomy, American Baptist missionaries aligned themselves with local aspirations for linguistic recognition and preservation. By supporting indigenous languages and advocating for linguistic rights, missionaries endeared themselves to the Assamese populace, further enhancing their influence and credibility within the community. Despite the challenges and opposition faced by missionaries in Assam, their commitment to their mission remained steadfast. The records and correspondences of Rev. Miles Bronson in Nagaon and the Guwahati churches provide insights into the hardships endured by missionaries and the resilience they demonstrated in the face of adversity.[47] These sources offer glimpses into the complexities and nuances of missionary engagement, highlighting both the triumphs and the tribulations experienced by early missionaries in Assam. While indigenous documentation regarding the missionary activities in Assam may be scarce, the available records offer valuable insights into the dynamics of missionary work in the region.[48]

The British rule in Mizoram was roughly over five decades, and was never really seen as being carried on with an imperialist mindset. The British extending their control towards the plains of Brahmaputra saw the raids from the neighbouring hill tribes as being merely problematic and often carried out retaliatory measures to resolve the situation. However, as they did not see satisfactory results, the governments of Assam and Bengal planned a joint military expedition in 1871 which is known to the Mizos as the *vailen*. It is interesting to learn that the Mizos associate the invasion with *Vaia*s; it was an encounter with an army who were mainly Gorkhas and Sikhs serving the British administration.[49] The actual period of rule was referred to as *sapin min awplai*, or the time 'when white men/sahibs ruled over us'. Zoremsiami Pachuau explains the significance of this phrase—*awpis* is also a word used for a hen incubating her eggs, signifying the contributory role the *sap* or whites had in 'hatching out' the Mizos.[50]

Ṭhimataengah, translated as 'from dark to light' is also a popular phrase describing the transitory period during

[47]Ibid.

[48]Ibid.

[49]Pachuau, Zoremsiami, 'History of the Gorkha Community in Mizoram from 19th-20th Centuries', 2022, Mizoram University, Doctor of Philosophy, Dept of History and Ethnography.

[50]Ibid.

this time. The period with the introduction of Christianity is often acknowledged as a mediation to bring the Mizos out of 'darkness towards the light'. Popular narratives often give an account of Bengkhuaia, the chief of Sailam village, as the main protagonist to lead one of the most noted expeditions against the British.

However, R.G. Woodthorpe, who wrote an account of the expedition, mentioned Bengkhuaia very little; instead he spoke of one of the most menacing chiefs of the Lushai—Lalburha. Many attempts were in fact carried out to retaliate and subjugate the Mizos even before 1871 when a joint attack to the Cachar plains was carried out by different chiefs. The story is popular as it involves the tragic incident of a young girl, who many Mizos later identified as a point of departure for the entry of Christianity among the Mizos. Bengkhuaia's men raided Alexandrapuri, a tea plantation where they eventually killed Mary Winchester's father, James Winchester, along with many other people. James Winchester was a manager for the British tea plantation and Mary stayed with him for 12 years. When her father decided that it was time for her formal education in Britain, a farewell party was held at the tea plantation, owned by Mr George Seller, a close friend of James Winchester.

Since the people present were mostly civilians, the Mizo sides saw the raid as a very successful one, killing and capturing many, including Mary Winchester. Being a little girl, and learning that she was an illegitimate daughter of a Kuki—their own hill people—they took great care of her giving her the Mizo name, Zoluti.

The British government launched their retaliatory attack on 8 October 1871. The British side had sophisticated military equipment and the Mizo arms were no match for their artillery; they advanced towards Sailam, suppressing and destroying villages in their way, burning them down to ashes. The right column of the campaign reached Sailam village on 21 January 1872. Bengkhuaia and Tom Lewin made a treaty of agreement known to the Mizos as *Sa ui tan.*[51]

In the process, the village was saved from being burnt down and it is said that Bengkhuaia was so boastful of his achievement to be able to have made peace with the British that he said, 'If I proclaim it to be; tell me who under heaven or earth can say it isn't so!'[52] Many Mizos often narrate this story as the most crucial point in history as many believed this was what brought the Mizo hills into the notification of the British. It is impossible to trace the origin of Christianity in this region without reference to this incident. Popular narrative gives way to many of the visual representations of Mizo history as opposed to precise historical accounts. Mizos often referred to Mizoram as *Pathianzawnchhuah ram*—'A country sought out by God himself'. A small region in the Northeast, which was surrounded by all major religious influences—Buddhism towards the east and Hinduism in the west—could probably be easily assimilated culturally and spiritually by neighbouring larger races.

The British first encountered the Nagas through interactions with the Burmese following the Anglo-Burmese War of 1759–1826.[53] The introduction of Western education by Christian missionaries introduced the Naga people to modern civilization, with the educated class serving as a bridge between the ruling authorities and the general population. Despite flaws in government educational policies, this system brought

---

[51]Woodthorpe, R.G., *The Lushai Expedition 1871–1872*, Hurst and Blackett Publishers, London, 1873.

[52]Ibid.

[53]Pau, Pum Khan, 'Small wars as 'savage warfare': rethinking colonial counterinsurgency operations in Northeast India and Northwest Burma (1826–1919)', *Small Wars & Insurgencies*, Vol. 34, No. 3 2023, pp. 571–596, https://tinyurl.com/5n6bc8b6. Accessed on 17 February 2025.

enlightenment to Naga society, revolutionizing its cultural ethos and instilling new values.[54] British colonial education facilitated a significant broadening of perspectives among the Nagas, allowing them to embrace societal changes.[55] Similarly, the arrival of Christianity among the Nagas and Kukis in Northeast India can be attributed to the efforts of American Baptist missionaries.[56]

In 1836, the Serampore missionaries, pioneers of evangelism in the Northeast, handed over their work to American Baptist missionaries based in Burma, a proposition that was accepted.[57] Among the first to venture into Assam were Rev. Nathan Brown, his wife, and O.T. Cutter. The foremost American Baptist missionary, Rev. Miles Bronson began his mission among the Nagas around 1842, lasting until 1852.[58] Bronson not only introduced Christianity to the Nagas but also taught them the cultivation of tea. His efforts were recognized and supported by the governor-general's agent, who recommended financial aid. Major Jenkins, the British commissioner at Sibsagar, was authorized to make small payments to Bronson for practical projects aimed at improving the Naga region and fostering habits of industry among its people. Bronson established a school in Namsang, Konyak, although the venture encountered limited success, leading Bronson to depart due to ill health.[59] Over time,

[54]Woodthorpe, R.G., *The Lushai Expedition 1871-1872,* Hurst and Blackett Publishers, London, 1873.

[55]Ghosh, Anupama, 'CONVERSIONS, EDUCATION AND LINGUISTIC IDENTITY IN ASSAM THE AMERICAN BAPTISTS MISSIONARIES, 1830S-1890', Proceedings of the Indian History Congress, Vol. 72, 2011, pp. 863–74, https://tinyurl.com/2dcpst9j. Accessed on 14 February 2025.

[56]Singh, K.R., 'Coming Of Christianity in the Naga Area of North East India', *IOSR Journal Of Humanities And Social Science (IOSR-JHSS),* Volume 20, No. 4, pp. 13–17. https://tinyurl.com/y7bdsn9z. Accessed on 14 February 2025.

[57]Ibid.

[58]Ibid.

[59]Ibid.

Christian missionaries played a significant role in reshaping the indigenous ethnic identity of the Nagas into a Christianized one. The Christian population in the Naga hills was minimal in the 1901 census, with only 579 individuals identified as Christians. In 1887, a new missionary effort emerged in Assam, known as the Naga Mission—distinct from the Assam Mission in the Brahmaputra Valley and the Garo Mission. This distinction aimed to underscore the specific focus on evangelizing and supporting the Naga community.

Additionally, Christianity played a pivotal role in shaping the Naga national movement for independence, instilling in Nagas a belief in a divine geo-political plan that distinguished them from 'Hindu India'.[60] The Federal Government of Nagaland's *Yehzabo* (constitution) acknowledged the sovereignty of the Christian God over Naga affairs, emphasizing divine sustenance during trials in 1956. The Naga National Council (NNC) led by Phizo mandated the inclusion of the Christian God in all practical aspects, even appointing pastors for war affairs. Later, the National Socialist Council of Nagaland (NSCN)—which emerged in 1980—promoted 'Christian Socialism' to unify Naga tribes, leading to mass conversions in previously untouched regions.[61] The adage 'Nagaland for Christ' remained influential, linking the church with the movement.[62]

Naga nationalism drew parallels with biblical accounts of Israel's deliverance, viewing adherence to God's decree as essential for political success. Numerous anecdotes bolstered the belief in divine protection, inspiring trust in God for achieving independence.

---

[60]Tohring, S.R., *Violence and Identity in North-East India: Naga-Kuki Conflict*, Mittal Publications, Delhi, 2010.

[61]Ibid.

[62]Singh, Prakash, *Nagaland*, National Book Trust, New Delhi, 1972.

Muslim Immigration in the Region—An Attempt at Islamization

The Assam problem is a long-drawn-out saga that began before India attained independence. In the late 1930s and early 1940s, Syed Muhammad Saadulla—the premier of the state who helmed the Muslim League government—undertook an extensive land settlement policy, called the Line System, as a part of his Grow More Food campaign, a scheme that aimed to increase the agricultural production of the state.[63] As part of this new land policy, lakhs of Bengali-speaking Muslim migrants from erstwhile East Bengal were settled as agricultural labourers in the districts of Lower Assam, particularly Barpeta and Goalpara, and Barak Valley.[64] The then viceroy, Lord Wavell, later wrote in his memoirs that Saadulla was more interested in 'growing more Muslims' than 'growing food crops'.[65]

Saadulla was also a member of the Executive Committee of the All India Muslim League which met in March 1940 to draft the 'Pakistan Resolution' and was a proponent of including Assam in the proposed East Pakistan. Jinnah aggressively campaigned for this demand stating that Assam was essentially a 'Muslim state'.[66]

Between 1940 and 1945, the Muslim League leadership did everything in their power to bring Assam under their control,

---

[63]Borthakur, Akunthita, and Ritu Thaosen, 'RETHINKING THE LINE SYSTEM IN ASSAM AND ITS POLITICS', *Proceedings of the Indian History Congress*, Vol. 73, 2012, pp. 545–52, https://tinyurl.com/ynmbhcva. Accessed on 14 February 2025.

[64]Casci, Simonetta, 'MUSLIM SELF-DETERMINATION: JINNAH CONGRESS CONFRONTATION, 1943-44', *Il Politico*, Vol. 63, No. 1 (184), 1998, pp. 67–85, https://tinyurl.com/4ub6m3ny. Accessed on 17 February 2025.

[65]Goradia, Prafull, 'Migration into Assam has roots in Jinnah's Pakistan plan', *The Sunday Guardian*, September 8, 2018, https://tinyurl.com/4jvrdc7. Accessed on 17 February 2025.

[66]Ibid.

despite having very little to no Muslim population in their appeal base.[67] Even without direct action, the ripples of this effect were felt on Assam during the early 1940s. The League was trying its best to include Assam among the territories they were planning to subsume under the newly formed state of Pakistan.

The decision of the Saadulla-led Assam government to enumerate the population in the 1941 census on the basis of community rather than religious affiliation was clearly a move to further reduce the numerical strength of the Hindu community in Assam in the official records, as a preparation for future Muslim League justification to demand the inclusion of Assam in Pakistan.[68]

By 1943, even Liaqat Ali Khan clearly argued that Assam was very much a part of Pakistan.[69] Presenting his general secretary's report in the Karachi session of the Muslim League in December 1943, he noted with satisfaction that the League was successful in forming the government and retaining power in all those provinces which would constitute the geographical area of Pakistan.[70] Assam was one such province and was keenly observed because it was essentially a non-Muslim majority province and yet was within the Muslim League's proposal. In every session of the League since 1940, Assam found mention in the presidential address of Muhammad Ali Jinnah and the

---

[67]Bhattacharjee, J.B., 'Presidential Address: WORLD WAR II AND INDIA: A FIFTY YEARS PERSPECTIVE', *Proceedings of the Indian History Congress*, Vol. 50, No. 1989, pp. 365–98, https://tinyurl.com/ywn7u42d. Accessed on 14 February 2025.

[68]Barpujari, H.K., 'PRESIDENTIAL ADDRESS', *Proceedings of the Indian History Congress*, Vol. 33, No. 1971, pp. 415–26, https://tinyurl.com/yc3k9v9a. Accessed on 14 February 2025.

[69]Casci, Simonetta, 'MUSLIM SELF-DETERMINATION: JINNAH CONGRESS CONFRONTATION, 1943-44', *Il Politico*, Vol. 63, No. 1 (184), 1998, pp. 67–85, https://tinyurl.com/4ub6m3ny. Accessed on 17 February 2025.

[70]Ibid.

general secretary's report of Liaqat Ali Khan.[71] The assumption of office by the Muslim League government in Assam was seen as the first step in making Assam a part of Pakistan.

The formation of this government in 1939 under Muhammad Saadulla marked a pivotal moment for the League's ambitions. A key issue at the time was the migration of Muslim peasants from Bengal, which was central to the politics of demographic transformation in Assam. These immigrants were seen as bolstering the League's claim to include Assam in its vision of Pakistan.

The issue gained further urgency as the League sought to incorporate Assam among its proposed 'five Muslim provinces'. Maulana Abdul Hamid Khan spearheaded public meetings across the province, particularly in the Assam Valley, where the League campaigned in favour of the Line System and celebrated Pakistan Day. Tensions began escalating between the League and rival Muslim organizations like the Jamiat Ulama-i-Hind, often leading to simultaneous gatherings and confrontations. These rivalries became a regular feature in the lead-up to the 1945–46 elections.

The League pursued a dual agenda—promoting Pakistan and supporting immigration—which were deeply intertwined. Immigrants were seen as the mass base for the League's political movement. Even Jinnah acknowledged the League's growing influence in Assam, noting it with satisfaction in a 1941 letter.[72] In Darrang district, Maulana Abdul Hamid Khan presided over meetings encouraging immigrants to forcibly occupy wastelands if their demands weren't met.

By 1941, communal tensions in East Bengal and Assam

---

[71]Ibid.

[72]Pirzada, S., *Quaid e Azam Jinnah's Correspondences*, East and West Publishers, Karachi, 1977, p. 15; see Jinnah's letter addressed to Maulana Abdul Hamid Khan, dated 8 December 1941.

had intensified. The League organized the Assam-Bengal Proja Conference in Goalpara, where Abdul Hamid Khan called for civil disobedience if the zamindari system was not abolished. Leaders from Bengal also addressed meetings in Shillong and Sylhet. During the Quit India Movement in August 1942, Muslim villagers in Assam remained largely unsupportive of the Congress-led protests, partly due to Congress-led boycotts of Muslim shops. In response, the League became active in places like Sylhet and Nagaon, mobilizing volunteers to protect Muslim interests.

While some areas like the Surma Valley remained relatively calm due to Muslim majorities, others saw rising tensions. In Mangaldoi, Muslim immigrants were called to defend shops, prompting protests from non-Muslims. Hindu-Muslim hostilities worsened as Hindu volunteers intercepted immigrant transports, evoking retaliation. The immigration issue and wartime food crisis dominated Assam's political landscape, with the League determined to connect immigration to its East Pakistan agenda.

The League's leadership, particularly Maulana Abdul Hamid Khan, intensified efforts in Assam and Bengal. Immigrants were urged to settle down on grazing reserves, sometimes using violence. In coordination with the Bengal Muslim League and other organizations, meetings condemned immigrant evictions and called the Line System illegal. The League's broader campaign addressed three key issues: Pakistan, eviction and famine. Secret meetings in mosques and homes coordinated resistance efforts.

The eviction issue became a symbolic rallying point for the League's Pakistan movement. After rejecting the Cabinet Mission Plan, the League prepared for 'direct action' in Assam, establishing militia units and raising funds. Maulana Abdul Hamid Khan reportedly distributed money and mobilized volunteers in places like Dhubri. Boycotts and communal tensions spread, particularly in areas like Sylhet and Lumding.

While some Assamese protested attacks on immigrants,

clashes between local communities and immigrants flared in places like Nalbari. By late 1946, political polarization between the Congress and the League reached a breaking point. The League expanded its National Guards, preparing for final efforts to establish Pakistan.

As Partition negotiations progressed, the focus shifted to determining which regions would be included. Though the Cabinet Mission grouped Assam with Bengal, the Congress argued that provinces should have the right to opt out. Assam, being Hindu-majority (with only about 30 per cent Muslims), resisted inclusion in Pakistan. However, the League remained adamant and the divide over Assam became a major point of contention.

Despite Congress resistance, the League continued recruiting volunteers, particularly from eastern Bengal. After the Punjab government banned the Muslim League National Guards, similar crackdowns occurred in Assam, though the League's activities intensified. Militant tones and religious leadership grew more prominent, especially in border areas.

In early 1947, large meetings were held in Mankachar and Maulvi Bazar protesting the Line System and zamindari. Training camps for militia were established near the Assam-Bengal border. A major 'East Pakistan Conference' at Rahumari-Mankachar drew over 10,000 participants, highlighting the growing scale of the League's campaign.

Leaflets and propaganda from League leaders spread throughout Dhubri and surrounding regions. Calls for jihad and resistance intensified. Secret meetings in Barpeta, led by local League leaders, encouraged reoccupation of grazing reserves. Plans were reported for sending Muslims from Bengal to occupy wastelands in Assam.

With increasing agitation, the situation grew volatile. By March and April 1947, major rallies were held in Chilmari and Sonahat, with some speeches framing the struggle as jihad.

A second training fort was built in Rangpur to prepare volunteers for entry into Assam. Alarmed by these developments, the Bengal government considered stricter controls on League activities.

The people of Assam, particularly in Goalpara and Kamrup, were increasingly concerned about the League's 'invasion' tactics. Demonstrations, flag-hoisting campaigns and riots in towns like Karimganj reflected rising tensions. When the League suspended talks, Assamese leaders threatened to expel all 'foreigners' from Upper Assam.

With the British Cabinet's decision to transfer power, the stage was set for Partition. On 3 June, the British prime minister announced the plan for Partition, including provisions for dividing Punjab, Bengal, and potentially Assam. Communal tensions peaked during the Sylhet Referendum and the eventual division of India on 14 August 1947.[73]

Considering the massive challenge posed by Islamic fundamentalism, coupled with Christian proselytization, it was only prophetic that a counter-revolution would soon begin.

A Saffron Spark

While continued social and political trouble was brewing in the Northeast, a young doctor was about to make an everlasting mark in Bharat. Losing both his parents to the plague at the tender age of thirteen, Keshav Baliram Hedgewar was determined to become a doctor and serve society. This was during the early 1890s when the British depredations were at its peak and Indians were deprived of basic healthcare and other facilities. It was during this time that a young Hedgewar broke colonial laws and sang 'Vande Mataram' in his school and was expelled. As is

---

[73]Dutta, Binayak, 'Pakistan Movement and Communalization of Peasants in Colonial Assam', *Vidyasagar University Journal of History*, Vol. 5, 2016–2017, pp. 107–118, https://tinyurl.com/47pz84xa. Accessed on 10 April 2025.

evident, he was a follower of Bankim Chandra Chattopadhyaya and soon followed his idol's philosophy to join the Anushilan Samiti in Kolkata.[74]

During his time in the revolutionary movement, he was deeply influenced by the works of V.D. Savarkar, Bal Gangadhar Tilak and Sri Aurobindo. They shaped his worldview and instilled the belief that a cultural renaissance was the means to true freedom and strengthened the tenets of renouncement, which are held sacred even today by *swayamsevak*s (volunteers). Additionally, Dr Hedgewar's involvement in both armed revolutionary struggle and Mahatma Gandhi's non-violent national movement made him realize the necessity of a disciplined, cadre-based nationalist organization to propagate strong patriotic values. Disillusionment with the pacifist tactics used by the Indian National Congress during the freedom struggle—exacerbated by the Hindu-Muslim riots post the Non-Cooperation Movement—reinforced this belief. He saw an urgent need to address the underlying issues rather than opting for temporary solutions to prevent any future colonization of India.[75]

As a result, on the auspicious occasion of Vijayadashami in 1925, a day that marks the victory of good over evil and of dharma over adharma, Dr Hedgewar and his compatriots founded the Rashtriya Swayamsevak Sangh, abbreviated as the RSS, in Nagpur.[76] While the RSS was just limited to men, Laxmibai Kelkar started the Rashtriya Sevika Samiti Sangh in 1936 to make women a part of the nation-making process.[77]

Together, the two organizations focused on the dual objective of 'man-making', or creating a dedicated cadre, and promoting the nationalist message in colonial India. This was done through a

---

[74]Saxena, Anurag, *Demystifying RSS*, BFC Publications, India, 2021.

[75]Ibid.

[76]Ibid.

[77]Ibid.

two-pronged approach: first, pracharaks or full-time 'propagators', and second, *shakhas* or branches.

Two years after the establishment of the Sangh, Dr Hedgewar organized an Officers' Training Camp (OTC), which has now evolved into the Sangh Shiksha Varg (SSV), focused on the objective of man-making. Through a combination of discipline, intellectual discourse (*baudhik*), physical training (*sharirik*) and service (*seva*), volunteers are inducted into the organization. People from different parts of the country and diverse backgrounds come together to stay in these camps.

We visited one of these Sangh Shiksha Vargs in Hojai, Assam, and found students—used to speaking in different dialects and languages, wearing different traditional clothes and having different food habits—chatting and laughing in broken Hindi while also trying to learn each other's languages, donning the iconic white shirt and khaki shorts, and sitting together on the same floor, irrespective of rank, eating the same *bhojan* (food) and cleaning their own plates.

This fosters unbreakable friendships and bonds of love and brotherhood, while promoting mutual respect for diversity and a common bond of national unity. Those who emerge from these camps become karyakartas, renouncing professional and family lives to dedicate themselves to the service of not just the Sangh but also the nation.

The second dice was expanding the institutional structure of the Sangh, not just within Maharashtra but throughout the country. Dr Hedgewar himself, the founder of the organization, was 35 years 'young' when he started its first shakha with a group of young boys on an open ground, where they played some interesting Indian games together.[78] The first pracharaks of the RSS were tasked with the responsibility of setting up as many shakhas as possible—first in Nagpur, then across Maharashtra,

[78]Ibid.

then in the Indian heartland, and later into the greater Indian landscape, such as the Northeast.

But what is a shakha? Simply put, a shakha is a daily gathering of swayamsevaks of different age groups at a predefined meeting place or ground for one hour. The daily routine includes physical exercises, singing patriotic chorus, group discussions on a varied range of subjects, and a prayer for the motherland. Even today, the most common mode of recruitment in RSS shakhas is the open playing field. The common theme running through all of these games is the importance of working together as a team and the sportsman spirit. A young boy slowly gets involved in this fun-loving group effortlessly. He also ends up learning the importance of discipline, time management and physical fitness. This is a daily activity, thus reinforcing good habits regularly.

The thought behind this unique set of tools or working style of the RSS through the daily shakhas is that a person should willingly dedicate at least one hour of their day to the nation. Once this thought becomes a part of his personality, he shall willingly increase his participation as the nation demands.

The third sarsanghchalak of RSS, the late Balasaheb Deoras, said:

> The RSS Shakha is not just a place to play games or parade, but an unsaid promise of the protection of the good citizenry, an acculturation forum to keep the young away from undesirable addictions; it is a centre of hope, for rapid action and undemanding help in case of emergencies and crisis that affect the people. It is a guarantee of the unafraid movement of women and a powerful deterrent to indecent behaviour towards them, also a powerful threat to the brutal and anti-national forces. But the most important aspect is [that] it is a university for training the appropriate workers to be made available for the requirements of the various fields of life of the nation. And the medium to

achieve all this is the games we play on the grounds of [the] RSS Shakha.[79]

These shakhas became the working units of the RSS in its early days.

The Philosophy of the Sangh—Decoding the Sangh Constitution

The Preamble of the Constitution of the Rashtriya Swayamsevak Sangh highlights the following:

'Whereas in the disintegrated condition of the country it was considered necessary to have an Organization:

(a) to eradicate the fissiparous tendencies arising from diversities of sect, faith, caste and creed and from political, economic, linguistic and provincial differences, amongst Hindus;
(b) to make them realise the greatness of their past;
(c) to inculcate in them a spirit of service, sacrifice and selfless devotion to the Hindu Samaj, as a whole;
(d) to build up an organised and well-disciplined corporate life; and
(e) to bring about an all-round regeneration of the Hindu Samaj;'

These five principles form the basis of the philosophy of the Sangh, an institution rooted in 'व्यक्ति निर्माण से राष्ट्र निर्माण' or man-making for nation-building, based on selfless service for national unity, religious renaissance.[80]

One figure, among all, was pivotal in shaping the philosophy of the Sangh—Madhav Sadashivrao Golwalkar, lovingly called

---

[79]Saxena, Anurag, *Demystifying RSS*, BFC Publications, India, 2021.

[80]'The Constitution of the Rashtriya Swayamsevak Sangh', Bodleian Library, Oxford University, https://tinyurl.com/2krvcsfs. Accessed on 06 May 2025.

Guruji, the second sarsanghchalak. Following Hedgewar's death in 1940, Guruji Golwalkar assumed leadership of the RSS and rapidly expanded it into a nationwide organization. He emphasized India as the sacred homeland of Hindus and advocated defending religion and culture as the means to attain freedom. Lamenting India's ancient glory being marred by successive foreign invasions, Golwalkar advocated for a 'national regeneration'.[81] He believed this revival could only occur by reinstating the Hindu identity.

Rejecting the idea of 'territorial nationalism', which equated statehood with territorial boundaries and granted equal citizenship rights to all inhabitants, Golwalkar argued that a nation was defined by its people, not its land.[82] For him, Hindus constituted the essence of the Indian nation. Golwalkar and the RSS fervently advocated for 'cultural nationalism', in stark contrast to civic nationalism. This distinction highlights their belief that cultural heritage and identity, particularly Hinduism, should form the cornerstone of Indian nationalism.

Guruji's charismatic aura and fiery speeches inspired many swayamsevaks to passionately promote the mission of the Sangh across the length and breadth of the country, inspiring the masses to adopt a cultural nationalism rooted in the universalist philosophy of the Sanatana Dharma.[83] A huge part of this outreach focused on reaching places that were hitherto considered unreachable and winning the hearts of people hitherto unwinnable, particularly in the Christian-majority areas. In fact, Golwalkar had strong opinions about conversions and actively encouraged his cadre to convince people to readopt their original faith. He once remarked:

'It is not conversion into Hinduism. It is only giving an

[81]Golwalkar, Madhav Sadashivrao, *Spotlight,* Rashtrotthana Sahitya, Bangalore, 1974.
[82]Ibid.
[83]Ibid.

opportunity for those who had been made to change the faith by force of circumstances in the past, to return to their ancestral faith. Is it not a fact that only a handful of Muslims and Christians came to our country from outside? All the rest have only changed their faith for well-known reasons. Returning to one's ancestral faith is not conversion at all. It is merely homecoming.'[84]

This led pracharaks into the Northeast, which fell under the Poorvanchal Kshetra (area/region), consisting of Bengal, Odisha and the Northeast, headquartered at Kolkata.

The Northeast in Sangh Imagination

In the face of existing challenges in the Northeast that we described above, the Rashtriya Swayamsevak Sangh extended its ideology into the region. However, as elucidated in great detail above, the Northeast was the toughest terrain for the Sangh to operate on. One of the primary methods employed by the RSS to spread its ideology in the Northeast was through grassroots organizing and the establishment of shakhas among local communities. In October 1946, three pracharaks—Dadarao Parmarth, Vasantrao Oak and Krishna Paranjpe—initiated the establishment of the inaugural RSS shakhas in Guwahati, Shillong and Dibrugarh, marking the organization's entry into Assam.[85] When we interviewed the earliest pracharaks who came to the Northeast during this time, which includes a nonagenarian, we were told about how apprehensive people were about the Sangh as an 'outsider' organization. Yet, this did not deter the first pracharaks and swayamsevaks who came here, determined to achieve two key objectives: first, counter Islamic

---

[84]Ibid.

[85]Gupta, Smita, 'How the RSS grew roots in the North-East', *The Hindu Business Line*, 09 March 2018, https://tinyurl.com/2s57k3rh. Accessed on 12 February 2025.

fundamentalism and prevent the Muslim League's total capture of Assam; and second, stop the high rate of forced conversions to Christianity.

To achieve the first goal, the Sangh vehemently backed the local Congress leadership helmed by Gopinath Bordoloi, who went on to become the first Chief Minister of Assam. The role of the Sangh Parivar and Hindu Mahasabha in preventing the total capture of Assam by the Saadulla-led Muslim League is well documented. The great freedom fighter Pushpalata Das said that Assam could not have been saved from being merged with East Pakistan by Gopinath Bordoloi alone if Dr Syama Prasad Mookerjee did not actively lend his support, strategize and fight to retain Assam in India.[86]

When Dr Mookerjee became the vice chancellor of Calcutta University in 1935, he introduced the Assamese language and hired Birinchi Kumar Barua to convene over the course.[87] He wanted the diverse cohort of the university to appreciate and learn the Assamese language, and read the state's rich indigenous history and culture, thereby promoting a sense of national belonging. In the later years, he travelled to several parts of Assam and stayed there, understanding the socio-political realities of the state. When partition became unavoidable, he advocated for the retention of Assam within the Indian Union and also worked for the resettlement of Hindu refugees coming in from erstwhile East Pakistan.

We interviewed one former pracharak—who later became a *grihasta* (householder)—Gurupada Bhowmick, whose family migrated to Assam during the partition.[88] He talked about the

---

[86]Bora, Mita Nath, 'Dr Syama Prasad Mookerjee: A Saviour of Assam & Protector of Hindus', Dr. Syama Prasad Mookerjee Research Foundation, 22 June 2022, https://tinyurl.com/3hpjp4re. Accessed on 06 May 2025.
[87]Ibid.
[88]Interview with Gurupada Bhowmick.

resettlement and how—due to the active work done by the Sangh for the protection of Hindu migrants—many young boys volunteered to join the RSS.[89] His elder brother, late Narayan Chandra Bhowmick, worked as one of the early pracharaks in Tinsukia district of Upper Assam, and came in contact with Thakur Ram Singh, who was given the responsibility of the Assam prant in 1949.[90] However, that is a story we shall tell later.

---

[89]Ibid.

[90]Ibid.

2

Early Days of the Republic

On the midnight of 15 August 1947, Jawaharlal Nehru declared India's 'tryst with destiny', marking the nation's emergence as an independent and sovereign republic. But a starkly different reality unfolded in India's northeast. Here, tales of exclusion, othering and victimhood permeated the political landscape. Particularly for the newly formed Indian state's Central leadership, the Northeast represented a distant frontier rich in resources but inhabited by perceived outsiders who held little political sway. Prime Minister Nehru's apprehensions in 1952 highlighted this sentiment, as he expressed concerns that the region lacked a 'feeling of oneness with the rest of India'.[91]

The narratives of exclusion persisted across generations, perpetuating a racial gaze that marginalized the Northeast in the collective imagination of the Indian nation. The Northeast became the 'other', relegated to the fringes of national consciousness. This sense of otherness manifested in the treatment of the region's diverse ethnic groups and the rigid, hierarchical dynamics characterizing interactions between the nation and its peripheries. Despite being an integral part

[91]Barooah, Nabaarun, 'Assam, Manipur, Mizoram, Nagaland And Yet More: What The Congress Still Has To Answer For In Northeast', *Swarajya*, 23 July 2023, https://tinyurl.com/5br42war. Accessed on 14 February 2025.

of the Indian state, the Northeast remained on the margins, grappling with the consequences of being cast as outsiders in their own homeland.

The Predicament of the Nagas

As a result of this lack of belonging, triggered by an abject lack of support from the Centre, the Northeast became a hotbed of secessionist movements.

The saga of the Greater Nagaland movement stands as one of the oldest insurgencies in Indian history with its origins going back to the 1920s. It was formalized in 1946 when the Naga National Council (NNC) was established under the Naga nationalist leader Dr Angami Zapu Phizo. A significant development came with the signing of the Nine-Point Agreement between NNC leaders and Assam's Governor, Sir Akbar Hydari.[92] This agreement granted the Naga community extensive rights over judiciary, executive, legislative, taxation, lands and autonomy; but a clause regarding the governor's special responsibility for ten years sowed seeds of discontent. Interpretations of this clause varied greatly between the Nagas and the Indian government, leading to simmering tensions, especially over the proposal of the ten-year-long 'experimental coexistence' with the Indian nation. The agreement was signed between Governor Hydari and the moderates of the NNC movement. However, this was done without taking into consideration the opinions of the main leaders, including Phizo. In addition, the confusion in interpretation of the ninth clause led to deep disagreements and thus the Nine-Point Phizo-Akbar Hydari Agreement was rejected, declaring Naga independence

[92]Srikanth, H., and C.J. Thomas, 'Naga Resistance Movement and the Peace Process in Northeast India', *Peace and Democracy in South Asia*, Vol. 1, No. 2, 2005, pp. 57–87, https://tinyurl.com/yub5e26r. Accessed on 14 February 2025.

on 14 August 1947, and organizing a plebiscite in 1951 to affirm Naga sovereignty.[93]

Initially, the movement was primarily political, marked by divisions between pacifists and extremists. However, the tides shifted dramatically in the 1950s, transforming the movement into a militant struggle for independence. The pivotal moment came in 1953, during a public rally addressed by Prime Minister Nehru and his Burmese counterpart U Nu. Members of the Naga National Council staged a walkout when the erstwhile deputy commissioner of Assam refused permission to an NNC delegation to meet Nehru.[94] A local adage describes how NNC members—donning their traditional attire—had walked out slapping their bare bottoms, enraging Nehru.[95] This singular event permanently damaged the relationship between the Central government and the Naga people, leading to the sending of armed troops to the Naga Hills. The Yengpang Massacre of 15 November 1954 ensued, marking a dark chapter in the Naga people's struggle. Further atrocities unfolded in 1960, including the Matikhrü Massacre where numerous Naga individuals were ruthlessly beheaded by the military.[96]

These incidents marked the genesis of the Nagalim insurgency which persists to this day. Radical factions within the NNC formed the Federal Government of Nagaland, including an underground Naga Army, intensifying the conflict.

---

[93]Ibid.

[94]Laba, Yambem, 'The Naga Question', *The Statesman*, 09 January 2017, https://tinyurl.com/2p9kk2uy. Accessed on January 24, 2025.

[95]Ibid.

[96]Katiry, Rev. Zhiwhuotho, 'Pochury Black Day and Massacre of Matikhrü Village by Indian Army On September 6th 1960', *Morung Express*, 05 September 2017, https://tinyurl.com/79kz9zus. Accessed on 17 February 2025.

The Mizo-Manipur Chapter

Before Mizoram attained statehood in 1987, Mizo-dominated areas were part of Assam's Lushai Hills district.[97] The Mizo Union and other organizations had long protested against the discriminatory treatment by the Assam government, advocating for a separate state for the Mizos. The discontent escalated when the Assam government imposed Assamese as the official language in 1960, disregarding the Mizo language, fuelling further dissent, protests and unrest among the Mizos.

In another case, in the year 1959, the Lushai Hills were struck by *mautâm*, an ecological phenomenon triggered by the flowering of a bamboo species.[98] This event led to a surge in the population of black rats due to the abundance of bamboo seeds. When the seeds were depleted, the rats ventured into human settlements, causing plagues and famines. Despite pleas from the severely affected Mizo people, the Indian government remained indifferent. In response, Pu Laldenga formed the Mizo National Famine Front, which later evolved into the Mizo National Front (MNF), an armed group that revolted against the apathetic Indian state.

The culmination of grievances led to the emergence of the MNF, which spearheaded a secessionist movement seeking independence from India. While the Mizo Union, the first political party of Mizoram which later merged with the Congress, initially aimed for a separate state within India, the MNF envisioned a sovereign Mizo nation. The extremist faction within the MNF advocated violence to achieve their goals, establishing the Mizo National Army and the Mizo

---

[97]Barooah, Nabaarun, 'Assam, Manipur, Mizoram, Nagaland And Yet More: What The Congress Still Has To Answer For In Northeast', *Swarajya Magazine*, 23 July 2023, https://tinyurl.com/5br42war. Accessed on 12 February 2025.
[98]Ibid.

National Volunteers. With support from East Pakistan (now Bangladesh), the MNF intensified its activities, recruiting volunteers and amassing weapons. Amidst the political turmoil, the MNF devised Operation Jericho to seize power in the Mizo district.[99] The plan involved capturing key establishments, neutralizing opposition, and hoisting the MNF flag in Aizawl. The MNF leaders hoped for international recognition of the Mizo territory as a sovereign nation. On 1 March 1966, the armed insurrection was set in motion, with simultaneous attacks planned on military posts.[100] The stage was set for a dramatic showdown between the MNF and the Indian state, as the struggle for Mizo autonomy reached its zenith.[101] By early 1966, the MNF had seized control of major towns and rural centres in Mizoram, such as Aizawl and Lunglei.[102]

Meanwhile, for over 1,900 years, the kingdom of Meitei, also known as Meitei Leipak or Kangleipak, had flourished as a sovereign entity, marked by both alliances and conflicts with neighbouring Burma.[103] However, its sovereignty was dealt a blow in 1891 during the Anglo-Manipur War.[104] Despite briefly regaining independence in 1947, thanks to the tumultuous events of the time—including the controversial Manipur Merger

---

[99]Joshi, Piravi, 'A Peaceful Resolution? Analysing Sustained Peace and Order in Mizoram', *E-International Relations*, 26 November 2022. https://tinyurl.com/5t57d5nd. Accessed on 08 May 2025.

[100]Chadha, Vivek, 'India's Counterinsurgency Campaign in Mizoram', In *India and Counterinsurgency: Lessons Learned*, Sumit Ganguly and David P. Fidler (eds.), Routledge, 2009, p. 41.

[101]Bareh, H.M., *Encyclopaedia of North-East India: Mizoram*, Mittal Publications, New Delhi, 2000, p. 179.

[102]Ibid.

[103]Patnaik, Jagadish Kumar, *Mizoram, Dimensions and Perspectives: Society, Economy, and Polity*, Concept Publishing Company, Delhi, 2008, p. 32.

[104]Singh, Pandit N. Khelchandra, 'The Historical, Archaeological, Religious & Cultural Significance Of "Kangla": The Ancient Citadel Of Manipur', E-Pao Books!, https://tinyurl.com/3j7svv5a. Accessed on 08 May 2025.

Agreement of 1949—its freedom was short-lived. During the nineteenth century, Hijam Irabot emerged as a key figure in Manipur, advocating for nationalism and challenging the monarchical rule in favour of democratic governance.[105] His actions laid the groundwork for a wave of demands, from self-determination to full liberation, rooted in the rejection of the merger agreement with India. Scholars like Paula Banerjee highlight how the agreement was viewed by Manipuris as an unlawful annexation.[106] Asserting the sovereignty of Manipur, Meitei and Pangal (a term used to refer to Manipuri Muslims) nationalists began rallying around the Manipur State Constitution Act of 1947 which outlined democratic governance.[107] It was argued that Maharaja Bodhchandra Singh lacked the authority to sign the merger agreement, further fuelling dissent against the integration with India.

Irabot, now a prominent leader of the Communist Party of Manipur, maintained close ties with the Communist Party of Burma to facilitate the training of his party's militant wing, the Red Guards.[108] Following Irabot's death, the movement fractured into multiple factions. The first separatist group to emerge during the second wave of the insurgency was the United National Liberation Front (UNLF), founded on 24 November 1964.[109] In 1969, during

---

[105]Ibid.

[106]Banerjee, Paula, and Sucharita Sengupta, 'New Capital, Emerging Conflicts and Social Governance in Northeast India; Nagaland and Manipur', 2017, https://tinyurl.com/nwzeun9d. Accessed on 08 May 2025.

[107]Sotinkumar, L., 'How Irawat became a communist', *The Sangai Express*, 30 September 2010, https://tinyurl.com/5c7vskxt. Accessed on 17 February 2025.

[108]Parratt, John, and Saroj Arambam Parratt, 'Hijam Irabot and the Radical Socialist Democratic Movement in Manipur', *Internationales Asienforum*, Vol. 31, No. 3-4, 2000, pp. 275-288, https://tinyurl.com/4dmsrt82. Accessed on 17 February 2025.

[109]Ganguly, Sumit, and David P. Fidler (eds.), *India and Counterinsurgency: Lessons Learned*, Routledge, 2009, p. 77.

a visit by Prime Minister Indira Gandhi to the state, protesters threw stones at her, leading to a violent crackdown by police that resulted in several deaths.[110] In the 1970s, discontent reached its peak with the formation of multiple secessionist organizations, including the People's Liberation Army of Manipur (PLA), the People's Revolutionary Party of Kangleipak (PREPAK), and the Kangleipak Communist Party (KCP), all of which soon joined the ongoing armed struggle.[111] The Naga nationalist movement, led by the National Socialist Council of Nagaland (NSCN) in the neighbouring state, also began to influence Manipur, where it garnered significant support, particularly among local groups such as the Kuki National Front.[112]

The Assam Episode

Between 1946 and 1958, Assam became home to over half a million Bengali refugees. However, the situation worsened after the 1964 East Pakistan riots, leading to a surge in the number of refugees arriving in Assam, reaching over a million by 1968.[113] Despite Assam's limited resources and capacity to accommodate such large numbers, the inflow of refugees continued, exacerbated by natural disasters like earthquakes and floods that diverted attention and resources towards disaster management.

The Central government's response to the refugee crisis was largely inadequate. Although the issue of immigration

---

[110]'History of Manipur Police', Manipur Police, https://tinyurl.com/yxc3nf5t. Accessed on 08 May 2025.

[111]Centre for Development and Peace Studies, 'Overview: Insurgency & Peace Efforts in Manipur', https://tinyurl.com/bdhr8brt. Accessed on 17 February 2025.

[112]Ibid.

[113]Mukhopadhyay, Kali Prasad, *Partition, Bengal and After: The Great Tragedy of India*, Reference Press, New Delhi, 2007, p. 134.

fell under the Union List, the government failed to establish proper mechanisms to address the influx of migrants into Assam.[114] Despite appeals from Assam's political leadership for legislation to prevent the entry of undesirable persons, the Central government remained passive. In 1950, after persistent efforts by Gopinath Bordoloi, the Immigrants (Expulsion from Assam) Act was passed to address the issue.[115] But it proved ineffective in practice due to a lack of proper machinery and support from the Centre.

Moreover, the directives regarding granting political rights to refugees further complicated the situation, with the Centre's relaxed approach blurring the line between genuine refugees and illegal immigrants. The refugee crisis became a source of friction between Assam and the Central government. By 1950, Assam had already provided shelter to hundreds of thousands of displaced individuals, straining its resources and exacerbating economic woes. However, Prime Minister Nehru's threat to withhold financial aid if Assam opposed further settlement of refugees demonstrated the Centre's disregard for the state's predicament.[116] Meanwhile, Assam's economic woes deepened with the diversion of crude oil to a refinery in Barauni, Bihar, instead of establishing refineries within the state.

This decision sparked widespread agitation in Assam in 1957, called the Refinery Movement, where '*Tej dim, tel nidiu*'

---

[114]Barpujari, H.K., 'GENERAL PRESIDENT'S ADDRESS: NORTH-EAST INDIA: THE PROBLEMS AND POLICIES SINCE 1947', *Proceedings of the Indian History Congress*, Vol. 56, 1995, pp. 1–73, https://tinyurl.com/54f5hjwe. Accessed on 14 February 2025.

[115]Sarma, Sanghamitra, 'IMMIGRATION ISSUE IN ASSAM (1947–1957) A HISTORICAL PERSPECTIVE', *The Indian Journal of Political Science*, Vol. 75, No. 3, 2014, pp. 531–542.

[116]Bhattacharya, Rajeev, 'Nehru ignored Assam's economic crisis to welcome refugees, threatened to halt financial aid', *The Print*, 26 December 2023, https://tinyurl.com/3jxw83km. Accessed on 12 February 2025.

(We will give blood but not oil) became a popular rallying cry for regionalist sentiments.[117] However, the Centre's neglect persisted, further exacerbated by the looming threat of the People's Liberation Army's advance through neighbouring Arunachal Pradesh, adding to Assam's concerns and challenges.

The RSS Intervention

The manifold challenges faced by the Northeast, compounded by the lack of robust state infrastructure and perceived neglect from the Central government, spurred the emergence of civil society organizations as pivotal actors in promoting welfare and addressing societal needs. Recognizing the vacuum left by inadequate governance, these organizations took on increasingly significant roles in advancing development initiatives and advocating for the rights of marginalized communities. Amidst this landscape, organizations such as the Rashtriya Swayamsevak Sangh extended their reach into the region, aiming to provide support and bolster the indigenous tribes.

The RSS extended its reach to Assam more than two decades after its foundation in 1925. The first RSS shakha in the Northeast was inaugurated in Guwahati, near the Brahmaputra River at the Shukreshwar Temple, on 28 October 1946.[118] According to RSS's own records, the establishment of RSS activities in Assam was attributed to the efforts of Keshav Dev Bawri, a young Marwari entrepreneur and proprietor of the Mahavir Byayam Sangh gymnasium in Fancy Bazar. Bawri, closely associated with Shankarlal Sharma, a member of Mahavir Byayam Sangh who

[117]Sarma, Sanghamitra, 'IMMIGRATION ISSUE IN ASSAM (1947-1957) A HISTORICAL PERSPECTIVE', *The Indian Journal of Political Science*, Vol. 75, No. 3, 2014, pp. 531–542.

[118]Nath, Nandalal, *Osom Kshetrar Sangh Karjyar Itihas*, Rouhin Deb and Nabaarun Barooah (trans.), Prachi Prakashan, Guwahati, 2020.

had some knowledge of the RSS, wrote to the RSS leadership in Delhi, urging them to establish a presence in Assam. Responding positively, the RSS sent three experienced pracharaks from Maharashtra—Dadarao Parmarth, Vasant Rao Oak and Krishna Paranjpe—to Guwahati on 27 October 1946.[119] Parmarth became the first pracharak of Assam, while his colleagues were delegated to Shillong, Silchar and Dibrugarh. Additional pracharaks like Bhau Mulkar, Dutta Bandisht, Kulkarni, Sahasrabhojne and Manohar Gurjar arrived subsequently to further RSS activities in the region.[120] During this period, Sylhet was a part of Assam, and Manohar Gurjar was designated as the pracharak there.[121] Guwahati's first significant event was the unification and assembly of these shakhas in October 1947.

However, in the aftermath of Mahatma Gandhi's assassination in 1948, the Rashtriya Swayamsevak Sangh was banned by the Central government, facing accusations of involvement in the heinous crime. The organization endured significant negative publicity, being portrayed as anti-Muslim, violent and culpable for Gandhi's murder. In response, RSS members—including 52 activists from the Assam unit, such as Keshav Dev Bawri, Girish Kalita, Shankarlal Tiwari and Prafulla Kumar Bora from Guwahati—launched a nationwide satyagraha in December 1948. Dadarao Parmarth was arrested and held in Shillong Jail.

Eknath Ranade, then the *sarkaryavah* (general secretary) of the RSS, earned the moniker of 'underground sarsanghchalak' as he navigated the turbulent waters of opposition. With conviction and steely determination, Eknath Ranade embarked on a mission to clear the RSS's name. He approached Sardar Patel, the deputy prime minister and a stalwart figure in India's political landscape.

---

[119]Ibid.

[120]Bhattacharjee, Malini, 'Tracing the emergence and consolidation of Hindutva in Assam', *Economic and Political Weekly*, Vol. 51, No. 16, 2016, pp. 80–87.

[121]Ibid.

Patel, known as the Iron Man of India, was struck by Eknath Ranade's resolve and integrity.

In a phone call with an unknown individual, Patel lauded Eknath Ranade's character, affirming his belief in the innocence of the RSS regarding Gandhi's assassination. Patel claimed, 'People call me Iron Man, but Eknath ji is not just a man of iron but also a man of steel. He is a man of unwavering conviction and I'm convinced that RSS had no hand in Gandhi assassination.'[122] Eknath Ranade's efforts bore fruit when the ban on the RSS was lifted in 1949. Undeterred by the challenges, he continued his service to society, taking on the role of the *kshetra pracharak* for the Poorvanchal Kshetra in Calcutta.

After the ban was lifted in July 1949, Dadarao Parmarth departed due to illness, and Dattopant Thengdi succeeded him. Manohar Rao Harekar, prant pracharak of Bengal, also oversaw RSS activities in Assam temporarily. Towards the end of November 1949, Thakur Ram Singh from Punjab was appointed as the prant pracharak of Assam. During this period, Bengal, Assam and Orissa were under the supervision of Eknath Ranade. It was here that he witnessed the plight of Partition refugees first-hand.

In the wake of the riots that ravaged East Pakistan after India's partition, the RSS saw an opportunity to extend its helping hand. Guruji Golwalkar visited Guwahati for the first time in 1949 to participate in the Press Milan programme. He entrusted Eknath Ranade with a crucial mission that included organizing relief camps for Bengali Hindu refugees who sought sanctuary in Assam and Bengal. Thus, the Vastuhara Sahayata Samiti was born, with its headquarters in Calcutta and operations spanning West Bengal and Assam.

Beyond providing basic necessities, the committee assisted refugees in finding employment, forging strong bonds with the displaced Bengali Hindu population, who became staunch

---

[122]Ibid.

supporters of the organization. As the years passed, the RSS continued its tireless efforts to serve and uplift communities in need. In 1957, a significant milestone was achieved with the organization of the first regional camp in Nagaon, where 308 dedicated swayamsevaks gathered, their hearts united in the spirit of service and compassion.[123] From the rubble of disaster and the plight of refugees, emerged tales of resilience, camaraderie and the commitment of the RSS to stand by those in distress.

On the night of 15 August 1950, an earthquake jolted the state of Assam, shaking its very foundations and leaving a trail of destruction in its wake.[124] As the tremors subsided, the people of Upper Assam found themselves grappling with the aftermath of nature's wrath, compounded by heavy floods off Brahmaputra—and its tributaries like the Dehang—engulfing the region. In the midst of the chaos, a glimmer of hope emerged. The Marwari Relief Society of Calcutta, closely affiliated with the RSS, effectively responded to the crisis, dispatching workers to aid in relief efforts.[125] Meanwhile, the Assam branch of the RSS mobilized its resources, establishing the Assam Bhukamp Pidit Sahayata Samiti, a society dedicated to providing aid to the earthquake-stricken populace. They proactively distributed essentials like food, clothing and shelter, offering solace to countless victims and earning the heartfelt gratitude of the local communities.

Subsequently, in 1951, Guruji Golwalkar attended another programme for RSS swayamsevaks in Guwahati, which also welcomed citizens. The event commenced with a *jan sabha* (general assembly), providing a platform for discourse and engagement, followed by a *karyakarta baithak* (functionary

[123] Ibid.

[124] Interview with Pravin Dabholkar.

[125] Kavishwar, Sandip, *Mrityunjay Veer*, Rouhin Deb and Nabaarun Barooah, Prachi Prakashan, Guwahati, 2022.

meet), where organizational matters were discussed. The city's learned citizens were invited to participate in this initiative.

However, socialist and Congress factions opposed to the RSS declared that the leader of an organization allegedly involved in Mahatma Gandhi's assassination would not be allowed entry into Guwahati. They threatened to block his arrival from the airport. In response to this, a firm stance was adopted against any attempts to obstruct the event under the resolute guidance of Prant Pracharak Thakur Ram Singh. This determination galvanized all swayamsevaks and supporters to ensure its success. They coordinated efforts to ensure timely execution of the event and ensure Guruji's safe arrival from the airport to Guwahati. Swayamsevaks, displaying unity and vigilance, encircled the event venue at Machkhowa Field, equipped with sticks to maintain security.[126] Despite facing challenges and opposition, the event took place according to schedule, showcasing the commitment and collective resolve of the RSS community to surmount obstacles and uphold their principles.

Upholding RSS's commitment, Guruji condemned the efforts of the Christian missionaries to convert people—particularly in tribal areas—and accused them of being part of a global plot to Christianize India. In a report dated 19 June 1950, the *Organiser* expressed concerns that Assam's tribal population, residing in both plains and hills, was becoming increasingly distant from the broader Assamese community, risking their cultural assimilation.[127] Publications affiliated with the Sangh Parivar asserted that many tribes in Assam were originally Indic and continue to adhere to Sanatan practices, despite their perceived 'primitive' religious beliefs. For instance, the Mikirs were said to chant the name of Lord Ram and revere the Tulsi plant, while

[126]Bhattacharjee, Malini, 'Tracing the emergence and consolidation of Hindutva in Assam', *Economic and Political Weekly*, Vol. 51, No. 16, 2016, pp. 80–87.
[127]Ibid.

refraining from killing or consuming cows. The RSS argued that Christian missionaries have systematically turned these 'simple mountain folk' against their own indigenous faiths, using strategic approaches such as establishing schools, hospitals and other welfare services to entice tribal communities away from their traditional beliefs.[128]

Between 1946 and 1950, Guwahati had just six RSS shakhas. In 1952, a swayamsevak called Vishnu Verma arrived in Assam. By this time, RSS shakhas had been established in major cities like Shillong, Dibrugarh, Kamrup, Nagaon and Silchar in Assam, and Imphal in Manipur. For the very first time in the year 1951, about five *jan siksharthi*s (teachers) went to Nagpur as part of the first year of training. From 1952 till 1960, siksharthis from Assam travelled to Nagpur and other states for first-, second- and third-year training.

In 1952, when the Sangh first made its mark among the Meitei people of Manipur, only three people attended the Sangh Siksha Varg (OTC). The first Sangh shakha of Khasi Hills, Shillong division, was started in 1952. The first pracharak was Sudarshan Sharma and the first *zila pracharak* was Srikant Joshi. Around the same time, the seeds of a significant movement were quietly sown in Tripura by Ganesh Deb Sharma. Despite his dedication, the progress was slow, hampered by a shortage of dedicated pracharaks committed to the cause. For nearly two decades, the work proceeded at a modest pace, building a foundation but struggling to gain widespread momentum.

The RSS established the Pahari Sewa Sangh in the 1950s, aiming for the 'economic, moral, and social upliftment' of tribal communities.[129] This body focused on fostering social

---

[128]Nath, Nandalal, *Osom Kshetrar Sangh Karjyar Itihas*, Rouhin Deb and Nabaarun Barooah (trans.), Prachi Prakashan, Guwahati, 2020.

[129]Bhattacharjee, Malini, 'Tracing the emergence and consolidation of Hindutva in Assam', *Economic and Political Weekly*, Vol. 51, No. 16, 2016, pp. 80–87.

connections; RSS volunteers were deployed in tribal areas, actively participating in the daily lives of tribals, constructing small temples, repairing roads and organizing religious gatherings. The Pahari Sewa Sangh's activities gained momentum when they were absorbed by the Vanavasi Kalyan Ashram. Although the Akhil Bharatiya Vanavasi Kalyan Ashram was founded in 1977, its Assam chapter began in 1978. Their initial efforts were concentrated on establishing hostels and medical facilities in tribal-dominated regions like Udalgiri, Diphu, Mayabagh, North Lakhimpur and Dhemaji. Over time, cultural centres, schools and preschools were also set up.

In the tense backdrop of the 1962 Sino-Indian War, China's covert ingress into Tezpur—amidst the looming shadow of the Cuban Missile Crisis—reverberated through the corridors of Indian leadership, stirring profound apprehension and urgency. As Prime Minister Nehru grappled with the unfolding crisis, the infiltration exposed an abject failure in India's defence strategy, casting a sombre cloud over the nation's security under his stewardship. When government officials stationed in Tezpur fled during the war, Sangh pracharaks and karyakartas went there to support the locals. They also went door to door, narrating stories of horror, oppression and massacre of Tibetan Buddhists, and the desecration of monasteries, convincing people to resist the Chinese. After the Chinese declared a ceasefire and withdrew, the Sangh began its operations in Arunachal, preventing it from following the path of Nagaland. This proactive stance ensured sustained efforts to bolster Indian identity and resist external influence, marking a crucial chapter in safeguarding India's territorial integrity and promoting national unity.

Another important RSS-affiliated organization founded around this time was the Vishva Hindu Parishad (VHP). Established by Guruji in 1964, the VHP quickly gained ground, establishing its Assam branch in Guwahati in 1966 under

Dadasaheb Aptekar. Venturing into the North Cachar Hills of Assam, the organization established a foothold in the small town of Haflong by inaugurating a residential school for 60 tribal students. By 1969, the VHP was active in approximately 45 villages, setting up hostels for tribal students, homoeopathic clinics, dispensaries, and arranging medical care.[130] It also initiated Ekal Vidyalayas (single-teacher schools) to instil 'Hindu values' in students from remote villages.[131]

Additionally, the VHP prioritized mass outreach, organizing *sammelans* to connect with various like-minded organizations and individuals. After its inaugural conference in Guwahati in 1967, the VHP organized its second conference in Jorhat in 1969, where it invited numerous tribal delegates from neighbouring states such as Arunachal Pradesh, Meghalaya and Nagaland. During the conference, a debate emerged regarding whether the *janajati*s could be considered Hindus despite their consumption of beef. Guruji addressed this by persuading the mathadheesh of Pejawara Matha of Udupi, H.H. Sri Sri Vishvesha Tirtha Swamiji, and other influential *satradhikar*s (leaders of satras or Vaishnavik monastic institutions) present that janajatis, inherently Hindu, lacked proper exposure to Hindu teachings due to societal isolation. He argued that their alienation from Hindu traditions, such as cow worship, was not their fault. Therefore, it was imperative to embrace janajatis as part of Hindu society without hesitation.

In the conclave, Guruji Golwalkar affirmed that janajatis are Hindus, attributing their beef consumption to economic necessity in remote hilly regions.[132] He criticized the lack of effort from culturally advanced individuals to educate these

[130]Ibid.

[131]Nath, Nandalal, *Osom Kshetrar Sangh Karjyar Itihas*, Rouhin Deb and Nabaarun Barooah (trans.), Prachi Prakashan, Guwahati, 2020.

[132]Ibid.

communities about Hinduism. Guruji reinforced this by sharing a meal with janajati leaders and urged Hindu unity, encouraging satradhikars to strengthen connections among themselves and with other Hindu leaders.

Establishing alliances against Christian missionaries, the VHP also collaborated with local tribal leaders, including Rani Gaidinliu, known for her resistance against British rule and Christian missionary influence on Zeliangrong Naga culture in Manipur.[133] In a small Manipuri village named Luangkao, in the year 1915, Gaidinliu was born into the Rongmei Naga tribe.[134] At the tender age of sixteen, she inherited the noble cause of her cousin, Haipou Jadonang, a revered spiritual leader of the Rongmeis. Jadonang envisioned the end of British rule, a revival of Zeliangrong religion, and the establishment of Naga self-rule.

Fearlessly stepping into his shoes, Gaidinliu led a valiant resistance against the British oppressors. Despite enduring a staggering fourteen years behind bars, she remained undaunted.[135] Even after India gained independence, Gaidinliu's battle continued, this time against Christian missionaries whom she saw as a threat to her people's cultural heritage. Under her guidance, a movement rooted in traditional nationalism emerged, challenging the dominance of Christianity-influenced Naga nationalism. Gaidinliu's spirit stood as a beacon of hope in the face of cultural erosion and ideological conflict. The Baptist Church was also opposed to her working for the revival of the traditional Naga indigenous faith Heraka. The NNC leaders considered her actions an obstacle to their own movement. The Baptist leaders deemed the Heraka revival movement anti-

---

[133]Longkumer, Arkotong, 'Religious and economic reform: The Gaidinliu movement and the Heraka in the North Cachar Hills', *South Asia: Journal of South Asian Studies*, Vol. 30, No. 3, 2007, pp. 499–515.

[134]Ibid.

[135]Nath, Nandalal, *Osom Kshetrar Sangh Karjyar Itihas*, Rouhin Deb and Nabaarun Barooah (trans.), Prachi Prakashan, Guwahati, 2020.

Christian and she was warned of serious consequences if she were not to change her stand. In order to defend the Heraka culture and strengthen her position, she went underground in 1960. In 1966, after six years of hard underground life in her old age, Rani Gaidinliu came out from her jungle hideout under an agreement with the government of India to work for the betterment of her people through peaceful, democratic and non-violent means. Years later, in the late 1960s and early 1970s, the Sangh worked in collaboration with Ranima to protect the Heraka faith in Nagaland, marking its entry in the state.

In October 1965, the ABVP, the student arm of the Sangh Parivar, initiated efforts for 'tribal welfare' in Assam. Led by Padmanabha Acharya, the volunteers arrived in Assam to study tribal life, engaging with youth from Meghalaya, Manipur, Nagaland and Arunachal Pradesh for nearly two months. Seeking to integrate the tribal youth with the mainstream Indian culture, an interstate living experience was introduced in 1966.[136] Selected students from the Northeast embarked on a Bharat *darshan* journey, meant to expose them to Hindu values and traditions. This initiative, known as Students Experience in Interstate Living (SEIL), aimed to foster long-term integration of tribals into Hindutva.[137] The project's success led to its institutionalization and evolution into an association that continues till today. Funded by the ABVP, SEIL has received tremendous success in the region.

In 1963, P.B. Acharya along with Dilip Paranjape embarked on a study tour of the north-eastern states.[138] They discovered a significant lack of emotional connection and cultural understanding between the people of the region and the rest of the country. Witnessing this disconnect first-hand, they realized

[136]Ibid.

[137]Ibid.

[138]Ibid.

the urgent need to strengthen the bonds of solidarity and unity. They observed that the limited exposure of north-eastern youth to other parts of India, and vice versa, contributed to this gap.[139] Motivated by their experiences, Acharya and Paranjape envisioned a programme that would facilitate the exchange of ideas and foster unity among youths from diverse backgrounds. This initiative aimed to bridge the gap and promote a sense of shared identity amidst the rich cultural diversity of India. Accordingly, in 1965, SEIL took shape, and within a year, 80 students from the north-eastern states—particularly from Arunachal Pradesh—embarked on a month-long study and cultural exchange tour to Mumbai. They explored historical sites, engaged in discussions with local students and faculty, and experienced homely hospitality from host families.

Over the following years, SEIL organized numerous tours and cultural exchange programmes annually. Each year, students from peripheral states visited bustling cities, while students from metropolitan areas ventured into the serene hinterlands of India, fostering mutual understanding and cultural exchange.

Language Movement

While linguistic movements existed across the Northeast, with ethnic groups across the Naga and Mizo belts demanding a separate state of their own, it was in Assam's Barak and Brahmaputra Valleys that linguistic conflicts led to the outbreak of violence.

For centuries, the Ahom dynasty ruled over Assam until the Treaty of Yandabo in 1826 transferred control to the English East India Company, placing Assam within the jurisdiction of the Bengal Presidency.[140] This transition was accompanied by

---

[139]Ibid.

[140]Phayre, Lt Gen. Sir Arthur P., *History of Burma,* Trubner & Co., Ludgate Hill, London, 1883, p. 257.

the British decision in 1836 to establish Bengali as the official language and medium of instruction. This move intensified existing tensions as it challenged the Assamese people's established governance and cultural traditions.

The integration into the Bengal Presidency and the imposition of Bengali language provoked resentment among the Assamese, leading to a significant societal shift and a decline in the usage of their native language. Conversing, reading and writing in Assamese became actively discouraged, resulting in a deterioration of Assamese literary culture. Furthermore, discriminatory employment practices favoured native Bengali speakers over Assamese, compounding the challenges faced by the Assamese population under colonial rule. This multifaceted impact of political and linguistic imposition not only altered the societal fabric but also marginalized the Assamese people, both culturally and economically. It underlined the complexities and struggles inherent in navigating colonial governance and its repercussions on indigenous identities and livelihoods in Assam.

In the midst of grappling with their place within the Bengal Presidency, the people of Assam found their identity imperilled at every turn, navigating a fragile existence. Their cherished traditions, culture and literature seemed to be stripped away, leaving them to adapt to rapid changes. American Baptist missionaries, seeking to spread Christian values among the indigenous population, took a stand against the new socio-political order by publishing newsletters in Assamese, advocating for their native language while expressing discontent.

It wasn't until 1872 that Assamese began to receive the recognition it deserved, with Lieutenant Governor George Campbell decreeing it as the language of education and administration for its speakers.[141] Subsequently, when Assam

[141]Chattopadhay, D.K., *History of the Assamese Movement since 1947,* Minerva Association Publication, Calcutta, 1990.

was designated as the Chief Commissioner's Province in 1874, Assamese was mandated as the sole medium of instruction in primary education institutions.[142] Despite these strides, the journey of the Assamese language remained tumultuous, constantly struggling with challenges to its status as a secondary language. Even during the Partition of Bengal, when the Chief Commissioner's Province was relocated to Eastern Bengal, Assamese faced a renewed struggle for recognition and usage rights.

Following the Partition of 1947, demands for separate states based on linguistic lines emerged across the subcontinent, including in Assam. With the enactment of the States Reorganisation Act in 1956, the Assamese language movement gained momentum. The Assam Sahitya Sabha, a non-profit organization dedicated to preserving Assamese culture, passed resolutions in 1950 and 1959 advocating for Assamese to be the sole official language in Assam.[143] However, opposition arose from non-Assamese-speaking citizens, culminating in a protest march in Shillong against this proposal. Tensions intensified, resulting in a volatile confrontation on 4 July 1960, where an Assamese student was killed and six others injured amidst clashes between opposing factions.[144]

In response to escalating tensions, the Assam government introduced the Assamese Official Language Bill on 10 October 1960.[145] The bill advocated for two official languages, Assamese and English (temporarily), and was approved on 24 October. However, protests in the Barak Valley turned violent, resulting in the tragic deaths of multiple students.[146] Consequently,

[142]Ibid.

[143]Ibid.

[144]Ibid.

[145]Ibid.

[146]Ibid.

the government amended the bill to include Bengali as an administrative language at the district level to address the grievances of the affected communities.[147]

Amidst the chaos of the Language Movement, Gurupada Bhowmick, a senior swayamsevak, found himself at the epicentre of a storm brewing in Assam. As a high-school student attending Cotton College, he had eagerly pursued his studies, the corridors of academia providing sanctuary from the tumult of the outside world. However, the winds of unrest soon swept through the city, disrupting the tranquillity of campus life. Riots erupted, casting a dark shadow over the once vibrant streets of Guwahati. Graffitis adorned the walls of the city, one of which read, 'Who ate all the fish? The Bengalis! So out with them.'[148] For the Sangh, the call to action was clear. Despite the risks, Bhowmick abandoned the confines of his college grounds and ventured into the heart of the turmoil. Sangh's mission: relief work among the besieged Bengali community.

In the Bengali-dominated neighbourhoods of Tinsukia where he resided, Bhowmick witnessed first-hand the strife tearing at the fabric of society. Yet, his resolve remained unshaken. With unwavering determination, he assumed the role of protector, standing as a stalwart defender of Assamese people amidst the chaos. Armed with nothing but leaflets and a fervent belief in the power of unity, Bhowmick and his fellow swayamsevaks embarked on a courageous campaign.[149]

They traversed the perilous streets, their voices echoing through the labyrinthine alleys as they implored their fellow citizens to rise above the fray. Leaflets fluttered in the breeze, bearing messages of peace and solidarity. 'Recognize that we are first Hindus,' they proclaimed, urging restraint in the face

[147]Ibid.

[148]Interview with Guru Bhowmick.

[149]Ibid.

of violence.[150] Door to door they ventured, engaging in *sampark abhiyan*, their words of reason serving as a balm to soothe the wounds of division.

In the midst of chaos, the RSS emerged as a beacon of hope—a guiding light amidst the darkness that threatened to consume them all. And though the road ahead remained fraught with peril, the Sangh marched onward, fuelled by a singular conviction: that in times of crisis, it is through compassion and solidarity that true healing begins.

Similarly, in 1967, Assam was engulfed in another wave of violence, particularly targeting the Marwari community, as it took the form of anti-Marwari violence. During this period, Bhowmick was a law student at Guwahati University and had also started working as a pracharak.[151] In the midst of the anti-Marwari violence, Bhowmick's work as a pracharak took on heightened significance. He had already witnessed the impact of communal tensions and the suffering inflicted upon innocent people. It was during this time that he felt compelled to take action, to advocate for peace and unity amidst the turmoil. Talking about the 2019 anti-CAA movement in Assam, he said, 'This pattern can be seen later as well when Muslims appropriated the anti-CAA movement to burn Kalakshetra. Tell me: why will an Assamese Hindu want to burn Kalakshetra?'[152]

Gurupada Bhowmick further mentions that in the 1960s the concerns of the RSS were echoed through the newsletter called *Alok*, where issues about the changing demographics of Assam were raised. The paper delved into research-backed pieces discussing the shifting population dynamics of the region. In 1969, a pivotal moment arose when the RSS recognized the necessity of fostering Hindu unity. To achieve this, the RSS organized a

---

[150]Ibid.
[151]Ibid.
[152]Ibid.

gathering of the four major satras of Majuli. Tirthanath Sarma from the VHP brought together the satradhikars of Auniati, Dakhinpat, Garamur and Kuruwabari for a Hindu Sammelan in Jorhat.[153] This event aimed to promote solidarity among Hindus and to welcome indigenous tribes into the Hindu community. Notable figures like Rani Gaidinliu attended, adding significance to the gathering.

The initiative didn't end there. In 1970, another Hindu Sammelan took place in Jorhat. Representatives from various religious organizations—including satras and other religious sects—came together to influence public opinion in favour of the Sangh.[154] This gathering was also graced by Guruji, emphasizing the importance of unity and mobilization in the face of challenges.

Seeds of Sampark

Bhaskar Kulkarni—now an octogenarian—was in his late twenties in 1965 when he boarded an evening train to Guwahati from Patna, right after attending his brother's wedding that morning. He arrived in Guwahati alongside Vinayak Kanitkar, Datta Shenolikar and Hari Mirajdar, and met Thakur Ram Singh, who urged Kulkarni to go to Silchar to oversee the Silchar Vibhag which—at the time—included Cachar, Manipur, Nagaland and Tripura.[155]

Thakur Ram Singh sent a letter to Vibhag Pracharak Ganesh Debsharma, informing him that Bhaskar Kulkarni from Maharashtra would be arriving at Silchar railway station and needed to be picked up.[156] Unfortunately, Debsharma did not

---

[153]Ibid.
[154]Ibid.
[155]Interview with Bhaskar Kulkarni.
[156]Ibid.

receive the letter in time.[157] Early next morning, Kulkarni arrived at the station only to find no one waiting for him. Unable to speak Bengali or Assamese, he faced a tough situation. He donned his black cap, hoping someone would recognize him as a pracharak, but no one did. After waiting for nearly thirty minutes, he approached a rickshaw.[158]

'RSS, RSS,' he said, but the rickshaw puller had no idea what that meant.[159]

'Narsingtola, RSS,' Kulkarni repeated.[160]

'Ah, Narsingtola!' The rickshaw puller exclaimed and took him to the Narsingtola Pond.[161]

'RSS,' Kulkarni pleaded. The rickshaw puller looked at him, perplexed.[162]

Meanwhile, Ganesh Debsharma, who had just received the letter, rushed out on his scooter and found Kulkarni near the Narsingtola Pond. Debsharma welcomed him and took him to the Sangh karyalaya.

Fate soon tested Kulkarni again. In early 1966, Guruji Golwalkar was scheduled to address a programme in Imphal and Kulkarni was tasked with making the arrangements. He took his first flight to Imphal, as no other mode of transportation was available. Upon landing, he asked a rickshaw puller to take him to Thangal Bazar.[163] Sensing that Kulkarni was not a local, the rickshaw puller dropped him in front of a cinema hall. Realizing it was Paona Bazar instead, Kulkarni asked again to be taken to the RSS karyalaya in Thangal Bazar, but the rickshaw puller

---

[157]Ibid.

[158]Ibid.

[159]Ibid.

[160]Ibid.

[161]Ibid.

[162]Ibid.

[163]Ibid.

insisted they were already there.[164] Amidst a crowd of filmgoers, a man in a dhoti and kurta appeared. It was Dhiresh Chandra Das, the local pracharak, who helped Kulkarni reach the RSS karyalaya.

Determined not to face such difficulties again, Kulkarni resolved to learn the local languages, Bengali and Meitei. He relocated to Imphal, taking charge of both the Manipur and Cachar vibhags. He bought children's alphabet books, sentence books, grammar books, and even handwriting books, diligently studying them. Within months, he became fluent, identifying places by reading local signs and communicating effectively with locals. Other pracharaks from Manipur, Cachar and Tripura held Kulkarni's linguistic skills in high regard. In Manipur, where he had established strong connections, locals affectionately called him 'K. Bhaskar Singh', with 'K' standing for the common Manipuri name 'Keisham', though it actually stood for Kulkarni.[165]

Kulkarni fondly recalls his time in Manipur, describing the people as simple and welcoming. He claimed it was the best time of his life, with work being relatively easier there than in other parts of the Northeast. 'The real Hindu way of life is in Manipur,' he exclaims, noting how, unlike in Maharashtra and Uttar Pradesh, schools in the valley required students to wear a sandalwood tilak on their foreheads.[166] Discussing the present situation in the state, Kulkarni attributes the rise of separatism in Manipur to rampant immigration and mass conversions in the hills. He recalls that in the 1960s, Sangh work and connections with local tribes progressed smoothly without these issues.[167]

---

[164]Ibid.
[165]Ibid.
[166]Ibid.
[167]Ibid.

Opposition and Solidarity

In the early 1960s, Assam's political landscape was a vibrant mosaic of ideologies and movements. One of the prominent figures steering this dynamic era was Dev Kant Barooah, a staunch leader of the Congress party and a formidable education minister of Assam, later becoming the first and only Assamese president of the Indian National Congress. His influence permeated the region, shaping policies and politics with a firm hand.

In 1962, the Rashtriya Swayamsevak Sangh planned a 25-day training programme in Nagaon district.[168] Despite their strong presence in Barhampur, securing a venue proved to be a Herculean task. However, a glimmer of hope emerged when a local school principal, sympathetic to their cause, agreed to host the event on school grounds.[169]

This arrangement, however, did not go unnoticed. Begum Afia Ahmed, the Muslim MLA of Jamunamukh in Nagaon district, was deeply offended by the idea of having Sangh activities in the district which had seen an unprecedented influx of Muslim migrants.[170] With a sense of urgency, she brought the matter to the attention of Dev Kant Barooah. Resolute and unwavering in his stance, Barooah swiftly issued an order banning the use of government schools for Sangh activities.[171] The principal received a direct threat, warning him of severe repercussions if he allowed the programme to proceed.

Yet, the principal's resolve was unshaken. Though the school could no longer serve as the venue, he pledged his unwavering support to the Sangh. This act of defiance ignited a spark of solidarity within the local community. The training programme,

---

[168]Ibid.

[169]Ibid.

[170]Ibid.

[171]Ibid.

now at risk, found new sanctuaries as the principal and residents united in their determination to see it through. The event unfolded in the nearby *namghars*, Shaheed Bhawans, and in the homes of supportive citizens.[172] This collective effort was a powerful testament to the community's resilience and unyielding spirit. Guided by the principal's leadership, the training sessions proceeded seamlessly, fostering a spirit of unity and perseverance.

The confrontation over a simple venue transformed into a narrative of communal strength and solidarity. It was a story of a community rallying together, driven by an unwavering belief in their cause and inspired by the determined leadership of a school principal who stood his ground against formidable odds. As Ulhas Kulkarni—the previous kshetra pracharak—explained while describing this incident in his interview, 'Sangh is not a uniform or a place where a shakha is held; it is a spirit.'[173]

Despite the numerous efforts and valuable services rendered to society by the RSS, the organization still struggled to gain acceptability in the Northeast. Perceived as an outsider group with a defined agenda, the RSS faced resistance and scepticism from local communities. Its ideology and methods were often misunderstood, contributing to its lack of traction in the region. However, the RSS remained undeterred and continued its work with dedication and perseverance. It would take many more decades, along with countless challenges, sacrifices and even loss of lives, before the RSS would finally find acceptance in the Northeast. The story of this arduous odyssey, marked by struggles and triumphs, shall unfold in the following chapters.

---

[172]Ibid.

[173]Interview with Ulhas Kulkarni.

3

An Organization behind Bars

India is Indira. Indira is India.

—Dev Kant Barooah[174]
(President, Indian National Congress, 1975–78)

In the journey of independent India, the end of the sixties and the beginning of the seventies marked the peak of India's first party system, with tremendous consolidation of power at the Centre. This chapter looks at how dissenting groups, such as the Sangh Parivar, negotiated with these pressures and conducted their work in the Northeast.

The second Indira Gandhi government—formed in November 1969—was the first minority government in independent India as the split between INC(R) and INC(O) made the former forty-one seats short of a majority. Prime Minister Gandhi and her Cabinet remained in power by relying on outside support from DMK, CPI and CPIM. However, knowing that this alliance might not be sustainable for long, she willingly dissolved the Lok Sabha on 27 December 1970 and President V.V. Giri called for fresh elections.

[174]Bobb, Dilip, 'India is Indira, and Indira is India. Who lives if Indira dies?', *India Today,* 01 May 2012, https://tinyurl.com/3bvxushc. Accessed on 17 February 2025.

In the general elections of 1971, she won a resounding majority—352 seats out of 518—rallying on her populist slogan *Garibi Hatao* (abolish poverty). Congress (R) became known as the 'real' Congress 'by the margin of its victory', historian Ramachandra Guha later noted, 'requiring no qualifying suffix'.[175] This marked the beginning of what can be termed as perhaps the darkest decade of Indian democracy.

The 1971 War and the Beginning of the Immigration Issue

In 1970, Pakistan held its general election and the results threatened the unity of West and East Pakistan as a singular sovereign entity. The Awami League, led by Sheikh Mujibur Rahman, won a staggering 167 out of 169 seats in the East Pakistan Legislative Assembly, comfortably crossing the majority-mark in the National Assembly against Zulfikar Ali Bhutto's Pakistan People's Party.[176] When Bhutto and President Yahya Khan refused to yield the premiership of the National Assembly to Sheikh Mujibur Rahman, the Awami League launched nationwide strikes and riots against the Pakistani state and its sympathizers.

In March 1971, Yahya Khan ordered a military crackdown on the Awami League, detaining many members and murdering sympathizers in the elite circles.[177] Sheikh Mujib himself was arrested and taken to West Pakistan. Termed as Operation Searchlight, the Pakistani military conducted an ethnic genocide of the Bengali population, slaughtering 50,000 to 200,000 people

[175]Mukul, Sushim, 'When Indira Gandhi broke "One Nation One Election" cycle', *India Today*, 17 December 2024, https://tinyurl.com/4kp3yy3s. Accessed on 12 February 2025.

[176]Naeem, Raza, 'The Watershed Moment in 1970 Elections That Broke Pakistan', *The Wire*, 07 December 2024, https://tinyurl.com/2ms5xrwb. Accessed on 12 February 2025.

[177]Ibid.

and raping two lakh to four lakh women.[178] This prompted Indira Gandhi to launch a war on Pakistan, despite the USA pressurizing her not to. The continued Indian offensives in East Pakistan angered President Nixon so much that he referred to her as an 'old witch', while Kissinger, who was the secretary of state, called her a 'bitch'.[179] Despite Western pressures, Indian troops launched a full-scale war on Pakistan after the Pakistani Air Force conducted aerial bombings on eight Indian airfields on 3 December 1971.[180]

In the next twelve days, the Indian Army reached up to Dhaka and encircled the capital.[181] At around 16:00 hours on 16 December, Indian armed forces issued an ultimatum to the East Pakistani Command to surrender within a thirty-minute time window. Upon hearing the ultimatum, the commander of the Pakistan Eastern Command, Lieutenant-General A.A.K. Niazi, surrendered without offering any resistance. On 16 December 1971, Pakistan ultimately called for unilateral ceasefire and surrendered its entire four-tier military to the Indian Army, ending the Indo-Pakistan war of 1971.[182] At 16:31 hours, A.A.K. Niazi signed the Instrument of Surrender of the Pakistan Eastern Command stationed in East Pakistan and handed it over to Lieutenant-General Jagjit Singh Aurora, the GOC-in-C of the Indian Eastern Command at the Ramna Race Course in

---

[178]Ahmed, Imtiaz, 'RECOGNISING THE 1971 BANGLADESH GENOCIDE: AN APPEAL FOR RENDERING JUSTICE', Ministry of Foreign Affairs, Government of the People's Republic of Bangladesh, 2022, https://tinyurl.com/5n79dpru. Accessed on 08 May 2025.

[179]Eisenberg, Carolyn Woods, *Fire and Rain: Nixon, Kissinger, and the Wars in Southeast Asia*, Oxford University Press, Oxford, 2023.

[180]Ibid.

[181]Ibid.

[182]Marwah, Onkar, 'India's Military Intervention in East Pakistan, 1971–1972', *Modern Asian Studies*, Vol. 13, No. 4, 1979, pp. 549–80, https://tinyurl.com/4xkjydaz. Accessed on 12 February 2025.

Dhaka, leading to the Independence of Bangladesh.

The 1971 War triggered a massive movement of people which changed politics in the east of India forever. The Indian government opened the East Pakistan-India border to allow approximately ten million East Bengali refugees to find safe shelter; the governments of West Bengal, Bihar, Assam, Meghalaya and Tripura established refugee camps along the border.[183]

The influx of refugees from Bangladesh placed immense strain on the resources and infrastructure of eastern India, particularly in the north-eastern states. Refugee camps were hastily set up to accommodate the displaced population, but they were often overcrowded and lacked basic amenities. The sudden influx of refugees also strained the social fabric of the host communities, leading to tensions and conflicts over resources and livelihoods.

The north-eastern states of India, already grappling with their own socio-political complexities, were particularly vulnerable to the influx of refugees from Bangladesh. Assam, in particular, bore the brunt of the refugee crisis, with millions of Bengali refugees crossing the border and settling in the state. This demographic shift exacerbated existing tensions between indigenous Assamese communities and Bengali-speaking migrants, culminating in the Assam Agitation of the 1980s, which we shall discuss in detail in the following chapter. The legacy of the Assam Agitation continues to shape politics in the state, with issues of immigration and identity remaining central to not just electoral discourse but also quotidian politics.

Tripura, located adjacent to Bangladesh, witnessed a significant influx of refugees during the Bangladesh Liberation War and its aftermath. The refugees—predominantly Bengali Hindus—sought

---

[183]Sarmin, Utsa, 'The Crisis of Public Health Among East Bengali Refugees in 1971', *Refugee Watch*, https://tinyurl.com/574amtjh. Accessed on 12 February 2025.

shelter in Tripura, leading to demographic changes in the state. The influx of refugees had profound social and economic consequences in Tripura, straining resources and infrastructure and exacerbating tensions between the indigenous tribal communities and Bengali-speaking settlers. The Tripura Tribal Areas Autonomous District Council (TTAADC) was established in 1982 to safeguard the rights of indigenous tribal communities in the state, reflecting efforts to address these tensions through political means.[184]

Meghalaya, with its predominantly tribal population, also experienced the impact of the refugee crisis, albeit to a lesser extent than Assam. The influx of refugees from Bangladesh contributed to demographic changes in certain areas of the state, leading to concerns among indigenous tribal communities about the preservation of their cultural and ethnic identity. The refugee crisis also had implications for Meghalaya's political landscape, contributing to the rise of regional political parties advocating for the rights of indigenous tribes. The Hill State People's Democratic Party (HSPDP) and later the United Democratic Party (UDP) have been prominent voices in Meghalaya's politics, advocating for the protection of tribal rights and interests.

The refugee crisis also had far-reaching economic and social repercussions in the Northeast. The sudden influx of refugees strained the region's economy, as resources were diverted to provide for their basic needs. Competition for jobs and resources heightened existing socio-economic inequalities, leading to resentment and conflict between host communities and refugees. Moreover, the cultural and linguistic diversity of the north-eastern states further complicated the integration of refugees into the local society.

---

[184]Debbarma, M., 'A STUDY ON THE CAUSES OF SEPARATE STATE DEMAND IN NORTH EAST INDIAN STATE OF TRIPURA', *The Journal of Multidisciplinary Research*, Vol. 4, No. 1, 2024, pp. 29–34, https://tinyurl.com/57md42pa. Accessed on 12 February 2025.

The Bangladesh Liberation War and its aftermath had significant political ramifications for India, particularly in the Northeast. India's support for the independence movement in Bangladesh strained its relations with Pakistan and other international actors. Domestically, the refugee crisis fuelled ethno-nationalist sentiments in the Northeast, leading to demands for greater autonomy and political representation for indigenous communities. The legacy of the refugee crisis continues to shape politics and identity dynamics in the region to this day.

Indigenous movements in the Northeast often emerged as a response to perceived threats to the cultural and ethnic identity of local communities. The settlement of Bangladeshi refugees, who often belonged to different linguistic and religious backgrounds, raised concerns among indigenous populations about the dilution of their distinct identities. Movements such as the Assam Agitation and the demands for tribal autonomy in states like Meghalaya and Tripura sought to preserve the cultural heritage and traditions of the region's native inhabitants.

The settlement of refugees led to increased competition for land and resources in the Northeast. Indigenous communities—who were already facing challenges related to land alienation and resource exploitation—viewed the arrival of refugees as exacerbating these issues. Organizations like the All Tripura Tribal Force (ATTF) in Tripura and various tribal organizations in Meghalaya articulated demands for land rights and control over natural resources as a means of safeguarding the socio-economic interests of indigenous populations.[185]

It also raised concerns about political representation and power-sharing in the north-eastern states. Indigenous movements

---

[185]Bhaumik, Subir, 'Insurgencies in India's Northeast: Conflict, Co-Option & Change'. *East-West Center*, 2007, https://tinyurl.com/5akn7nhs. Accessed on 13 February 2025.

advocated for greater political autonomy and decision-making powers for local communities, challenging the dominance of mainstream political parties and institutions. The emergence of regional political parties such as the Asom Gana Parishad (AGP) in Assam and the United Democratic Party (UDP) in Meghalaya reflected the aspirations of indigenous populations for self-governance and greater control over their political destiny.

What was more concerning was that existing tensions and conflicts between different ethnic and linguistic groups in the Northeast heightened. Indigenous movements sought to address these conflicts and promote peace and stability in the region. However, in some cases, these movements also resorted to violence as a means of asserting their demands and confronting perceived threats. Organizations like the National Liberation Front of Tripura (NLFT) and the United Liberation Front of Assam (ULFA) in Assam emerged as militant outfits advocating for separatism and ethnic nationalism in response to perceived injustices and grievances arising from refugee settlement.[186]

New Frontiers, New Horizons

Shankar Das, the current *baudhik pramukh* of RSS in Assam, recalled that Guruji Golwalkar visited the Northeast in 1971 and stayed here for quite some time, travelling from village to village in the border areas of Assam, Tripura and Meghalaya.[187] He—along with local pracharaks and swayamsevaks—convinced people to help in the resistance process and also held village-level baithaks about the immigration issue, which is discussed in detail below.

In the midst of the 1971 war, a unique scene unfolded in the north-eastern region of India. Amidst the tension and

---

[186]Baruah,Sanjib, *In the Name of the Nation: India and Its Northeast*, Stanford University Press, California, 2020.

[187]Interview with Shankar Das.

uncertainty of conflict, canteens operated by the RSS became a beacon of hope and camaraderie for Indian soldiers. Although private organizations are typically not permitted to operate within military zones during wartime, the Sangh's longstanding commitment to societal service and nation-building earned it a rare exception. The canteens, set up near the frontlines, offered much more than just food; they became places where weary soldiers could find a moment of solace and warmth.

They buzzed with activity, as soldiers from all across the Northeast gathered there, seeking respite from the rigours of war. The volunteers of the Sangh, driven by a sense of duty and patriotism, worked tirelessly to provide not only meals but also comfort and encouragement. They served as reminders of the unity and strength that bound the nation together, even in the face of adversity. Through their selfless service, the Sangh volunteers forged a unique bond with the soldiers, who found a home away from home in the canteens. This small yet significant gesture of support and solidarity left an indelible mark on the hearts of those who experienced it, embodying the spirit of service and sacrifice that defined the times. This sense of solidarity built a new inroad for the tough times that lay ahead.

One of the most important changes that marked the Northeast in the beginning of the seventies decade was the passage of the North-Eastern Areas (Reorganisation) Act, 1971, in December.[188] As a result, in January 1972, the following changes were enacted:

i. Reduction in the size of territory and administrative authority of the state of Assam
ii. Creation of the new state of Meghalaya, with Shillong (former capital of undivided Assam) as its capital

[188]India Code, 'The North-Eastern Areas (Reorganisation) Act, 1971', https://tinyurl.com/2e8ctb9a. Accessed on 17 February 2025.

iii. Statehood to the Union Territories of Manipur and Tripura
iv. Carving out the Union Territories of Mizoram (from Lushai Hills) and Arunachal Pradesh (from North East Frontier Agency)

This was a result of a decades-long struggle of the hill tribes, particularly Khasis, Jaintias and Garos, to have an autonomous state of their own, free from the influence of the Assamese intelligentsia. A senior Kalyan Ashram leader, who has spent over three decades working in Meghalaya, says that the movement for a separate state was possible because the Bengalis threw their weight behind the Khasis, seeing an avenue to assert their own power once the Assamese were sidelined.[189] By the dawn of 1972, the Assamese populace, feeling the ground shifting beneath their feet, began to depart en masse, leaving behind vacant streets and hollowed homes. Like a tide receding, their exodus marked the turning point for the Bengalis, who wasted no time seizing the reins of authority. Government offices in Shillong echoed with the sound of Bengali dialects, as they swiftly filled the void left by their departing rivals.

Yet, amidst the euphoria of new-found power, the Khasis found themselves betrayed. The promises of partnership and shared governance soon rang hollow as they realized that they had merely traded one master for another. It was against this backdrop of shattered dreams and smouldering resentment that the events of 1978 unfolded. The Khasis, feeling betrayed and embittered, lashed out in an explosion of violence that shook the region to its core. Durga Puja, a festival once celebrated in harmony, became a battleground as blood spilled onto the streets. The conflict—a senior karyakarta of Kalyan Ashram argues—was not a simple dichotomy of Hindu versus Christian, but rather a

[189]Interview with Kumar Rajiv (name changed).

complex interplay of tribal identity versus Bengali hegemony.[190]

Ages ago, when the memory of colonization was fresh, the Bengalis and tribal communities had shared a bond forged through mutual respect and cooperation. However, the winds of change had blown cold, ushering in an era of Westernization and Christianity which had disproportionately targeted the tribals and eroded the bonds of camaraderie. For three harrowing days, the hills echoed with the sounds of chaos and terror. Thirty-two lives were extinguished, each death a tragic testament to the depths of human folly. Even the sanctity of the Ramakrishna Mission—a bastion of peace and enlightenment—was violated, as a bomb tore through the tranquillity of a karykarta Gokla Nandy's room.[191]

Morarji Desai, the erstwhile prime minister of India, issued a clarion call for peace, urging an end to the bloodshed that threatened to engulf the land. In response, the might of the Indian Army descended upon the troubled region, their boots crushing dissent as they sought to restore order. After this, many Bengalis, traditionally supporters of the RSS, did not support the Sangh's seva in Khasi areas. Many Bengali swayamsevaks claimed, '*Saap ko doodh pila rahe ho*' (You're feeding milk to snakes).[192] In turn, the Sangh turned to an individual who had spent the decade of the 1970s engaged in the academic world, conducting research on Khasi indigenous faith and writing fire-brand literature on the need to preserve the same—H. Onderson Mawrie, an intellectual ideologue from the Seng Khasi Movement, which was founded on 23 November 1899 by another intellectual, U Babu Jeebon Roy, to fight the British and their Christian proselytization efforts.[18]

Moving on to Nagaland, this was the decade that actually saw the Sangh make inroads into its most difficult terrain possible.

---

[190]Ibid.

[191]Ibid.

[192]Ibid.

As discussed in the previous chapter, the Naga National Council had taken a violent turn in the 1960s under the leadership of Phizo. After prolonged struggle, a section of Naga rebels signed the Shillong Accord in November 1975, while other extremists collectively got together and formed the National Socialist Council of Nagaland (NSCN), a militant secessionist outfit inspired by both Maoism and Christian evangelism.[193]

Around this time, Rani Gaidinliu's efforts to preserve the indigenous tribal faith of the Naga people, particularly the Zeliang tribe, took shape in the form of Zeliangrong Heraka Association, set up in 1974.[194] Kalyan Ashram then joined hands with Ranima and started working in Nagaland under this association and helped counter the Baptist missionary nexus in the state.

In the 1970s, the tranquil hills of Nagaland witnessed the arrival of a man on a mission. Krishnarao Sapre, the first Kalyan Ashram pracharak to set foot in the region, brought with him a fervent dedication to understand and document the intricate dynamics of the tribal communities.[195] His focus? The subtle yet profound influence of Christian missionaries on the indigenous pagan tribes. Armed with a thirst for knowledge and a sense of purpose, Sapre embarked on an ambitious journey of research and exploration.

His efforts were not in vain; he meticulously conducted fact-finding exercises, delving deep into the fabric of tribal life to uncover the nuances of proselytization. Each report he compiled was not merely a collection of data but a testament

---

[193] Das, Suranjan, 'Sectional President's Address: ETHNICITY AND NATION-BUILDING IN INDIA: THE NAGA EXPERIENCE', *Proceedings of the Indian History Congress*, Vol. 64, 2003, pp. 677–740, https://tinyurl.com/4nr8xk7w. Accessed on 13 February 2025.

[194] Longkumer, Arkotong, 'Religious and economic reform: The Gaidinliu movement and the Heraka in the North Cachar Hills', *South Asia: Journal of South Asian Studies*, Vol. 30, No. 3, 2007, pp. 499–515.

[195] Interview with Sandip Kavishwar.

to his unwavering commitment to the cause. Sapre's pioneering work laid the groundwork for future endeavours by the Kalyan Ashram. In 1978, the organization's founder Balasaheb Deshpande and Northeast Organizing Secretary Vasant Rao Bhatt followed in his footsteps, bringing with them a renewed sense of purpose and direction.[196] Their arrival coincided with a significant development in the indigenous faith movement, as former Congress MP N.C. Zeliang retired from active politics to join forces with Kalyan Ashram.

The seeds of change planted by Ranima in 1974 found fertile ground in Zeliang's commitment about five to six years later, further fuelling the indigenous faith movement. Kalyan Ashram's endeavours gained momentum, culminating in the establishment of the Zeliangrong Heraka School in Tening, Peren district, in 1984–85.[197] As we shall see later, this educational institution became the nucleus of Kalyan Ashram's activities, fostering a sense of pride and cultural resurgence among the local populace.

In Arunachal Pradesh, a different organization from the Sangh Parivar had cemented its roots. This movement found its genesis in the vision of Eknath Ranade, a visionary leader whose passion for education and community development ignited the flame of change. Founded in 1972 under the aegis of the Vivekananda Kendra, this movement embarked on a journey of enlightenment and empowerment, guided by the teachings of Swami Vivekananda.[198] The seeds of this endeavour began to sprout with the arrival of A. Balakrishnan and his cohort of sixteen dedicated pracharaks in 1974 in Shillong, eight to ten of whom were dispatched to Arunachal Pradesh, a land ripe with potential yet plagued by the absence of basic amenities.[199]

[196]Ibid.

[197]Ibid.

[198]Interview with Pravin Dabholkar.

[199]Ibid.

The pivotal moment in the organization's history occurred during the inauguration of the Vivekananda Rock Memorial in 1970. It was here that Eknath Ranade crossed paths with K.A.A. Raja, the esteemed first lieutenant governor of the North-East Frontier Agency (now Arunachal Pradesh).[200] In a meeting fuelled by patriotic fervour and a shared commitment to uplift the masses, Ranade and Raja deliberated on the pressing need for quality education and healthcare facilities in the region. Impressed by Ranade's nationalist ideals and unwavering dedication, Raja was swayed into allowing swayamsevaks to integrate into government schools as teachers. This landmark decision not only laid the foundation for the establishment of Vivekananda Kendra Vidyalayas (VKVs) but also paved the way for a second wave of Kendra karyakartas, led by Nivedita Bhide, to enter government schools as educators.[201]

Whispered rumours of Ranade's influential advocacy reached the highest echelons of power, even swaying the opinion of the formidable Indira Gandhi herself. This purported dialogue bore fruit in 1977 with the official establishment of VKVs as fully-funded government institutions, offering free education to the eager minds of Arunachal Pradesh. The VKVs—funded jointly by the Central government and the Arunachal Pradesh administration—emerged as beacons of hope in a landscape marred by the shadows of neglect.[202]

With transportation and communication infrastructure still in its infancy, most students found sanctuary in the hostels provided by VKVs, fostering a sense of community and camaraderie. The school curriculum also incorporated Hindu prayers and hymns to Bharat Mata—among other rituals—promoting a feeling of national unity. In the early years, Vivekananda Kendra's focus

[200]Interview with Pravin Dabholkar.
[201]Ibid.
[202]Ibid.

remained singularly dedicated to education, recognizing it as the cornerstone of societal progress.

The Darkest Days of Indian Democracy

In the summer of 1975, India found itself teetering on the edge of chaos. Political turmoil simmered beneath the surface as dissent and unrest threatened to engulf the nation. In Gujarat, Morarji Desai, the embodiment of Gandhian principles, led a crusade against corruption and maladministration in the state government headed by Chief Minister Chimanbhai Patel, galvanizing public opinion against the ruling establishment.[203] Meanwhile, in the dusty by-lanes of Bihar, Jayaprakash Narayan—or JP as he was affectionately called—ignited the flames of revolution with his call for Total Revolution.[204] The movement reached its zenith in 1974 with the historic Bihar Movement, a non-violent uprising that brought the state to a standstill and forced the Congress government to accede to JP's demands and lead to the dissolution of the state assembly.[205]

As the pressure mounted, Gandhi faced a pivotal legal battle that would determine her political future. Raj Narain, a firebrand socialist leader and staunch opponent of Prime Minister Indira Gandhi, filed a petition challenging her election to the Lok Sabha from the constituency of Raebareli in the 1971 general elections.[206] Narain alleged widespread electoral malpractice

---

[203]Kidwai, Rasheed, *Leaders, Politicians, Citizens: Fifty Figures Who Influenced India's Politics*, Hachette India, 2022.

[204]Chisti, Seema, 'Jayaprakash Narayan: Reluctant messiah of a turbulent time', *The Indian Express*, 11 October 2017, https://tinyurl.com/mr5wv5j9, Accessed on 12 February 2025.

[205]Ibid.

[206]Yadav, Shyamlal, '1977 Lok Sabha elections: Emergency imposition, first non-Congress Govt, and a promise belied', *The Indian Express*, 04 May 2024, https://tinyurl.com/4mesymxs. Accessed on 12 February 2025.

and misuse of government machinery by Gandhi's election campaign, including the use of state resources and intimidation tactics to secure victory. The case—heard by the Allahabad High Court—garnered nationwide attention as it pitted a formidable political leader against the might of the ruling establishment. In a historic judgement delivered on 12 June 1975, the Allahabad High Court ruled in favour of Narain, declaring Gandhi's election null and void, and unseating her from the Lok Sabha.[207] The court's damning verdict sent shockwaves through the corridors of power, threatening to topple the mighty edifice of the ruling establishment.

In the heart of India's capital, New Delhi, Ramlila Maidan stood witness to the unfolding drama of democracy. A deluge of protestors—led by JP—had assembled to demand the resignation of Gandhi on 25 June 1975. As the sun dipped below the horizon, casting long shadows upon the gathered throngs, Prime Minister Indira Gandhi made a fateful decision. On 26 June 1975, the nation awoke to a jarring announcement by then President Fakhruddin Ali Ahmed—Emergency had been declared.[208] It is interesting how two Assamese politicians became such important actors in this move—President Ahmed and Congress Party Chief Dev Kant Barooah.

As civil liberties were suspended, the press was censored and political opponents were arrested en masse, India transformed into a police state overnight, shrouded in fear and uncertainty. Gandhi justified her actions as a necessary step to restore law and order, citing the need to combat internal disruption and external threats. Yet, beneath the veneer of stability lay a darker

---

[207]Ibid.

[208]ET Online, '1975 Emergency explained: A look back at India's "dark days of democracy"; Govt designates day as "Samvidhaan Hatya Diwas"', *The Economic Times*. 12 July 2024. https://tinyurl.com/yc3c74mp. Accessed on 12 February 2025.

truth—Emergency was a calculated manoeuvre to consolidate power and silence dissent. The months that followed were marked by a climate of fear and repression. Political opponents languished in jail, dissenting voices were silenced, and fundamental freedoms were curtailed. Key opposition voices—such as Morarji Desai, Jayaprakash Narayan, Atal Bihari Vajpayee, L.K. Advani, George Fernandes, among others—were put behind bars. The Rashtriya Swayamsevak Sangh was banned. The vibrant tapestry of Indian democracy seemed to unravel as authoritarianism tightened its grip on the nation.

In the month of June 1975, amidst the tranquil surroundings of North Guwahati's Auniati Satra, the Sangh Siksha Varg camp for all of Northeast was being organized in the presence of Eknath Ranade.[209] Little did the participants anticipate the seismic shift that would soon engulf the nation. As dawn broke on 26 June, the customary wake-up call at 4.00 a.m. was accompanied by an eerie silence, shrouding the air with a foreboding sense of apprehension. The feeble summons from the instructors to rouse the siksharthis seemed but a mere whisper against the backdrop of impending doom. The news, when it came, struck like a thunderbolt—on the preceding night, Prime Minister Indira Gandhi had declared a state of internal emergency across the country.

Even in such trying circumstances, the ongoing programmes of the camp did not stop for three days, until the gravity of the situation necessitated its premature conclusion on 29 June. As the convocation address unfolded amidst the hallowed halls of the temple, a sudden encirclement by law enforcement personnel sent ripples of tension through the congregation. Bhumidev Goswami, who was heading the camp as the *prant karyavah*, found himself in a tête-à-tête with the Superintendent

---

[209]Chauthaiwale, Shashikant, *Mor Pracharak Jatra* (translated from Assamese), Prachi Prakashan, Guwahati, 2023.

of Police, Mr Priya Goswami, as the temple grounds brimmed with apprehension.[210] Amidst this whirlwind of uncertainty, a group of prominent Sangh workers covertly crossed the Brahmaputra river to Guwahati, evading the watchful gaze of law enforcement.

Although no arrests were made that day, the participants of the camp found themselves subjected to interrogation and photographic documentation, their allegiances scrutinized under the unrelenting gaze of authority. The police asked everyone only one question: 'What is your opinion of PM Indira Gandhi?' The participants from Manipur—who understood little Hindi and English—answered, 'She is very beautiful.'[211]

The following day marked a pivotal moment in the annals of history as Balasaheb Deoras—the then sarsanghchalak—was apprehended in Nagpur. A call to action reverberated through the ranks of volunteers, urging them to increase public awareness and maintain peace amidst the tempestuous storm of repression. What followed was a series of arrests all across the Northeast. Interestingly enough, Eknath Ranade—then formally affiliated with the Vivekananda Kendra—avoided arrest. When the RSS was banned on 4 July 1975, he wrote a letter to Indira Gandhi stating, 'I am an RSS pracharak but give me six months before you arrest me. I need to work on my new organization Vivekananda Kendra. Without me this baby organization will fail. After six months, I will offer myself to you.'[212] Indira Gandhi trusted Ranade so much, particularly because of his great work during the Rock Memorial inauguration, that she neither banned the Kendra nor arrested him.[213] Others weren't so lucky.

---

[210]Chauthaiwale, Shashikant, *Mor Pracharak Jatra* (translated from Assamese), Prachi Prakashan, Guwahati, 2023.

[211]Ibid.

[212]Interview with Pravin Dabholkar.

[213]Ibid.

Amidst the looming shadows of the Emergency era, the life of Gurupada Bhowmick, a dedicated RSS pracharak and seasoned lawyer, unfolded against a backdrop of uncertainty and turmoil. In the confines of his rented chamber in Dibrugarh, fate cast its ominous shadow as the police descended to affect his arrest. Though absent from the court, news of Gulap Borbora's wrongful incarceration had reached Bhowmick, signalling the looming threat that now encroached upon his own doorstep. An acquaintance within the police force relayed the grim tidings—warrants had been issued for his and Ashim Dutta's arrest.[214]

Yet, amidst the chaos, a plea for respite was voiced—to inform clients and secure their affairs before the inevitable incarceration. With steely resolve and a hint of desperation, Bhowmick bargained for time—a mere two days to orchestrate the handover of responsibilities—before the jaws of justice snapped shut. After informing his clients of the state of affairs, and helping them find replacement lawyers, he honoured the pact of voluntary surrender to the authorities, sealing his fate on the fateful day of 5 July 1975, within the confines of the Dibrugarh Police Station.[215]

Under the ominous shadow of the controversial Maintenance of Internal Security Act (MISA), Bhowmick's freedom dwindled to a mere illusion, ensnared in the web of political intrigue and repression that defined the first phase of the Emergency.[216] Yet, hope flickered faintly, an ember of optimism that whispered of swift release and imminent liberation. But fate had other plans. He got bail from the clutches of MISA after a year's incarceration, but this brief taste of freedom was quickly snatched away, swallowed by the gaping maw of the Defence of India Act (DIR). Alongside 180 others in Dibrugarh, he became a prisoner once

[214]Interview with Gurupada Bhowmick.

[215]Ibid.

[216]Ibid.

more, thrust into the second phase of the Emergency, where shadows deepened and freedoms waned.

Several hundreds in Assam, mostly businessmen, were also arrested under the Conservation of Foreign Exchange and Prevention of Smuggling Activities Act (COFEPOSA), 1974, for shady economic 'crimes'. Over 80,000 swayamsevaks were booked under various sections across the country. More than 350 Sangh activists were also jailed in Northeast India.[217]

When in jail, many swayamsevaks were brutally tortured. Madanji Sinhal, Sharat Kalita, Motilal Jalan, Manju De, Haricharan Jindal and Banwari Sharma had to bear a lot of beatings and other humiliating tortures.[218] Some satyagrahis were stripped of their clothes and beaten up while cold water was poured on them. Shankar Das told us that his seniors were forced to sleep tied to ice slabs till they melted. Jyoti Gogoi of Dibrugarh suffered from severe jaundice while in jail.[219]

The incarcerated members of the Sangh would often share jokes amongst themselves, fostering a sense of camaraderie and inspiration within their ranks. In Jorhat Jail, a fellow prisoner from the Congress party queried a Sangh member, asking, 'Masterji, how much longer must we endure this confinement?' In response, the Sangh member reassured him, saying, 'Why worry, sir? Even Veer Savarkar endured 25 years of Kala Pani.'[220]

Amidst the darkness of confinement, amidst the gnawing uncertainty of prolonged incarceration, a semblance of normalcy emerged. Shakhas were organized in these jails, prayers whispered in furtive tones, and the rhythmic thwack of shuttlecocks filled the stagnant air as badminton became a refuge from the suffocating

---

[217]Chauthaiwale, Shashikant, *Mor Pracharak Jatra*, Tirthankar Das (trans.), Prachi Prakashan, Guwahati, 2023.

[218]Ibid.

[219]Interview with Shankar Das.

[220]Interview with Gurupada Bhowmick.

reality of prison life. In the company of intellectuals, politicians and ideological-adversaries-turned-comrades, Bhowmick navigated the treacherous waters of imprisonment, bound by a common fear of the unknown that lingered in the air like a palpable spectre of dread. Yet, despite the pervasive atmosphere of distrust that gripped society, amidst whispered conversations and sidelong glances, a spirit of resilience simmered beneath the surface.

Whispers of Defiance

Shashikant Chauthaiwale, a senior pracharak, said that against the backdrop of repression, a silent revolution simmered beneath the surface, as Sangh functionaries embarked on a mission of enlightenment and empowerment.[221] Through covert channels and discreet meetings, the seeds of dissent were sown, nurturing a burgeoning sense of defiance that refused to be quelled. As the days turned into weeks, and the weeks into months, a network of clandestine operations took shape, with Sangh workers operating under pseudonyms and adopting disguises to evade the watchful eye of the authority.

The spirit of resistance burned bright, fuelled by the collective determination to reclaim the freedoms that had been usurped by tyranny. In the corridors of power, voices of dissent grew louder as prominent figures from diverse ideological backgrounds united in their condemnation of the Emergency regime. Letters of protest were penned, petitions circulated and alliances forged in the pursuit of a common goal—the restoration of democracy and fundamental rights. On the streets, whispers of resistance echoed through the alleys and byways, as ordinary citizens found courage in solidarity, rallying behind the banner of freedom and justice. Despite the ever-present threat of reprisal, the spirit of

---

[221]Chauthaiwale, Shashikant, *Mor Pracharak Jatra,* Tirthankar Das (trans.), Prachi Prakashan, Guwahati, 2023.

defiance remained unbroken, a testament to the indomitable resilience of the human spirit.

In Assam, leaflets were published by the names of *Varta Patra, Satyavarta, Lokvani,* etc.[222] Initially, printing was a problem. No printing press dared to print the leaflets. Therefore, with the help of two photo frames, mesh cloth and glass, a homemade machine was created. Also, there was no roller for printing. Only a *belan* (roti roller) was used for the purpose.[223] Every fifteen days, a leaflet was published to inform people about the unspeakable government repression and the challenges that lay before them. Leaflets were distributed in various ways—by direct meetings, by putting them in homes at night, or by post.

A young pracharak, Deepak Ranjan Sharma, distributed many such leaflets from one house to another. They also used to go to the houses of the opposition leaders to give them the news on contemporary developments in the country, because all other sources of contact among the leaders had ended.[224] Financial assistance was also provided to the families of many jailed persons by visiting their homes with utmost caution.

Another defiant hero of this time in Tripura was Bhaskar Kulkarni. When the Emergency was announced, Bhaskar Kulkarni, who was in Tripura at the time, went into hiding. Adopting the alias 'Narayan Sharma', he became a key figure in leading the anti-Emergency underground movement in the state.[225] His efforts included the covert distribution of leaflets that reached even the remotest corners of Tripura. For four months, he skilfully evaded arrest, but on the fateful day of

[222]Ibid.

[223]Ibid.

[224]Interview with Deepak Ranjan Sharma.

[225]Interview with Bhaskar Kulkarni.

25 October 1975, his luck ran out.[226]

Kulkarni was staying with an acquaintance in Dharmanagar, a person he would later regret trusting. This acquaintance betrayed him to an SIB inspector.[227] As Kulkarni was about to board a bus in Dharmanagar, carrying a bag full of leaflets destined for Manipur, the inspector approached him.

'Who are you and where are you headed?' The inspector enquired.[228]

'Narayan Sharma,' Kulkarni replied confidently. The inspector, however, pulled out a photograph and pointed at him. 'You are Bhaskar Kulkarni, and you are from the RSS.'[229]

Kulkarni was arrested on the spot, with all his leaflets and contacts seized. Charged under the Defence of India Act (DIR), he was sent to Silchar Jail.[230] Upon his arrival, Kulkarni was greeted with garlands by many of the inmates, who were young college students sympathetic to the RSS and familiar with his work. Instantly, Kulkarni became a hero among the prisoners, which included several socialist leaders.

In jail, Kulkarni initiated regular Sangh shakha activities. He led the inmates in reciting prayers, engaging in intellectual discussions (baudhik), and performing yoga and physical exercises (sharirik).[231] His actions inspired great enthusiasm among pracharaks across the country. Even Sarsanghchalak Balasaheb Deoras—who was imprisoned in Pune—wrote letters to Kulkarni, praising his resilience and spirit.

Kulkarni's influence became such a menace to the authorities that they decided to transfer him to Nagaon. However, his indomitable spirit could not be contained there either. The jailers

[226]Ibid.
[227]Ibid.
[228]Ibid.
[229]Ibid.
[230]Ibid.
[231]Ibid.

in Nagaon found it equally challenging to suppress his activities. As a result, Kulkarni was extradited to Nasik Jail in his home state of Maharashtra, where his continued defiance and dedication further fuelled the resolve of the anti-Emergency movement.[232]

The Emergency also saw the mass incarceration of 60–70 pracharaks and Sangh karyakartas in Manipur, bringing the RSS's three-decade-long sampark to a total end. It was only in December 1981 that Bhaskar Kulkarni could return to Manipur to re-establish sampark and continue its work, along with a renewed and stronger cadre consisting of people such as M.M. Asokan, who later became the prant pracharak.[233]

At the national level, prominent people like Nanaji Deshmukh of Jana Sangh, Dattopant Thengadi of Sangh, socialist ideologue Ravindra Verma and others started correspondence with Indira Gandhi through the Lok Sangharsh Samiti to end the Emergency. But the repression did not stop. As all the efforts failed, the Samiti decided to start a satyagraha. Meanwhile, Nanaji Deshmukh was also arrested. Moropant Pingle of the Sangh, Dattopant Thengadi and Ravindra Verma visited Assam.

Information about the satyagraha was shared in small meetings. In such meetings, maximum attendance was of the swayamsevaks of the Sangh. It was decided to hold satyagrahas in every province from 14 November 1975 to 20 January 1976.[234] It was urged that the first satyagraha of the opposition parties would be held in Assam. Despite not being completely prepared for the event, the first satyagraha took place in Guwahati on 14 November. Gradually satyagrahas were organized in other districts as well.[235]

Chauthaiwale writes about two acts of resistance. In

---

[232]Ibid.

[233]Ibid.

[234]Chauthaiwale, Shashikant, *Mor Pracharak Jatra,* Tirthankar Das (trans.), Prachi Prakashan, Guwahati, 2023.

[235]Ibid.

Dibrugarh, three swayamsevaks who worked at All India Radio were presenting a programme which was filtered by the government. In the middle of the programme, they started raising slogans against the Emergency.[236] They were obviously arrested. The second example is that of the Lawyers' Conference organized by the Congress Party in Guwahati. The then All India President of Congress, Dev Kant Barooah, and Rajni Patel of Delhi were invited to the programme. Before either of them reached the venue, while the speeches of other local leaders were going on, some swayamsevaks started distributing leaflets and began raising slogans in the hall itself. The police closed the doors of the auditorium and caught hold of all the satyagrahis. They were beaten up.[237]

However, as the tide of public opinion turned against the oppressive regime, cracks began to appear in the facade of authoritarian rule. From the halls of academia to the corridors of power, dissent simmered beneath the surface, awaiting the opportune moment to erupt into full-fledged rebellion. Ultimately, it was the collective will of the people that proved to be the undoing of the Emergency regime. Through acts of courage and defiance, ordinary citizens and dedicated activists alike paved the way for the restoration of democracy and the rule of law.

And when the shackles of oppression finally fell away in December 1977, the Sangh pracharaks and swayamsevaks emerged as phoenixes reborn from the ashes of adversity, their paths forever altered. Many of them, such as Deepak Ranjan Sharma and Gurupada Bhowmick, campaigned for the Janata Party coalition. The RSS, with its vast network of dedicated workers, embarked on an extensive campaign across the length and breadth of the nation. They traversed villages and towns, spreading the message of change, of a brighter tomorrow where democracy

[236]Ibid.

[237]Ibid.

would reign supreme. Through fiery speeches and impassioned pleas, they ignited the flames of dissent, rallying the masses to rise against oppression.

In the midst of this tumultuous landscape, the 1977 elections loomed large. The RSS threw its weight behind the Janata Party, aligning itself with like-minded individuals who shared their vision for a free and democratic India. Together, they forged an alliance that would shake the very foundations of the political establishment. With unwavering determination, RSS volunteers fanned out across the country, leaving no stone unturned in their quest to secure victory for the Janata Party. They canvassed tirelessly, knocking on doors and engaging in spirited debates, all in a bid to sway the hearts and minds of the electorate.

Their efforts bore fruit on that fateful day when the nation went to the polls. The echoes of change reverberated through the ballot boxes as millions of voters cast their votes in favour of the Janata Party. It was a landslide victory, a triumph of democracy over despotism. As the results poured in, the nation held its breath, poised on the cusp of history. And when the final tally was announced, there was jubilation in the streets as it became clear that the undemocratic reign of Indira Gandhi had come to an end.

In the corridors of power, a new dawn broke as Morarji Desai ascended to the highest office in the land, his hands clasped in gratitude to the countless volunteers of the RSS who had fought tirelessly for this momentous victory. And as the sun set on that historic day, it cast its warm glow over a nation reborn, united in its quest for freedom and justice.

4

Tales of Bullets and Blood

Save Assam today to save Bharat tomorrow.

—ABVP[238]

(Slogan raised during the Assam Agitation, 1979–85)

Just as the Sangh emerged out of the shadows of the Emergency, dark clouds gathered over their heads again. In the tranquil state of Assam, the rhythm of life was dictated by the mighty Brahmaputra River. This serene facade, however, concealed a growing unease—a storm brewing beneath the surface, born of decades-long tensions and fears.

The late 1970s marked a period of increasing demographic pressure on Assam that threatened to erode its very identity.[239] The roots of this crisis lay deep in the region's history, marked by waves of migration dating back to the colonial era (as described in the first chapter). The situation worsened further during the Bangladesh War of 1971.[240] The influx, often undocumented, brought about significant demographic changes, particularly in Assam's rural and border areas.

---

[238]Interview with Gulab Chand Kataria.

[239]Basumatary, Kumud Ranjan, 'A critique on the history of creation of tribal belts and blocks in Assam', *Asian Journal of Research in Social Sciences and Humanities,* Vol. 10, No. 7, 2020, pp. 8–16.

[240]Ibid.

By the mid-twentieth century, the indigenous Assamese communities began to feel overwhelmed and marginalized; their political power seemed diluted and their cultural heritage threatened by the sheer number of new settlers. The landscape of Assam was changing—not just physically, but demographically and culturally too. Fields that once grew rice and tea were now home to new settlements, and the Assamese language found itself competing with Bengali in schools, offices and marketplaces.

The situation reached a boiling point in 1978 during the by-election in Mangaldoi.[241] As officials prepared the voter rolls, they discovered that a significant number of voters were illegal immigrants. Chief Election Commissioner S.L. Shakdher admitted that the practice of enlisting foreigners in electoral rolls did happen, sending shockwaves across the state.[242] In 1979, draft enrolments in Mangaldoi by-polls showed 47,000 doubtful entries out of which 26,000 were confirmed to be outsiders.[243] This revelation was a lightning rod for the Assamese population. It wasn't just about numbers; it was about identity, land and the future of Assam. The fear that the Assamese would become a minority in their own land was palpable and pervasive.

In universities and colleges, the young minds of Assam—witnessing the erosion of their cultural and political influence—began to stir. Among these young leaders, the All Assam Students' Union (AASU) emerged as a potent force. Formed in 1967, AASU had grown in prominence by the late 1970s, becoming the vanguard of the movement against illegal immigration.[244] Under the leadership of dynamic and articulate figures, the AASU began organizing meetings, rallies and discussions, spreading

[241]Ibid.

[242]Ibid.

[243]Ibid.

[244]Sharma, Protim, 'Identity consciousness and students' movement: The role of AASU', *Unheeded Hinterland*, Dilip Gogoi (ed.), Routledge India, 2016, pp. 133–143.

their message far and wide. The call to action was clear: the identification and deportation of illegal immigrants to preserve Assamese identity.

As the message of the AASU resonated, a collective consciousness began to emerge among the Assamese people. From the bustling streets of Guwahati to the remote villages nestled in the hills, a sense of unity and purpose took hold. The movement was not just about politics; it was about survival and self-preservation. It was about ensuring that future generations could grow up in an Assam that still felt like home.

The streets and fields of Assam began to echo with the fervent cries of the movement. Slogans demanding the preservation of *Asomiya Ashmita* (Assamese self-respect/pride) rang out in public gatherings, uniting people across different communities and walks of life.[245] The Brahmaputra, once a symbol of life and continuity, now mirrored the turbulence that gripped the state. The placid waters seemed to hold within them the reflections of a people on the brink of a historic struggle.

Thus, the stage was set for the Assam Agitation, an epic struggle that would test the resilience and resolve of Assam and its people. The tranquil land of lush greenery and serene rivers was about to be engulfed in a storm of passionate protests and fierce demands, driven by the unyielding spirit of its people determined to reclaim their identity and secure their future.

The Protests

The first signs of unrest in Assam were subtle. Students boycotted classes, small gatherings formed in town squares, and hushed conversations took place in tea stalls. These were the early rumblings of what would soon become a powerful mass movement. By 1979, the Assam Agitation had erupted

[245]Ibid.

with a force that shook the entire state. The All Assam Students' Union (AASU) and the Gana Sangram Parishad (GSP) emerged as the vanguards of the movement, channelling the collective frustration into a structured campaign demanding the detection, disenfranchisement and deportation of illegal immigrants.

The streets of Guwahati, the state's bustling capital, became the epicentre of agitation. Protesters, carrying banners and placards, filled the avenues, chanting 'Foreigners go back!' and 'Save Assam!'[246] These protests quickly spread to other towns and villages, uniting people across different demographics—students, farmers, intellectuals and ordinary citizens alike. The movement became a tapestry of shared grievances and hopes, woven together by a common fear of losing cultural and political autonomy.

Frequent strikes (known locally as *bandh*s) and road blockades brought everyday life to a standstill. The once-busy markets, schools and offices of Assam found themselves deserted. The state-wide bandhs were a show of solidarity and resistance, paralysing transportation and commerce. Villagers joined hands to block major highways and railway lines, cutting off Assam from the rest of the country. The *rail roko* (block the trains) campaigns were particularly symbolic, highlighting the blockade of foreign influence and the protection of their land.

Educational institutions transformed into hubs of political activism. Universities and colleges buzzed with fervent discussions and debates. Lecture halls were replaced by protest stages, and classrooms became planning rooms for the next demonstration. Students—many of whom had never before engaged in political action—found themselves on the front lines, driven by a deep-seated desire to protect their heritage. Their youthful energy and idealism injected a vigorous spirit into the movement.

---

[246]Interview with Ashish Chauhan.

The Central government—viewing the protests as a threat to national integrity and stability—responded with increasing force. First, the Indira Gandhi-led Union government passed the Illegal Migrants (Determination by Tribunals) (IMDT) Act in 1983, making it even more difficult to deport illegal Bangladeshi Muslim immigrants.[247] The Act was pushed through mainly on the grounds that it provided special protections against undue harassment to the 'minorities' affected by the Assam Agitation.[248] Under the IMDT Act, the burden of proving citizenship rested on the accuser and the police, not the accused.

Second, police and paramilitary units were dispatched to Assam to maintain order, but their presence often led to violent clashes. The streets of Guwahati and other towns became battlegrounds. Tear gas filled the air, and the sound of gunfire echoed through neighbourhoods.[249] Baton charges and mass arrests became common, and the images of students being dragged away by police officers were broadcasted across the nation, further fuelling the anger and resolve of the protestors. Despite the oppressive measures, the spirit of the movement remained unbroken. Leaders of the AASU and GSP continued to rally their supporters, organizing marches and sit-ins that defied curfews and bans on public gatherings.

Meanwhile, the migration crisis continued, further exacerbated by the IMDT Act. Only while analysing the migration data in hindsight do we realize the sheer scale of unchecked immigration. Data shows that a total of 19.8 lakh foreign immigrants came into Assam from 1951, out of which 13.04 lakh or 45.26 per cent were illegal.[250] The decadal growth rates of Bengali Muslims

---

[247]Guha, Archit, 'The "Illegal Immigrant" Identity and Its Fragments–From "Enemy Foreigner" to "Bangladeshi Illegal Immigrant" in (Post) Colonial India', *Socio-Legal Review*, Vol. 12, No. 1, 2016, pp. 108–132.

[248]Ibid.

[249]Interview with Ashish Chauhan.

[250]Barooah, Nabaarun, 'In Assam, Hindutva Has Helped BJP Build an

during 1971–1991 was a staggering 77.42 per cent, the result of a combination of high total fertility rate (TFR) as well as unchecked illegal immigration on a tremendous scale.[251] On the contrary, the same was 42 per cent for other indigenous communities of the state. According to Census data, only three out of the fourteen districts of Lower Assam have a non-Muslim majority. This sparked fears and concerns among the local population, often leading to violent reactions such as riots.[252]

One of the darkest moments of the Agitation came in 1983 with the Nellie massacre. In a tragic and brutal outbreak of violence, over 2,000 Bengali-speaking Muslims were killed in and around the village of Nellie over alleged grooming, kindapping and the gangrape of Tiwa girls by 'immigrant Muslims'.[253] However, in the aftermath of the incident, the Tiwa community was vilified and attacked. During this testing time, the Sangh backed and supported the Tiwas when the entire community faced racial abuse. The massacre exposed the deep-seated communal tensions that lay beneath the surface of the agitation. It was a grim reminder of the dangerous potential for violence when ethnic and communal fears are stoked.

Despite such setbacks, the leadership of the agitation pressed on with their demands. Negotiations with the Central government began, but the process was slow and fraught with mistrust. The Assamese leaders were adamant: no settlement would be acceptable without a concrete solution to the immigration issue. The Central government—on the other hand—was wary of setting a precedent that might ignite similar movements in other states.

Impossible Consensus', *The Wire*, 3 April 2023, https://tinyurl.com/2m4jcaub. Accessed in 08 May 2025.

[251]Ibid.

[252]Ibid.

[253]Interview with Mohini Pator (name changed).

In the tumultuous year of 1983, Assam was a battleground of electoral violence, with the Lakhimpur and Dhemaji areas experiencing some of the worst clashes. The state was in turmoil, and the people in these regions found themselves caught in the crossfire. In response to the escalating crisis, the Sangh took a decisive step by forming the Sangharsh Peedit Sahayata Samiti, a committee aimed at providing relief to those affected by the violence. The committee's mission was clear: to bring aid and solace to the suffering population.[254] However, the formation of this committee did not sit well with everyone. AASU vehemently opposed the Sangh's initiative. The opposition was so intense that it forced all the committee members to resign, effectively dismantling the Sangharsh Peedit Sahayata Samiti before it could fully implement its relief efforts. The resignation of the committee members left a void in the much-needed relief operations, adding to the despair of the affected communities.

Recognizing the urgent need for continued relief efforts despite the political opposition, Deepak Borthakur, a swayamsevak, displayed remarkable resilience and leadership. He took the initiative to form an alternative committee, undeterred by the challenges that lay ahead. His newly formed committee took up the responsibility of providing relief in the strife-torn areas of Lakhimpur and Dhemaji. Under Borthakur's leadership, the committee carried out extensive relief work, bringing much-needed support to the affected populations.[255] His efforts not only alleviated the immediate suffering but also exemplified a spirit of perseverance and humanitarianism.

The agitation continued for six long years, marked by periods of intense protest interspersed with moments of uneasy calm. It was a time of great upheaval in Assam—socially, politically and economically. The state's economy suffered as

[254]Interview with Shankar Das.

[255]Interview with Brahmaji Rao.

strikes and blockades disrupted trade and industry. Educational institutions faced closures, and the constant state of unrest took a psychological toll on the populace. It is estimated that 860 Assamese citizens, mostly youth, were martyred. Yet, through it all, their determination to safeguard the Assamese identity remained steadfast.

The Assam Agitation was more than just a protest; it was a profound assertion of regional identity and self-determination. The passion and resilience displayed by the people of Assam during these years became a testament to their unwavering commitment to their land and culture. As the protests raged on, they sought to not only change policies but also etch their struggles and aspirations into the collective consciousness of the nation.

The Role of ABVP

The story of the Assam Agitation cannot be fully understood without acknowledging the significant role played by the Rashtriya Swayamsevak Sangh (RSS) and its student wing, the Akhil Bharatiya Vidyarthi Parishad (ABVP). The roots of their involvement stretch back to 1950, when the ABVP began its operations in Assam with a nationalist agenda.

From its inception, the ABVP focused on mobilizing youth around issues of national importance. In Assam, their activities initially centred on educational reforms and cultural preservation, echoing the broader goals of the RSS, which had had a long-standing presence in the state. The RSS's ideological emphasis on national unity and cultural integrity found fertile ground in Assam, a region where identity and demographic changes were becoming increasingly contentious issues. However, the acceptance of ABVP within the Assamese student-fold hadn't occurred for nearly three decades. The Assam Agitation changed that.

By the late 1970s, the demographic crisis in Assam, spurred by the influx of illegal immigrants, had reached a critical point.

The ABVP and RSS recognized the potential for this regional issue to escalate into a national crisis. They began to frame the immigration issue not just as a threat to Assamese identity but also as a challenge to India's sovereignty and cultural fabric.

With the eruption of the Assam Agitation in 1979, the ABVP and RSS intensified their involvement. They strategically positioned themselves as key allies of the AASU and the Gana Sangram Parishad, providing organizational support and amplifying the movement's message. They saw the agitation as an opportunity to reinforce their nationalist ideology and highlight the importance of protecting India's borders and cultural integrity.

One of the significant contributions of the ABVP was its ability to take the movement to a national platform. They launched a nationwide campaign, bringing the plight of the Assamese people to the forefront of national discourse. Slogans like 'Not just Assam's problem but India's problem' and 'Save Assam today to save Bharat tomorrow' echoed across campuses and cities throughout India.[256] The ABVP united students from different states, highlighting the common cause of protecting the nation's integrity.

ABVP activists organized rallies, protests and awareness campaigns in major cities, from Delhi to Mumbai. They mobilized students on campuses, emphasizing the idea that the struggle of Assam was a struggle for India. Slogans such as 'Mumbai *ho ya* Guwahati, *apna desh apni mati*' (Mumbai or Guwahati, our country our land) underscored the pan-Indian solidarity with the Assamese cause.[257]

In a particularly impactful move, the ABVP facilitated the travel of Assamese students to other states, such as Rajasthan, to share their stories and experiences.[258] This not only fostered

[256]Interview with Ashish Chauhan.
[257]Interview with Ashish Chauhan.
[258]Interview with Gulab Chand Kataria.

a sense of unity but also educated people in other parts of the country about the specific challenges faced by Assam. One such student interaction in Rajasthan left a lasting impact on a young man named Gulab Chand Kataria, who would later rise to become the governor of Assam. His empathy for the Assamese struggle and his commitment to their cause highlighted the far-reaching influence of the movement.

The involvement of ABVP and RSS also brought with it significant sacrifices. In 1980, during a major protest at Judges' Field in Guwahati, ABVP workers faced brutal repression. The *lathi* charge by the police left many injured, and stories of torture and arrests became emblematic of the struggle's intensity. Despite the violence and the risks, the commitment of these activists did not waver. Their efforts ensured that the Assam Agitation remained in the national spotlight, pressuring the Central government to take the issue seriously.

The combined force of regional passion and national solidarity gave the Assam Agitation a unique character. It was not merely a localized protest but a significant chapter in India's ongoing narrative of identity and autonomy. The involvement of national organizations like ABVP and RSS showcased the potential for regional issues to resonate on a larger scale, uniting diverse communities under a common cause. Their involvement was instrumental in bringing the Assamese struggle to the attention of the entire nation, ensuring that the voices of Assam were heard loud and clear across India.

As the Assam Agitation continued to rage throughout the early 1980s, its impact began to reverberate across the social, political and economic landscapes of the state and the nation. The movement, marked by intense protests, violent clashes, and deep communal divides, left a lasting legacy that shaped Assam's future in profound ways.

The most immediate and significant consequence of the

Assam Agitation was the signing of the Assam Accord on 15 August 1985. This historic agreement between the leaders of the Agitation and the government of India stipulated several key provisions:

i. Detection, deletion and deportation of all illegal immigrants who had entered Assam after 24 March 1971.[259]
ii. Constitutional, legislative and administrative safeguards to protect the cultural, social and linguistic identity of the Assamese people.[260]
iii. The assurance of the government to halt the influx of illegal immigrants and prevent future inflows through enhanced border security.[261]

The Assam Accord was a significant political victory for the leaders of the agitation, particularly for the AASU and the GSP. It marked the culmination of their demands and the official recognition of their concerns. The implementation of the accord, however, proved to be a complex and contentious process. Despite the initial euphoria, the practical challenges of identifying and deporting illegal immigrants led to prolonged debates and legal battles. The National Register of Citizens (NRC) update, intended to enforce the accord's provisions, became a protracted and controversial exercise, stirring fresh disputes and anxieties among different communities in Assam.

The Assam Accord also had broader political repercussions. It led to the formation of the Asom Gana Parishad (AGP), a regional political party born out of the agitation. The AGP, capitalizing on the widespread support it had garnered during

---

[259]Barooah Pisharoty, Sangeeta, *Assam: The Accord, The Discord*, Penguin eBury Press, India, 2019.
[260]Ibid.
[261]Ibid.

the movement, won a decisive victory in the 1985 state elections. Political scientists give the anecdote of how student leaders shifted overnight from their university hostel to Dispur to assume power. The party's rise to power marked a significant shift in Assam's political landscape, as it brought a regionalist agenda to the forefront of governance. The AGP's tenure, however, was fraught with challenges, including economic difficulties, continued ethnic tensions and insurgent activities by groups such as the United Liberation Front of Assam (ULFA), which emerged in the aftermath of the agitation.

The Assam Agitation deeply affected the social fabric of the state. The movement, which had united people across various demographics, also sowed seeds of division and mistrust, particularly along ethnic and communal lines. The exodus of many Bengali speakers, including Bengali Hindus, and Hindi speakers, including Marwari businessmen, Bihari migrants and other communities who felt targeted by the agitation, altered the population dynamics in several regions. The fear of being labelled an illegal immigrant and the subsequent social ostracization pushed many to leave Assam, seeking safety and stability elsewhere.

Despite these fractures, the Assam Agitation also fostered a renewed sense of Assamese identity and pride. The movement reinforced the cultural and linguistic heritage of Assam, leading to efforts to preserve and promote Assamese language, literature and traditions. Educational reforms and cultural initiatives aimed at strengthening Assamese identity became more prominent, shaping the state's cultural policies for years to come.

The movement also exposed the fragility of social cohesion and the complexities of addressing deep-seated demographic issues. Most importantly, it brought the RSS into the centre-stage of Assamese socio-political debate.

The Other Side of Sub-Nationalism: Rise of Robin Hoods

The regionalism and sub-nationalism that emerged in the tail-end of the 1970s led to another faction of nationalists that advocated for violent revolution. It was 7 April 1979. The fires of the Assam Agitation still blazed, and a group of passionate young radicals gathered in secret in the Ahom monument of Rang Ghar in Sibsagar.[262] Led by the fiery Paresh Baruah, Arabinda Rajkhowa and Anup Chetia, they formed the United Liberation Front of Assam (ULFA).[263] Unlike the peaceful protests that had defined the Assam Agitation, these young revolutionaries believed that only through armed struggle could Assam achieve true sovereignty. They viewed the political process as a dead-end, incapable of addressing the deep-seated grievances of their people.

In the beginning, ULFA operated in the shadows, building their strength and gathering followers. They found eager recruits among the disillusioned youth who had lost faith in the slow-moving promises of the Assam Accord. For these young men and women, ULFA's mission offered a sense of purpose and a way to fight for their homeland. ULFA's early days were marked by bold, almost romantic acts. They targeted wealthy Hindi-speaking businessmen, seen as symbols of economic exploitation and cultural dominance. These businessmen, prospering while the local Assamese struggled, became prime targets. ULFA's leaders justified their actions by claiming they were taking from the rich outsiders to help their own impoverished people. The money they extorted funded their operations and supported poor Assamese youth, paying for

---

[262]Hazarika, Sanjoy, *Strangers of the Mist: Tales of War and Peace from India's Northeast*, Penguin Books India, Delhi, 1994.
[263]Ibid.

education and basic needs. This Robin Hood-like strategy resonated deeply with many Assamese, who saw ULFA not as criminals, but as protectors and avengers. The narrative of fighting against economic exploitation and standing up for Assamese identity won them significant popular support.

In those early years, ULFA's actions struck a chord. Robberies and targeted extortion were viewed as acts of defiance against a system that had long marginalized the Assamese. The wealth they redistributed helped local communities, further enhancing their image as modern-day Robin Hoods. In villages and towns across Assam, ULFA was seen as a force for good, standing up to the powerful and giving hope to the downtrodden. ULFA's early successes in challenging the status quo and providing tangible benefits to the local populace helped solidify their support base. Many locals viewed ULFA as the only group willing to take decisive action to protect their interests and fight against external economic dominance. The romanticized image of ULFA as champions of the Assamese cause cemented their place in the hearts of many.[264]

As ULFA grew in strength and confidence, their operations became more sophisticated and their political goals clearer. They began to articulate a vision of a sovereign Assam, free from Indian control. This radical vision continued to attract recruits and maintain their support base among those who felt marginalized. However, even in these early years, ULFA's methods drew criticism from some quarters. While their Robin Hood-like operations earned them admiration, the inherent violence of their approach raised concerns. In the early days of ULFA, the group turned its ire toward Marwari businessmen, whom they

---

[264]Baruah, Sanjib,. 'The State and Separatist Militancy in Assam: Winning a Battle and Losing the War?', *Asian Survey*, Vol. 34, No. 10, 1994, pp. 863–877, https://tinyurl.com/4apn3zhb. Accessed on 13 February 2025.

viewed as exploiters of Assamese resources and culture.[265] ULFA cadres extorted money from these businessmen, using threats and violence to extract funds for their cause. Shops owned by Marwaris were frequent targets; they were attacked, looted and often vandalized. One striking tactic involved painting over English signboards with black paint, a symbolic act of defiance against what they perceived as cultural imperialism. ULFA demanded that all signboards be written in Assamese, asserting local language and identity. Simultaneously, Bihari migrant labourers, seen as outsiders taking away jobs meant for the locals, faced brutal aggression. These labourers were attacked, harassed and driven out of their settlements, further stoking ethnic tensions and fostering an atmosphere of fear and division. Yet, for many Assamese, the group's promise of a better future and their role as protectors of Assamese identity kept support strong.

The creation of ULFA was a direct response to the unfulfilled promises and lingering frustrations of the Assam Agitation. This early phase, marked by a romanticized image of defiance and protection of Assamese culture, garnered significant popular support. The narrative of ULFA as defenders of Assamese rights and autonomy set the stage for their evolution into a more militant organization before they became a dreaded terrorist group.[266]

Tangled Paths of Sangh and ULFA

In the early years of ULFA's rise, an unexpected and complex relationship began to form between ULFA and the RSS. Both organizations, despite their differing ideologies and methods, found common ground in their shared anti-infiltrator agenda. They sought to protect the Assamese identity and culture from

---

[265]Interview with Prabir Thakur (name changed).

[266]Ibid.

what they perceived as the threat of illegal immigration and demographic changes.

Shankar Das, the baudhik pramukh, recalls how there was limited but notable cooperation between RSS and ULFA during this period. Both groups were deeply embedded in local rural communities, spreading awareness about the demographic problems and the dangers posed by unchecked immigration.[267] Das emphasizes that their interactions were primarily based on mutual respect for their shared goals, even though their ultimate visions for Assam diverged.

In the early 1980s, the Assamese countryside was a hotbed of activism and ideological fervour. ULFA's fiery rhetoric and bold actions struck a chord with many locals who felt marginalized and threatened by the influx of outsiders. Similarly, the RSS, with its disciplined cadres and focus on cultural nationalism, found a receptive audience among those who wanted to preserve their indigenous heritage. The synergy between these two groups was palpable in the early days, as both were seen as protectors of Assamese identity in different ways.

Brahmaji Rao, who served as the Jorhat Zila Pracharak in the late 1980s, provides a vivid picture of the grassroots dynamics.[268] He recounts how people in rural Assam often supported both ULFA and RSS for different but complementary reasons. ULFA was revered for its staunch pro-Assamese stance, while RSS garnered respect for championing the cause of the indigenous populations.[269] Rao recalls with a mix of nostalgia and irony how, in many households, it was common to find an RSS worker and an ULFA member sleeping under the same roof, united by their common cause despite their differences.

These shared nights, where an RSS volunteer and an ULFA

---

[267]Interview with Shankar Das.

[268]Interview with Brahmaji Rao.

[269]Ibid.

member would break bread and share stories under the same roof, symbolized a rare and delicate harmony.[270] Families saw ULFA as the fiery warriors standing up against economic exploitation and cultural erosion, while they viewed the RSS as steadfast guardians of traditional values and local interests. This coexistence was not just a political alignment but also a social phenomenon, reflecting the deeply intertwined lives and shared struggles of the Assamese people.

However, this fragile camaraderie was not destined to last. As ULFA's methods grew increasingly violent, their perspective on the RSS began to shift. ULFA started to view the RSS as an organization primarily composed of Marwaris and Bengalis—communities they began to see as part of the problem rather than the solution.[271] This shift in perception marked the beginning of a darker phase in their relationship.

The turning point came as ULFA's operations became more aggressive and indiscriminate. This evolution in tactics caused a rift between ULFA and many of its earlier supporters, including the RSS. ULFA began to perceive the RSS not as allies in the fight against demographic change, but as representatives of the very communities they blamed for Assam's problems.

The animosity soon manifested in violent confrontations. ULFA started targeting RSS shakhas and members, disrupting their meetings and harassing their workers. The once-cooperative atmosphere turned hostile, with ULFA accusing the RSS of undermining Assamese interests. This schism reflected the broader unravelling of ULFA's early support base, as their turn to violence alienated many who had initially seen them as defenders of Assamese identity.

In 1981, the city of Guwahati witnessed a significant event—the Hindu Sammelan, where Madhukar Dattatraya Deoras, the

---

[270] Ibid.

[271] Ibid.

then sarsanghchalak, delivered a stirring address. He emphasised the importance of organizing Hindu Sammelans across various regions to instil faith and unity among Hindus. Inspired by his call, the Sangh took steps to implement this vision, scheduling the first such event in the town of Nagaon. The preparations for the Nagaon Sammelan were meticulous. A grand pandal was erected, and the town buzzed with anticipation. However, not everyone welcomed the initiative. As the event drew closer, a wave of resistance began to build. Many who opposed the sammelan saw it as a threat and planned to disrupt it. On the day of the event, a group of agitators descended upon the pandal, intent on destruction.

The tension was palpable as these individuals, driven by hostility, moved towards the venue. In response, the Sangh members remained steadfast. They confronted the agitators with a surprising plea: 'First, go and take the blessings of your parents and family.'[272] This unexpected approach, grounded in respect and tradition, momentarily halted the aggressors. Yet, the intensity of their resolve did not wane. The situation escalated as more agitators joined in, determined to dismantle the pandal and halt the sammelan.

With stringent resolve, Prafulla Bora, a swayamsevak, stepped forward and placed himself between the pandal and the angry crowd. In a powerful gesture, he raised his voice and announced, 'Cut me with the spade before destroying the pandal.'[273] His words resonated with a blend of defiance and sacrifice, embodying the spirit of protection and devotion to the cause. His bravery galvanized the Sangh members and inspired the onlookers. The aggressors—faced with such unyielding determination—hesitated. Bora's act of valour highlighted the profound belief that the ideals of unity and faith were worth

---

[272] Ibid.

[273] Ibid.

defending, even at the loss of one's life.

Rao recounts another poignant example from Jorhat, where an RSS shakha was attacked by ULFA militants.[274] The shakha—which had once been a place of community gathering and cultural activities—was vandalized, and its members threatened. This incident shocked many in the community who had supported both organizations.[275] It marked a clear signal that ULFA had begun to view the RSS as adversaries, not allies.

This relationship became so intense that it resulted in atrocities against the pracharaks. This comes from the personal story of Sunita Haldekar, the Akhil Bharatiya Sampark Pramukh of the Rashtra Sevika Samiti. In 1989, she was sent to Guwahati as a *pracharika*, where she encountered intense anti-Bharat sentiments and witnessed the brutal killings of fellow karyakartas.[276] The following year, she received a threatening letter from ULFA.[277]

One evening, Sunita Haldekar was invited to dinner by a woman who had quietly admired the RSS's efforts.[278] This woman, despite her husband's pro-ULFA stance, felt a connection to the work Haldekar was doing and wanted to show her support in a small but meaningful way.[279] As Sunita Haldekar arrived at their home, she was warmly welcomed. The aroma of freshly cooked Assamese cuisine filled the air, and the children of the house looked at her with curious, innocent eyes. However, this atmosphere of quiet camaraderie was abruptly shattered when the woman's husband returned home. A staunch ULFA supporter, he had no tolerance for the RSS and its affiliates, whom he viewed as outsiders and enemies of the Assamese cause. As soon as he realized that Sunita Haldekar was in his home, his demeanour

[274]Ibid.
[275]Ibid.
[276]Interview with Sunita Haldekar.
[277]Ibid.
[278]Ibid.
[279]Ibid.

changed drastically. His face contorted with rage and he began hurling insults at her, his voice rising with each word.

'How dare you bring this Marwari party into our home?' He shouted at his wife, his eyes blazing with anger. 'You know very well that they are against our people, against Assam!' Haldekar sat calmly, her eyes reflecting a quiet resilience.[280] She had faced such hostility before, and she knew that responding with anger would only escalate the situation. Instead, she chose to maintain her composure, hoping that her calmness might help diffuse the man's fury.

But her silence seemed to fuel his rage even more. He turned his verbal assault directly at her, calling her a 'Bengali sympathizer' and 'anti-Assamese'.[281] His words were like venom, each one meant to wound and humiliate. His wife, now cowering in a corner, looked on helplessly as her husband's tirade continued. He even lashed out physically, thrashing her in a fit of blind rage. The man's accusations cut deep, not because they held any truth, but because they showcased the deep-seated hatred and fear that ULFA had managed to instil in the hearts of many Assamese people.[282]

The pro-ULFA sentiments ran deep, fuelled by a sense of betrayal and the fear of losing one's cultural identity. Sunita Haldekar's experience was not an isolated one; it was a narrative replayed in many homes across Assam. Despite these terrifying experiences, her work continued undeterred.

In one of the large camps in Tezpur, Samiti volunteers from across the region had gathered to participate. The camp was set up with meticulous care; the *dhwajsthan* (flagpole) and the prayer grounds were prepared to inspire and motivate the participants.[283] However, not everyone in Tezpur welcomed

---

[280]Ibid.

[281]Ibid.

[282]Ibid.

[283]Ibid.

their presence. As the sun dipped below the horizon, the camp's atmosphere of camaraderie and purpose was abruptly shattered. A group of AASU members, emboldened by their numbers and driven by a deep-seated mistrust, descended upon the camp. What started as verbal taunts quickly escalated into physical aggression. Haldekar, caught in the fray, found herself face to face with one of the attackers. In that moment she was slapped, the sting of the blow momentarily blinding her. The shock and pain radiated through her, but Haldekar's spirit remained unbroken. Her colleagues, witnessing the assault, were galvanized into action. They retaliated, attempting to defend their fellow worker and the sanctity of their camp. The confrontation grew chaotic, a swirl of shouts and scuffles in the gathering dusk.[284]

In the midst of the melee, the AASU members turned their attention to the dhwajsthan and the prayer area, symbols of the RSS's presence and purpose. They desecrated the sacred spaces, tearing down the flagpole and trampling over the prayer grounds.[285] The destruction was not just physical but deeply symbolic, an attempt to undermine the very essence of what the camp represented. As the dust settled, the camp's participants were left to reckon with the aftermath of the attack. The desecration of the dhwajsthan and the prayer area was a profound blow, but it also steeled their resolve.

Sunita Haldekar and her colleagues knew they could not let this act of aggression go unanswered. The decision was made to file FIRs against the attackers. It was a step that required courage, as they were up against a formidable and influential force in the region.[286] Yet, they were undeterred. They went to the local police station, determined to seek justice for the

---

[284]Ibid.

[285]Ibid.

[286]Ibid.

violence and desecration they had endured. The legal process was arduous, fraught with challenges, but it also brought the issue to the forefront, drawing attention to the unprovoked aggression they had faced.

Haldekar recounts a few more incidents. Back when Guwahati's streets rarely saw vehicles, she boldly rode around on a scooter. One day, in 1990 in Athgaon, she was stalked by a man who grabbed her scooter, pulled a knife, and asked her to leave Assam. In the same year, while travelling from Manipur to Silchar, militants hijacked her night bus, leading to a horrifying forty-hour hostage crisis during which sixteen men were shot to death before her eyes.[287] In fact, every pracharak we interviewed was attacked during this phase, including prominent figures like Shankar Das.[46] We got to hear one such fear-defying story of resilience from Ulhas Kulkarni, former kshetra pracharak of Purvanchal.

Ulhas Kulkarni recalled, 'I, along with Dhananjay ji and Mahendra ji, were forcibly taken from Nagaon city and crammed into a Maruti van, surrounded by heavily armed ULFA militants.'[288] Their destination was the remote village of Gumutha, situated about eight kilometres away. As the van sped through the rough terrain, the captives pondered their uncertain fate.[289]

Upon arriving in Gumutha, the three men were led into a house. Serendipitously, this house belonged to Pabitra Zamindar, the village headman.[290] More than just a local leader, Zamindar was a staunch supporter of the Sangh.[291] This unexpected connection cast a shadow of doubt and unease over the kidnappers.

Determined to assert their dominance, the militants began

---

[287]Ibid.

[288]Interview with Ulhas Kulkarni.

[289]Ibid.

[290]Ibid.

[291]Ibid.

to interrogate Ulhas Kulkarni with accusatory fervour. 'Why is the Sangh spreading communalism against Muslims?' One militant demanded, his voice laced with hostility.[292]

Undeterred, Ulhas Kulkarni responded with calm conviction, 'We are not spreading communalism, communalism is not a recent development. They date back to the eleventh century, with a history marked by numerous atrocities. The Ahoms had fought innumerable times against Mughals, even having to give up the Ahom Princess once. The Kamakhya Temple was destroyed by Kalapahar, a general of Sulaiman Karrani. So many other attacks have been launched. How are we responsible for communalism?'[293]

Taken aback by his composed demeanour, the militants pressed on with their questioning. 'What is your contention with Christians? They are doing noble work by building schools and hospitals. Look at Mother Teresa.'[294]

Ulhas Kulkarni's eyes sparked with determination as he replied, 'Service is indeed commendable, but what about the conversions that the Christian community is orchestrating? Is that something their dharma teaches them?'[295]

The militants, unable to counter Ulhas Kulkarni's unwavering logic and conviction, found themselves at a loss for words.[296] Their initial intent had been to intimidate the men, to instil fear and submission. However, they quickly realized that their captives possessed an unshakable resilience.

As the hours dragged on, the insurgents' resolve began to wane. By midnight, they decided to release the three men. Ulhas Kulkarni and his comrades walked free, their spirits unbroken.[297]

---

[292]Ibid.

[293]Ibid.

[294]Ibid.

[295]Interview with Ulhas Kulkarni.

[296]Ibid.

[297]Ibid.

News of their ordeal quickly spread, transforming into a tale of resilience and inner strength. The kidnapping, initially meant to be an act of terror, inadvertently showcased the power of conviction and the unyielding spirit of those who stand firm in their beliefs. The brave Sangh karyakartas returned to their community, not as victims, but as symbols of fortitude and courage. Their story became a testament to the enduring power of faith and resilience in the face of adversity.

Baying for Saffron Blood

The strained relationship between the Sangh and ULFA was marked by escalating violence against the former. This period saw increased tensions and confrontations as the Sangh began solidifying its political influence. Several pracharaks, who were at the forefront of this conflict, lost their lives. Murli Manohar was one of them. He was born as G. Narayanan on 29 March 1951, in the village of Venmani, nestled in Alappuzha, Kerala.[298] From a young age, Narayanan had dedicated his life to the selfless service of a cause much larger than himself. The pivotal year was 1968 when Narayanan, still in his adolescence, encountered the Sangh.[299] It was a meeting that would shape the rest of his life. Drawn to the Sangh's ideals and vision, Narayanan immersed himself in its philosophy of volunteerism, committing to its principles with an earnest fervour that would persist till his last breath.

Narayanan found his calling in the RSS and rose through the ranks, starting as the head teacher of a shakha.[300] His responsibilities grew as he took on the management of the

[298]Kavishwar, Sandip, *Mrityunjay Veer*, Rouhin Deb and Nabaarun Barooah (trans.), Prachi Prakashan, Guwahati, 2022.
[299]Ibid.
[300]Ibid.

division, showcasing his organizational acumen and leadership skills. Murli Manohar—or Murli ji, as he was affectionately called when he came to Assam—was more than just a figurehead; he was a teacher, a mentor, and a strategist. He was well-versed in the traditional disciplines of punishment, warfare and hierarchical structures, which were integral to the Sangh's training and ethos. Narayanan's magnetic teaching style and his warm, affectionate demeanour drew scores of young individuals to the Sangh shakhas. These branches flourished under his guidance and became vibrant hubs of youthful energy and nationalist zeal. He had an innate ability to connect with the youth, inspiring them with stories of valour and dedication, and instilling in them a sense of duty towards their country and community.

The dawn of a new chapter in Narayanan's life as a pracharak began when he was entrusted with the significant responsibility of the Uttar Kamrup district, with its *kendra* (centre) at Nalbari. Embarking on this journey with an open heart and dedication, he swiftly embraced his new role. His days were filled with tireless work and genuine efforts to connect with the local community. Recognizing the importance of language as a bridge to understanding, Narayanan immersed himself in learning Assamese and became fluent in the language within a remarkably short period of time. Murli Manohar's warm and amiable personality—and the simplicity and purity of his mind and intent—quickly endeared him to the people of Kamrup. He integrated seamlessly into the local society, gaining the trust and affection of those he served. His ability to understand and address the concerns of the people further solidified his standing in the community.

Basistha Bujarbaruah, the present kshetra pracharak, told us that whenever Narayanan would visit their village for sampark, he would focus on making friends among the young school and college-going students. As a result, the RSS recruited many youngsters. Once when Murli Manohar saw two boys fishing for an hour, he remarked, 'You would rather waste the whole day waiting for one fish than toil hard under the sun in fields or do manual labour.'[301] He urged everyone to work hard and not import migrant labourers. Looking back, Basistha Bujarbaruah remarks, 'This is why I joined the Sangh. Here was a man from Kerala who came all the way to Assam, learnt Assamese, embraced young Assamese people, roaming from village to village, wanting to genuinely solve our problems. Why? Just for the Hindu cause. I wanted to be a part of the same cause.'[302]

As a result, Narayanan came to loggerheads with ULFA. Once when Bujarbaruah and others were passing by a village which was an ULFA stronghold, some ULFA cadres stopped them, 'Don't come to our village again.' Bujarbaruah responded, 'If people here do not want us to come, we won't come. Unless they have a problem, we will keep coming. We won't stop coming because of your threat.'[303] As such clashes increased, it became imminent that all hell would break loose.

And so it did, on 5 October 1990.[304] On what seemed like an ordinary day, Murli Manohar and his companion, Hemen Medhi, set out from Balitara to Dhamdhama on a motorcycle. The journey, intended to be routine, turned into a nightmare when they were ambushed by three ULFA insurgents. The sudden attack was brutal and swift, leaving no time for escape or defence.[305] The aftermath was a chaotic blur of fear and confusion, as Narayanan was forcibly taken away by the assailants. The news of the ambush spread rapidly, igniting a wave of shock and despair. Narayanan's disappearance left a void that was felt

---

[301]Interview with Basistha Bujarbaruah.

[302]Ibid.

[303]Kavishwar, Sandip, *Mrityunjay Veer*, Rouhin Deb and Nabaarun Barooah (trans.), Prachi Prakashan, Guwahati, 2022.

[304]Ibid.

[305]Ibid.

deeply by the community. Immediate efforts to locate him were launched, with Sangh workers and local authorities mobilizing to search every conceivable place where he might have been taken. Days turned into weeks, and weeks into months, but every lead ended in frustration. The relentless search yielded no results, and hope began to wane.

As the days passed, the gravity of the situation sunk in and the anxiety of not knowing Narayanan's fate began to gnaw at the hearts of his followers and loved ones. The uncertainty was excruciating, but it also galvanized the community into action. In a powerful display of solidarity and resolve, a massive protest march was organized in Guwahati. Several people from Nalbari, Guwahati and other surrounding regions came together and marched on the Dispur Secretariat, their collective voice echoing a thunderous demand for Narayanan's release.[306] This was perhaps Guwahati's first and largest anti-ULFA demonstration of that time. The rally was even flanked by ULFA sympathizers in bikes, but to no avail. The sheer scale of the gathering was a testament to the impact Narayanan had made in his time as a pracharak. Despite the intensity of the protests and the continuous efforts of the authorities, there was no breakthrough and the organization's morale was at an all-time low.

This incident created a climate of fear and uncertainty. In response, the RSS sought a way to mobilize and inspire a demoralized youth, and so the Hindu Yuba-Chattra Parishad was born in 1991. Unlike the traditional shakhas—where discipline, structure and ideology were paramount—the Hindu Yuba-Chattra Parishad took a different approach. It relaxed the rigid framework of the shakhas and infused Bollywood-style charisma into its activities to appeal to the youth.

Open jeeps, emblazoned with the symbolism of youth and vigour, roamed the streets to attract the next generation. The

---

[306]Ibid.

aesthetic of freedom, fun and purpose was designed to captivate those who had grown indifferent or hesitant to join more conventional shakhas. The Parishad became an entry point for thousands of young people, igniting curiosity and engagement at a time when fear had dulled both.

The effect was noticeable. Though the number of shakhas initially dwindled as the Parishad flourished, it brought about an unexpected benefit. A surge in sampark emerged among the youth, who now found themselves part of a shared cause. The psychological impact on the broader community was even more profound: fear diminished. The sight of energetic youths on open jeeps, defiantly celebrating their heritage, helped restore confidence among people who had been intimidated by political instability.

To mark the significance of the event that had spurred this movement, the RSS organized the Smriti Sammelan on 5 October 1991. Over 5,000 youths gathered to commemorate the kidnapping of Murli Manohar, with Vinay Katiyar—a fiery leader—serving as the chief guest. It was a symbolic moment of defiance, signalling that the era of fear was over and that the community had rediscovered its sense of purpose.

As confidence returned, the need for the Hindu Yuba-Chattra Parishad waned. Shakhas resumed and their traditional discipline and ideological rigour made a quiet comeback as the perceived threats to the community receded. With its role fulfilled, the Parishad gradually faded, its contributions etched into the memories of those who had been part of it.

Months of uncertainty finally culminated in a tragic revelation in March 1993.[307] The news that everyone had feared—but been fervently hoping against—came through: Narayanan had been killed by his captors.[308] The confirmation of his

---

[307]Kavishwar, Sandip, *Mrityunjay Veer*, Rouhin Deb and Nabaarun Barooah (trans.), Prachi Prakashan, Guwahati, 2022.

[308]Ibid.

untimely demise sent ripples of sorrow through the community. The initial shock gave way to a profound and pervasive grief, as the reality of their loss settled in. Narayanan's death was not just a personal loss to his family and friends but also a significant blow to the larger cause he had devoted his life to. However, his legacy lived on. The dedication, sacrifice and love he had shown for his work—and the people of Kamrup—left an indelible mark. Narayanan's life and untimely death became a poignant reminder of the challenges faced by those who work selflessly for the betterment of society.

A similar fate was met by another pracharak, Omprakash Chaturvedi. From a young age, Chaturvedi was drawn to the teachings and principles of the RSS.[309] His involvement with the Sangh began in his formative years and grew deeper with time. The Sangh's emphasis on discipline, spirituality and service resonated with him, moulding his aspirations and values. Chaturvedi's academic journey led him to the prestigious Banaras Hindu University (BHU), where he pursued his post-graduation.[310] The intellectual environment of BHU further fuelled his passion for learning and his commitment to the Sangh. Despite the pressures and challenges of academic life, Chaturvedi remained steadfast in his devotion to studies and spiritual pursuits. His parents, recognizing his dedication and potential, gave him their blessings as he chose a path of service and preaching in late 1976.[311]

Chaturvedi embarked on a journey that would define the rest of his life.[312] In 1989, Chaturvedi's journey took a pivotal turn when the Sangh called upon him to venture into Assam.[313]

[309]Ibid.
[310]Ibid.
[311]Ibid.
[312]Ibid.
[313]Ibid.

The task was daunting: he was to campaign in the districts of Dhubri and Kokrajhar, areas known for their complex social fabric and historical challenges. These districts were home to diverse tribes and communities, each with its own unique cultural identity. However, the region was also grappling with significant issues, such as infiltration and religious conversions.[314] During this period, Assam's political landscape was in a state of flux. Ethnic tensions, demands for autonomy and socio-economic challenges created a volatile environment.

In early 1990, Prant Sanghchalak Rajnikant Dev Sharma passed away.[315] His death left a deep void in the hearts of those who knew him, and on the thirteenth day following his demise, tribute programmes were organized by all branches of the province to honour his memory. One such solemn occasion took place in the village of Vidyapur, located in Kokrajhar district, where Chaturvedi was scheduled to attend a programme in the evening shakha.[316] The day began with an air of reverence and anticipation. Dedicated children and young swayamsevaks had been diligently preparing for the event since the early morning. Across the river, some young swayamsevaks were engrossed in the task of cooking, while others indulged in playful activities, their laughter mingling with the soothing sounds of nature. As the afternoon sun cast its gentle glow over the gathering, Chaturvedi assembled everyone in a large circle for a discussion. In this peaceful setting, the twelfth chapter of the Srimad Bhagavat Gita was recited.[317] Following the recitation, heartfelt prayers were offered for the peace of Rajnikant Dev Sharma's soul. The atmosphere was filled with a sense of unity and collective mourning, as everyone present reflected on the legacy of their departed leader.

---

[314]Ibid.

[315]Ibid.

[316]Ibid.

[317]Ibid.

However, the tranquillity of this sacred moment was shattered by an act of unimaginable violence. Two young men, their faces concealed with handkerchiefs, approached Chaturvedi with malicious intent.[318] The serene ambiance was pierced by the chilling sight of guns in their hands, and before anyone could react, they fired two fatal shots at Chaturvedi.[319] Panic erupted as the sound of gunfire echoed through the gathering. Volunteers, who had been playing and cooking just moments before, now scrambled to protect Chaturvedi. In the ensuing chaos, some tried valiantly to shield him from further harm, but the assailants, driven by cold and calculated malice, managed to flee across the river, disappearing into the forest that lay beyond.

As the smoke cleared, the sight of Chaturvedi lying on the ground, his life ebbing away, was a heart-wrenching scene. Despair hung heavy in the air, and the sense of loss was palpable. Yet, in a final act of brutality, one of the youths returned and fired another bullet at the fallen leader, sealing his fate with merciless finality. Desperate attempts were made to rush Chaturvedi to the hospital.[320] In the absence of a proper vehicle, a handcart was used to transport him, a stark symbol of the helplessness that gripped the Sangh and its members during that decade. Upon arrival, the doctors could do nothing more than confirm the worst. Chaturvedi was declared dead, his life cut short by a senseless act of violence.[321]

The news of his death sent shockwaves through the community, casting a pall of sorrow over the gathering. The event that was meant to honour the memory of one beloved leader had now become the tragic scene of another. Chaturvedi, a man

---

[318]Ibid.

[319]Ibid.

[320]Ibid.

[321]Ibid.

dedicated to the service of his people and the teachings of the Sangh, was no more. The senseless act of violence robbed the community of a cherished and devoted member. Chaturvedi's passing left a profound void that words could scarcely convey. His life, marked by humility, dedication and an unwavering commitment to the principles he held dear, was abruptly ended. Yet, even in the face of such tragedy, his legacy endured in the hearts and minds of those who had the privilege of knowing him.

Another figure at the forefront of spreading the Sangh's ideology was a pracharak named Pramod Dixit. Growing up alongside his two brothers, Prakash and Praveen, Pramod embraced the values of seva from a young age, taking on roles as both a teacher and a *shakha sarkaryavah* in the Sangh.[322] Dixit's dedication to the Sangh's principles and his natural leadership abilities were evident from early on. His journey within the Sangh culminated in a significant milestone in 1973 when he completed the third-year Sangh education class, qualifying him to become a pracharak.[323] This achievement marked the beginning of a lifelong commitment to the Sangh's mission of fostering cultural and national unity.

In the tumultuous years following the Emergency, Dixit responded to a higher call of duty. Guided by the vision of Sarsanghchalak Rajjubhaiya, he embarked on a journey to Assam in 1979. Dixit's first assignment in Assam was as the Guwahati Mahanagar Pracharak. Immersing himself in Assamese culture, he demonstrated an exceptional ability to connect with people from all walks of life.[324] His approach was inclusive and empathetic, and he quickly gained the trust and respect of the local community. One of his most impactful initiatives was organizing blood-donation camps, which rallied thousands

[322]Ibid.
[323]Ibid.
[324]Ibid.

Vasant Fadnavais, who came to Assam in 1946 and laid the foundation of the RSS in Jorhat and Silchar.

Source: Archives of RSS

Lalit Bordoloi of Dibrugarh, one of the first local *pracharaks* from Assam in the 1950s.

Source: Archives of RSS

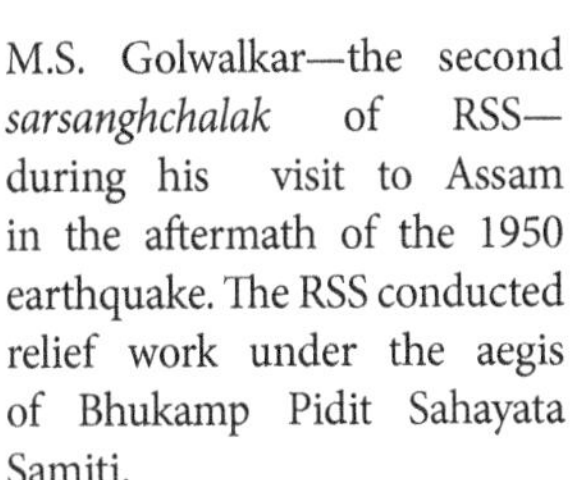

M.S. Golwalkar—the second *sarsanghchalak* of RSS—during his visit to Assam in the aftermath of the 1950 earthquake. The RSS conducted relief work under the aegis of Bhukamp Pidit Sahayata Samiti.

Source: Archives of RSS

Swayamsevaks providing relief aid to Chakma refugees.

Source: Archives of RSS

Balasaheb Deoras—the third sarsanghchalak of RSS—being felicitated at Judges' Field, Guwahati, in 1977 after coming out of a 19-month-long imprisonment during the Emergency.

Source: Archives of RSS

People along with swayamsevaks gathered to mark the event of Balasaheb Deoras' felicitation programme.

Source: Archives of RSS

Rajendra Singh Tomar, the fourth sarsanghchalak, meets Rani Gaidinliu.

Source: Archives of RSS

Members of the Good Will Mission who came to Assam after the 1983 communal clashes. Sridhar Pathak, Avinash Brahma and Narendra Devshastri along with Professor Kedarnath Poddar, Professor Omprakash Kohli, Professor S.V. Seshgirirao, journalist Rampal Singh, Justice T.V. Mehta and others. The man on the far left is the then Akhil Bharatiya Vidyarthi Parishad Sangathan Mantri and present RSS Sarkaryavah Dattatreya Hosabale.

Source: Archives of RSS

Relief work by Sangharsha Peedit Sahayata Samiti in Assam in 1983.

Source: Archives of RSS

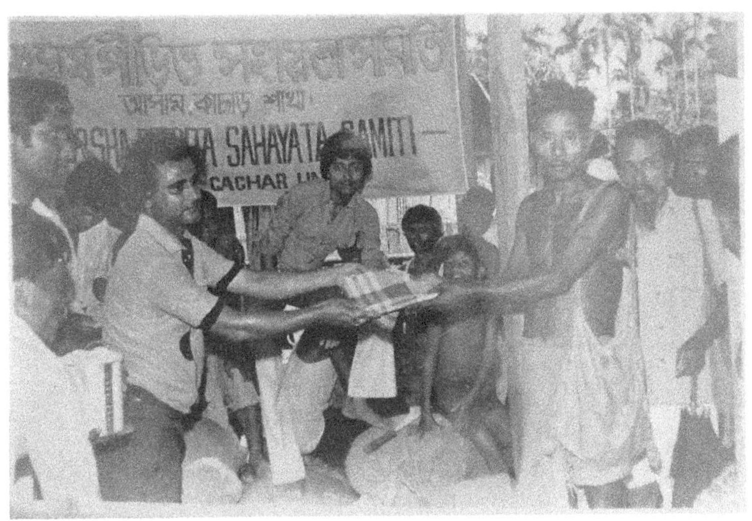

Relief work by Sangharsh Pidit Sahayata Samiti in Cachar in 1983.

Source: Archives of RSS

G. Narayanan (also known as Murli Manohar), who was a pracharak in Nalbari, providing flood relief. He was later kidnapped and killed by the ULFA in 1990.

Source: Archives of RSS

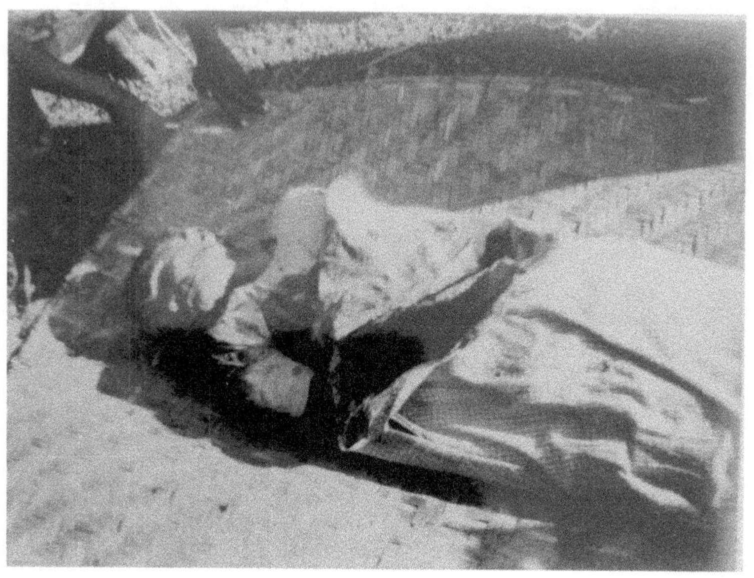

The assassination of Omprakash Chaturvedi, the Kokrajhar Zila Pracharak, by militants in 1991.

Source: Archives of RSS

Thakur Ram Singh, the first *prant pracharak* of Assam (1949–71), addressing a public meeting in 1996 to mark the golden jubilee of the RSS in the state. To his left is Assam's then prant sanghchalak, Birinchadhar Buragohain.

Source: Archives of RSS

Swayamsevaks present at the golden jubilee celebrations of the RSS in Assam in 1996.

Source: Archives of RSS

Lakshyadhar Chowdhury speaking at the inaugural function of the birth centenary celebration of RSS founder Dr K.B. Hedgewar held in the District Library, Guwahati. Prant Sanghchalak Rajnikant Dev Sharma, Akhil Bharatiya Baudhik Pramukh K.S. Sudarshan and Prant Karyavah Bhumidev Goswami are present on stage.

Source: Archives of RSS

Dr Satyendra Nath Sharma addresses the closing ceremony of the Dr Hedgewar Birth Centenary Celebration Committee at B. Borooah College, Guwahati. Sarsanghchalak Balasaheb Deoras, Prant Sanghchalak Rajnikant Dev Sharma, the satradhikar prabhu of Sri Sri Auniati, and Prant Karyavah Bhumidev Goswami are present on stage.

Source: Archives of RSS

First temple dedicated to Rangfrah built by the locals of New Changlang on 4 November 1997.

Source: Rajesh Deshkar

The oil painting of Rangfrah that was chosen out of 172 entries to be the first representation of the deity.

Source: Rajesh Deshkar

Sarsanghchalak Mohan Bhagwat addresses the Luitporiya Hindu Samavesh at Guwahati on 21 January 2018.

Source: RSS.org

Janajati leaders at Luitporiya Hindu Samavesh at Guwahati on 21 January 2018.

Source: RSS.org

Sarsanghchalak Mohan Bhagwat with Seng Khasi members at U Lum Sohpetbneng on 27 September 2022.

Source: *Organiser*, RSS

A group of 15 Mizo girls meet Narendra Modi, Gujarat's erstwhile chief minister, on an educational tour organized by Rashtra Sevika Samiti in 2013. The tour was led by Samiti member Melita Lingdoh.

Source: NarendraModi.in

Sarsanghchalak Mohan Bhagwat at the Poorvottar Sant Manikanchan Sammelan in Majuli, Assam, a religious congregation of 104 seers from 48 satras and 37 other religious institutions from all over the Northeast, on 28 December 2023.

Source: *Organiser*, RSS

A swayamsevak during the closing ceremony of the Sangh Siksha Varg at Geetashram, Hojai, in June 2023.

Source: Authors

of youths to join the cause. These camps were more than just events; they were a testament to the power of collective action and solidarity.

Dixit's service extended beyond Guwahati to the districts of Kamrup, Goalpara and Barpeta. In each place, he forged meaningful connections with students, professors and local leaders. His approach was characterized by genuine care and a willingness to listen, which won over even those who initially opposed his presence. Dixit's ability to build bridges and foster dialogue was a key factor in his success. In Kamrup, Dixit's efforts focused on integrating the local youth into the Sangh's activities. He organized workshops and seminars that emphasised the importance of cultural preservation and national unity.[325] His charismatic leadership inspired many young people to take pride in their heritage and contribute to their community's welfare.

Goalpara presented a different set of challenges, with its diverse communities and socio-economic issues. Dixit approached these challenges with sensitivity and respect for the local traditions. He worked tirelessly to address the concerns of infiltration and cultural erosion, advocating for the preservation of the region's unique identity. His initiatives in Goalpara included health camps, educational programmes and cultural festivals that celebrated the area's rich heritage while promoting unity and cooperation.[326] In Nalbari, Dixit's inclusive approach and dedication to service left a lasting impact. He engaged with local leaders and community members to understand their needs and aspirations. His work in Nalbari was marked by a series of successful community projects that improved living conditions and fostered a sense of collective responsibility. Dixit's ability to inspire and mobilize people was evident in the tangible improvements seen in the area.

---

[325]Ibid.

[326]Ibid.

The summer of 1991 was particularly intense for Dixit. As the Barpeta Zila Pracharak, he was constantly on the move, organizing events, mentoring youth and spearheading initiatives that brought people together. His latest project involved the distribution of *Raksha Bandhan* leaflets, an effort to reinforce the bonds of unity and brotherhood among the community, which ended up being his undoing.

On the fateful day of 16 August 1991, Dixit had just returned from a successful *pravas* (trip).[327] Accompanied by a student worker called Nimai and his trusted colleague Kamlesh, Dixit had spent the day reaching out to people, spreading the message of Raksha Bandhan and inviting people to participate in the upcoming festivities.[328] The air was thick with monsoon humidity, but Dixit's spirits were high as he believed in the power of these small yet significant gestures to bring about change.

Back at the Barpeta karyalaya, Dixit, Nimai and Kamlesh were greeted by youth activist Amarjit Das.[329] The office, a modest building that buzzed with the activity and enthusiasm of swayamsevaks, was a hub of planning and strategy. As they settled in, the conversation flowed easily, filled with reflections on the day's work and plans for the future. Their camaraderie and shared vision was palpable, a testament to the strong bonds Dixit had nurtured. Unbeknownst to them, danger loomed nearby. Three individuals on a motorcycle circled the karyalaya—their movements barely noticed by those inside, engrossed in their discussion.[330] The motorcycle stopped and the men dismounted, their intentions masked by the normalcy of the day. When they entered the office, Dixit's welcoming demeanour shone through, as it always did with visitors. He greeted them with warmth,

[327]Ibid.

[328]Ibid.

[329]Ibid.

[330]Ibid.

unaware of the sinister motive behind their visit.

The atmosphere shifted abruptly as the men's conduct became hostile. In a sudden violent outburst, they forcibly expelled Amarjit from the room. The tension was palpable as Dixit, Nimai and Kamlesh tried to make sense of the unfolding chaos. Dixit—always the diplomat—attempted to de-escalate the situation, but his words fell on deaf ears. In a blink, the fatal moment arrived. One of the men drew a gun and fired. The bullet struck Pramod Dixit in the chest.[331] The deafening sound of the gunshot echoed through the office, signalling a tragic end. He fell to the ground, lifeless, as the assailants fled the scene on their motorcycle.

Nimai and Kamlesh rushed to Dixit's side, their hands trembling and hearts heavy with shock and sorrow. The man who had been their guide, mentor and friend, had been shot dead. Despite their desperate attempts to save him, it was clear that Dixit's wounds were fatal. The news of Dixit's assassination spread like wildfire, casting a dark shadow over Barpeta and beyond. The community he had so passionately served was plunged into mourning, the loss of such a dedicated and inspirational leader leaving an indelible mark on all who knew him. His sacrifice was a stark reminder of the dangers faced by those who stand up for unity and peace in the face of violence and hatred.

A similar misfortune struck Shukleshwar Medhi. Born as Shukra in the village of Balitara in Nalbari district, he was the fifth child of Ramanath and Sanupriya Medhi, a humble, farming couple.[332] Life in the Medhi household was modest, yet enriched with the warmth of family and the values of hard work and devotion. Shukra, along with his two brothers and two sisters, grew up in a nurturing environment where simplicity was cherished and community bonds were strong.

[331]Ibid.

[332]Ibid.

From a young age, he displayed an insatiable curiosity and a love for learning. His early education began in the local school, where he excelled in his studies despite the limited resources. The close-knit community of Balitara recognized the spark in Shukra, and his parents—though bound by the constraints of farming life—encouraged his academic pursuits. Their support bore fruit when Medhi completed his BSc in physics in 1990.[333]

But Medhi's life was not defined solely by academic success. Deeply influenced by the teachings of the Sangh, his spiritual and ideological journey began early. The village Sangh shakha became his second home, and Medhi found a path that resonated with his values. The Sangh's emphasis on discipline, selfless service and cultural pride struck a chord with him, shaping his worldview and aspirations. A pivotal figure in Medhi's life was Murli Manohar, the pracharak of Nalbari district at the time.[334] Also known as Narayanan, his dedication and wisdom left a profound impact on Medhi, who saw in him a role model of service and humility. Inspired by Narayanan, Medhi's involvement with the Sangh deepened. He transitioned from a dedicated participant in the village shakha to taking on more significant responsibilities, including teaching at the Balitara M.E. School. His role in the Sangh was multifaceted, extending from grassroots organization to district-level leadership.

In his village, he was not only a respected Sangh worker but also a beloved secondary school teacher. His passion for education and ability to connect with students made him a favourite among the children. Medhi's classroom was a place of learning and inspiration, where he imparted knowledge with patience and enthusiasm. His teaching went beyond textbooks; he instilled values of integrity, respect and curiosity in his

[333]Ibid.
[334]Ibid.

students. However, Medhi's talents were not confined to the realms of education and social service. He possessed a flair for the theatrical, a gift that he utilized to convey profound messages through art. His involvement in theatre was particularly evident during the annual celebrations of Srimanta Sankardev's *tithi*. Each year, Medhi meticulously crafted and staged plays that depicted religious and social themes. His productions were more than mere entertainment; they were powerful narratives that captivated audiences across villages, leaving them with lasting impressions.

The villagers eagerly anticipated Medhi's plays, knowing they would witness stories brought to life with passion and authenticity.[335] Through his theatrical endeavours, Medhi addressed issues close to his heart, promoting unity, moral values and a deeper understanding of their cultural heritage. His life was a blend of personal fulfilment and dedicated service, each aspect reinforcing the other. His work with the Sangh extended beyond mere involvement; it was a lifeline for many in Nalbari.

ULFA, who were at the peak of their power at the time, saw Medhi as a significant obstacle owing to his influence in the region. Threats from the group were not uncommon, yet Medhi's response was as unexpected as it was remarkable. One evening, an emissary from ULFA arrived at Medhi's modest home to intimidate him.[336] Instead of reacting with fear or hostility, Medhi welcomed the visitor with genuine warmth. He extended traditional Assamese hospitality, offering food and shelter for the night. The agent was taken aback by this unexpected kindness. This act of humanity in the face of danger was a testament to Medhi's character, illustrating his belief in the power of compassion over conflict.

---

[335]Ibid.

[336]Ibid.

However, Shukleshwar Medhi's story took a tragic turn on the morning of 30 August 2005.[337] The day began like any other, with the first light of dawn casting a serene glow over the village of Santipur, where he had spent the night for Sangh-related work. After completing his morning rituals, Medhi set out for his home, his thoughts already turning to his responsibilities as a secondary school teacher. Returning to Balitara, he followed his routine meticulously and prepared for his day at school, where he was a beloved figure among students and colleagues. His journey to the school included a brief stop at a local tea stall, a small but cherished part of his daily routine.[338]

As he sipped his tea and greeted familiar faces, two unfamiliar youths approached him. They struck up a conversation, their demeanour casual, yet something about them seemed out of place. Medhi, ever the approachable and warm-hearted man, engaged with them openly, unaware of the danger that lurked beneath their friendly facade. In a sudden horrific moment, one of the youths drew a gun and fired a shot at Medhi's chest.[339] The sound of the gunfire shattered the morning calm, sending shockwaves through the quiet street. The assailants fled, leaving behind chaos and a gravely wounded Medhi. People rushed to his aid, their hearts heavy with shock and sorrow. An ULFA commander—who later became an MP—claimed responsibility for the act.

Despite the desperate efforts to save him, Medhi succumbed to his injuries. The news of his death spread rapidly, plunging the community into profound mourning. The streets of Nalbari, usually bustling with life, were enveloped in a sombre silence as the reality of their loss set in.[340] Shukleshwar Medhi's life

---

[337] Ibid.

[338] Ibid.

[339] Ibid.

[340] Ibid.

had been a beacon of hope and resilience in a region often overshadowed by violence and fear. His unwavering commitment to the Sangh and his community had made him a target, but it had also made him a hero. His actions, whether confronting danger with kindness or dedicating himself to education and service, left an indelible mark on everyone he touched.

As a result, the opposite of what ULFA had hoped for, happened. Instead of demoralizing people, it galvanized them. While Narayanan's death led to fear, Medhi's led to public outcry as people from all walks of life condemned this act of violence against a humble teacher. Unlike his predecessor, Medhi was a native of the region.[341] His assassination was an attack not on an outsider but on a son of the soil. As a result, anti-ULFA sentiments peaked among the people.

Sangathan Stands Strong

These brutal killings were like a haunting scar on the Sangh, shaking the organization to its core. The loss of dedicated leaders like G. Narayanan, Omprakash Chaturvedi, Shukleshwar Medhi and Pramod Dixit, who had tirelessly championed the Sangh's ideals, was a profound blow.[342] These were not just individual tragedies but attacks on the very spirit and fabric of an organization committed to the service of the nation. However, even in the face of such atrocities, the Sangh's resolve remained unbroken. Their commitment to their ideology and mission only grew stronger, becoming a testament to the resilience and unwavering dedication of its members.

The Sangh had always faced adversity with courage and determination. Yet, the targeted assassinations of pracharaks were particularly painful. These leaders were not just administrators;

---

[341]Ibid.

[342]Ibid.

they were visionaries who had inspired thousands. Their loss was deeply felt across the organization and among the communities they served. In the immediate aftermath of these killings, there was a palpable sense of grief and anger. Sangh offices across the country became centres of mourning as members gathered to pay their respects and reflect on the loss. Prayer meetings were held and tributes poured in from all quarters. These gatherings, however, were not just about mourning; they were about reaffirming the Sangh's commitment to its ideals. The Sangh leaders emphasised that these sacrifices should not derail the organization's mission but rather inspire it to work harder towards its goals.

One of the most remarkable aspects of the Sangh's response was its emphasis on non-violence and constructive action. Despite the provocations, the Sangh leaders urged their members to channel their grief and anger into positive action. This was a critical moment for the organization, as it chose to uphold its principles of peace and service rather than retaliate with violence. This stance not only helped maintain social harmony but also reinforced the moral high ground that the Sangh aspired to hold.

The Sangh's work continued unabated. In fact, the organization intensified its efforts to expand its reach and deepen its impact. New initiatives were launched, focusing on education, health and rural development. Sangh workers were encouraged to engage even more closely with local communities, understanding their needs and addressing their concerns. This grassroots approach helped build stronger bonds between the Sangh and the people, making it harder for any opposition to undermine the organization's efforts.

In the face of adversity, the Sangh's message of unity and service resonated even more strongly. The organization's commitment to its core values of selfless service, discipline and patriotism helped it navigate through these challenging times. Years after the tragic events, the Sangh continued to grow and evolve. The sacrifices of leaders became an integral part of the organization's lore, inspiring countless members to dedicate themselves to the cause. The stories of their bravery and commitment were shared widely, becoming a source of inspiration for new recruits and seasoned workers alike.

Amidst the chaos and violence, the Sangh also embarked on a bold and compassionate initiative to mend the fractured society and reclaim these lost youths. By 1991, the Sangh's efforts began to take on a more structured and proactive form. Sunita Haldekar and her colleagues recognized the need to address the root of the problem: the estrangement of young men from their families and communities.[343] They decided to conduct an outreach programme targeting the families of ULFA cadres, hoping to bridge the gap and reintegrate these young men into society.

The Rashtra Sevika Samiti embarked on a door-to-door campaign, visiting homes across various districts, explaining their mission to anxious parents and relatives. Their message was clear: it was possible to bring the youth back to the mainstream, to offer them a chance at a peaceful and productive life. This was not merely a political strategy but a deeply humane endeavour rooted in the belief that every individual had the potential to change and contribute positively to society. The task was monumental. Many families had resigned themselves to believing that their sons were irretrievably lost to the insurgent cause. Convincing them otherwise required patience, empathy and a great deal of persuasion. Yet the Samiti persevered, slowly but surely winning the trust of the families they visited.

One of the most poignant stories emerged from the district of Dhemaji. A *sevika* had been tirelessly working to connect

[343]Kavishwar, Sandip, *Mrityunjay Veer*, Rouhin Deb and Nabaarun Barooah (trans.), Prachi Prakashan, Guwahati, 2022.

with the local families. Her own son had joined the ULFA and she was determined to bring him back. Her personal struggle added a layer of authenticity and urgency to her mission. She spoke from the heart, sharing her own pain and hope with other parents. Her story resonated deeply and she became a beacon of hope for many. Her efforts culminated in a dramatic and emotional encounter. She managed to establish contact with her son, who had been living in the dense forests with other ULFA cadres.[344] She appealed to his sense of duty towards his family and community, urging him to abandon the path of violence. It was a tense and heart-rending moment when, after much deliberation and internal struggle, her son agreed to come home.

Inspired by her example, other families began to take similar steps. Processions were organized, where parents and siblings of ULFA members marched through towns and villages, calling for their loved ones to return.[345] These processions were powerful displays of collective will and compassion, illustrating the deep bonds of family and community that transcended the allure of insurgency. Sunita Haldekar and her colleagues continued their outreach, supporting families through these challenging transitions. They provided counselling, organized community meetings, and facilitated dialogues between returning youths and local leaders. These efforts helped to create a supportive environment for reintegration, reducing the stigma associated with abandoning the insurgent cause.

The impact of this initiative was profound. By the mid-1990s, numerous young men had returned home, reuniting with their families and reintegrating into society. These success stories had a ripple effect, encouraging more families to come forward and seek help.

In the years that followed, the Sangh's outreach efforts

---

[344]Interview with Sunita Haldekar.

[345]Ibid.

continued to expand, reaching more districts and touching more lives. The story of the sisters of the Sevika Samiti and the countless others who participated in this initiative became a testament to the power of grassroots activism and the enduring strength of familial and communal bonds. This initiative not only helped to reduce the strength of the ULFA but also fostered a sense of unity and purpose within the communities affected by insurgency. It highlighted the importance of addressing the underlying social and emotional issues that drive young men towards insurgency, offering them a path back to peace and productivity.

Another interesting story of peaceful co-existence comes from Meghalaya. Apart from being political, this is also a story of love and romance. In the turbulent 1980s, when insurgency and ethnic nationalism reached their zenith in the Northeast, the beautiful state of Meghalaya was not exempt from its influence. It was during this time that Dr Vishwamitra arrived from Ranchi—a dedicated physician with a mission to serve society through the Kalyan Ashram.[100] He set up an affordable, low-cost clinic, determined to provide medical care to those in need, regardless of their financial means. Despite his noble intentions, Dr Vishwamitra faced immense hostility from the local populace.[346] They viewed him as an outsider and subjected him to relentless harassment. The doctor's resolve, however, remained unshaken. He continued to treat patients with compassion, slowly but surely making a difference in their lives.[347]

In a twist of fate, Dr Vishwamitra found an unexpected ally in a local woman who was deeply impressed by his dedication and selflessness.[348] She saw the good he was doing for her community and admired his courage. Their mutual respect blossomed into love, and they decided to marry. This union was more than a

[346]Ibid.

[347]Ibid.

[348]Ibid.

marriage; it was a bridge between two worlds.[349] With his local wife by his side, Dr Vishwamitra's relationship with the deeply matrilineal and matrilocal community began to change. The locals started to see him as one of their own. His wife's support and endorsement played a significant role in this transformation.[350] Gradually, the harassment diminished and trust began to grow.

Dr Vishwamitra's clinic became a place of hope and healing. He continued to offer medical care at a very low cost, ensuring that even the poorest could afford treatment.[351] His relentless service and dedication earned him the respect and love of the community. Over time, he became an integral part of their lives, and the clinic stood as a testament to his commitment. In the face of adversity, he forged a path of compassion and unity, ultimately becoming one with the people he had set out to serve. This story symbolizes what the Sangh truly is. Even in the face of seemingly insurmountable challenges, compassion, persistence, community support and love can pave the way for healing and reconciliation, and this is exactly the secret that helped them rise in the next phase of their journey.

---

[349]Ibid.

[350]Ibid.

[351]Ibid.

5

Echoes of the Old Gods

If the Northeast of the 1980s was dominated by political narratives surrounding ethno-regionalism, the 1990s saw politics being gripped by religious issues across the whole of India. The Hindu community in India faced a growing wave of religious conversions, particularly in the southern state of Tamil Nadu, in Meenakshipuram.[352] The situation had reached a critical point, threatening the cultural and spiritual fabric of the region. In response, the Vishwa Hindu Parishad (VHP) launched a significant initiative to counter these conversions and restore faith among Hindus and unite the community. This initiative was the Ekad Mat Rath Yatra, organized under the auspices of the Sanskriti Raksha Nidhi.

Several chariot processions were launched simultaneously across different parts of India under the Ekad Mat Rath Yatra campaign. In the Northeast, the processions began from three significant cultural and religious sites—Parshuram Kund in Assam, Shree Govindajee Temple in Manipur and Tirthamukh in Tripura. These sacred places were chosen for their deep spiritual significance and their ability to draw large crowds. More importantly, they highlighted the unity and oneness of Bharat.

[352]India TV News Desk. 'Flashback: How 800 Dalit Hindus in Meenakshipuram were converted to Islam 33 years ago', *India TV News*, 12 December 2014, https://tinyurl.com/mtwm9hav. Accessed on 13 February 2025.

As the chariot processions rolled through towns and villages, they received an overwhelming response from the masses. The processions, adorned with vibrant decorations and filled with chanting devotees, became powerful symbols of faith and unity. Communities came together, drawn by the common cause of protecting their cultural heritage and spiritual identity. The sight of the processions, with their sacred images and the sound of devotional songs, instilled a renewed sense of pride and purpose among the people.

A few years later, in the autumn of 1990, the Indian subcontinent stood on the brink of a political and cultural upheaval. It was a time of burgeoning aspirations and rising tensions, when the echoes of ancient history began to influence contemporary politics. In the midst of this charged atmosphere, L.K. Advani, a former pracharak of the RSS and a senior leader of the Bharatiya Janata Party, embarked on a journey that would alter the course of Indian history—the Ram Rath Yatra.

The journey commenced on a crisp September morning from the historic temple-town of Somnath in Gujarat. This choice of starting point was laden with symbolism, for the ancient, eponymous temple—that had been rebuilt after multiple destructions—epitomized resilience and religious revival. Advani's destination was Ayodhya in Uttar Pradesh, a town revered as the birthplace of Lord Ram, and the focal point of a contentious debate over the disputed religious site where the Babri Masjid stood.

Advani's vehicle for this odyssey was not a mere van, but a specially modified Toyota, decked out to resemble a grandiose *rath* (chariot) from Hindu mythology. With saffron flags fluttering and a portrait of Lord Ram adorning the vehicle, Advani stood as a modern-day charioteer, steering the Sangh Parivar towards its ideological goals. The chariot itself was an emblem of Hindu pride and a rallying point for millions of supporters.

As the Rath Yatra wended its way through the vast expanse

of India, it became a moving spectacle of fervour and devotion. Everywhere it went, throngs of people gathered, chanting 'Jai Shri Ram' (Victory to Lord Ram) and other slogans that echoed the call for a Ram temple in Ayodhya. The journey covered nearly 10,000 kilometres, passing through states like Maharashtra, Madhya Pradesh and Bihar, drawing unprecedented crowds that turned each stop into a massive rally.[353] The Yatra was meticulously planned, with daily routes and speeches designed to maximize impact and media coverage.

The Ram Rath Yatra of 1990 was more than a political campaign; it was a defining moment that reshaped India's socio-political landscape.[354] It heralded the rise of Hindutva and changed the way people thought about their identities. It not only changed the decade of the 1990s but the times that followed, altering the course of history in the subcontinent.

The Northeast Story

Even in the north-eastern part of India, the call of 'Jai Shri Ram' found its way. *Karsevaks*, inspired by this call, stepped forward to join a movement that transcended geographical boundaries and cultural differences. The roots of such massive support for the movement can be traced back to the 1990s when the RSS planted its seeds of influence through welfare programmes—particularly in education—across the tribal-dominant states of Arunachal Pradesh, Nagaland, Meghalaya and Mizoram. These initiatives aimed not only to uplift the socio-economic status of the indigenous populations but also to foster a sense of cultural pride and identity. Amidst Christian-dominated regions, the Vanvasi Kalyan Ashram emerged as a hope, promoting the cause

[353]Nag, Kinshuk, *The NaMo Story: A Political Life,* Roli Books Private Limited, New Delhi, 2013.

[354]Ibid.

of local icons who were depicted as stalwarts resisting the tide of Christian conversions.[355]

Through grassroots efforts and community engagement, they sought to preserve indigenous traditions and beliefs, weaving these into the fabric of the larger cultural narrative. Participation particularly peaked in the state of Assam, reaching a crescendo during the Ram Janmabhoomi movement. The state's VHP chapter conducted *shilapujan*s (literally: rock worship) in over 20,000 villages.[356] Each village became a sanctum—adorned with the echoes of chants—as communities gathered to pay homage to their revered deity, Lord Ram. Through these rituals, the narrative of Ram's *janmabhoomi* (birth place) transcended from being a distant legend to becoming a palpable reality, binding hearts and minds in a shared sense of purpose and devotion.[357]

During the movement, the arrival of the Ramjyoti from Ayodhya to North Lakhimpur signified a potent declaration of faith and identity. This flame, symbolizing the spirit of Lord Ram, journeyed across the heartland of India, bringing with it a message of unity and devotion. However, its progress in Assam was met with fierce resistance from the ULFA, which viewed the movement as a threat to their own regional aspirations.[358] Their response was brutal, unleashing violence upon the peaceful marchers, resulting in the tragic loss of innocent lives.

Amidst this turmoil, the Sangh recognized the grave threat posed by ULFA and took a bold and unconventional approach to keep the spirit of the movement alive.[359] They saw potential in the strength and resolve of the village women, who remained steadfast in their faith and commitment despite

---

[355]Interview with Sandip Kavishwar.

[356]Ibid.

[357]Ibid.

[358]Ibid.

[359]Ibid.

the chaos. These courageous women, galvanized under the leadership of Brahmaji Rao, embodied the indomitable spirit of their community. They organized processions, carrying the sacred flame of the Ramjyoti from the namghars to the *mandir*s (temples), spreading the message of the Ram Mandir across villages.[360]

Their presence was not just powerful, but also deeply symbolic and proved to be a significant deterrent to the ULFA insurgents, who, despite their previous violent actions, found themselves unable to harm the women. The insurgents, accustomed to dealing with male protesters, were taken aback by the sight of the women. Their courage and conviction stood as a formidable shield, one that the insurgents found difficult to penetrate. The women, with their fearless actions, ensured that the Ramjyoti continued to burn brightly, unimpeded by the threats surrounding them.[361]

The women's processions moved from village to village, each step echoing their resolute spirit. They sang *bhajan*s, chanted prayers, and carried the sacred flame with an unwavering grip, their faces glowing with determination.[362] The sight of these women, steadfast in their devotion, inspired many to join the movement, strengthening the resolve of the entire community.

One memorable procession started from a namghar in a small village. The women, dressed in traditional *mekhela chador*s, carried the Ramjyoti with pride. As they moved, villagers joined them, creating a growing wave of devotion and solidarity. They reached the mandir at dusk, the flame of the Ramjyoti flickering yet steadfast. The villagers gathered around, their faces lit by the sacred light, as prayers were offered and the message of the Ram Mandir was shared.

[360]Interview with Brahmaji Rao.

[361]Ibid.

[362]Ibid.

In another village, the women's procession faced a direct threat from the ULFA, who—armed and intimidating—blocked their path. But the women, undeterred, continued their march. They sang louder, their chants of 'Jai Shri Ram' resonating through the air.[363] Members of the ULFA, confronted with such unwavering faith and courage, faltered. The women passed through—their heads held high and resolve unbroken.

Their bravery not only protected the sacred flame but also galvanized the community, creating a wave of support for the Ram Janmabhoomi movement across Assam.[364] The story of these women became a powerful narrative of faith, resilience and the unyielding spirit of the people. Their courage and conviction lit a path for others to follow, ensuring that the flame of devotion burned brightly in the hearts of all who witnessed their journey.[365]

People from all walks of life in the Northeast, who were affiliated with the RSS, joined the *karseva*. Sunil Mohanty, an RSS pracharak at the time and now the kshetra prachar pramukh, recalled the various phases of this *andolan*. He reopened his old diary from 1990.[366] Its pages had turned yellow with age, but each line and paragraph vividly rekindled the memories of those bygone days.

On 13 October 1990, Mohanty—along with a small group of inmates from the East Hostel at Ravenshaw College—embarked on a mission to raise awareness.[367] They went room to room, selling calendars, stickers and badges featuring images of Lord Ram standing before the proposed Mandir. This campaign had a dual purpose: to awaken people to the cause of Shri Ram and to support the Mandir's construction through the small purchases

---

[363]Interview with Brahmaji Rao.

[364]Ibid.

[365]Ibid.

[366]Interview with Sunil Mohanty.

[367]Ibid.

of these items.[368] Surprisingly, everyone in the hostel bought the items without any opposition, showing unanimous support for the cause. The next day, 14 October 1990, the Ramjyoti Rath, which had started from Ayodhya, arrived in Cuttack.[369]

Mohanty and his fellow volunteers from the college joined the massive procession to welcome the rath at the outskirts of Cuttack, proudly wearing badges of Lord Ram and Lord Hanuman. The *shobhayatra* (procession), filled with a huge number of Ram *bhakts*, passed through Chhatra Bazar to Kathjodi. Drums and bells echoed as they welcomed the Ramjyoti Rath. The volunteers formed a cordon with lathis around the rath to control the enthusiastic crowd. Mohanty noticed that even the police on duty were offering *pranam* (salutation) to the sacred flame, overwhelmed with devotion.[370] The line between common ladies in sarees and lady police officers in uniform blurred, unified in intense Ram *bhakti*.

At the Badambari bus-stand, Mohanty climbed atop a bus to witness the vast ocean of uncountable heads rushing towards the rath with electrifying bhakti.[371] Many had tears streaming down their faces, which indeed was a heart-touching scene. The rath journeyed through Dolamundai, Ranihat, Bakshi Bazar, Choudhury Bazar, High Court and Shaikh Bazar. Despite the strain, Mohanty and his fellow volunteers remained motivated, reaching their final stop near Chandi Mandir. After the procession, Mohanty faced the long walk back to Ravenshaw campus, another five kilometres.[372]

Fortunately, he managed to catch a running trekker and reached Ranihat, where he had his hostel dinner. In the

---

[368]Ibid.

[369]Ibid.

[370]Ibid.

[371]Ibid.

[372]Ibid.

East Hostel's common room, they watched the TV, feeling overwhelmed as they saw the Ramjyoti Rath Yatra news. However, the newspapers of the day were filled with negative news about the nationwide Ram Mandir movement, with various statements and speculations from political parties.[373] Despite the media's portrayal, the spirit of the movement remained unshaken for Mohanty and the countless devotees who had participated.

In 1992, the Assamese people embarked on a pilgrimage to Ayodhya to contribute to the construction of the Ram Mandir.[374] Bhaskar Kulkarni was tasked to recruit people from all around Northeast to join the karseva. For his stellar work during the Ram Janmabhoomi movement, Bhaskar Kulkarni was briefly appointed the organizing secretary of Vishwa Hindu Parishad Assam during the Jaipur Sammelan. Additionally, the Ram Paduka Yatra, spanning the length and breadth of Assam, emerged as a unifying force, rallying support from cities and villages alike for the establishment of the Ram Mandir.

The account of another pracharak called Deepak Ranjan Sharma stands as a testament to the fervour and unity that defined those historic days. Leading a team of 400–500 karsevaks from Assam to Ayodhya, he found himself amidst a sea of humanity converging upon the sacred city.[375] Karsevaks from various states joined them on the train along the way. As they arrived in Ayodhya on the eve of the karseva, the sight that greeted them was awe-inspiring. Lakhs of people from every corner of the nation had gathered, their makeshift tents dotting the landscape. Despite the colossal crowd, there was an air of orderliness, with everyone lending a helping hand to settle in. The resounding chants of 'Jai Shri Ram' echoed through the atmosphere, infusing the environment with a palpable energy and

[373]Ibid.

[374]Interview with Bhaskar Kulkarni.

[375]Interview with Deepak Ranjan Sharma.

spirit.[376] An evening meeting was convened by K.S. Sudarshan, the then *sah sarkaryavah* of the RSS, where he gave a call to be ready to march towards the revered spot of Ram Janmabhoomi by 3.00 a.m.[377]

On the fateful morning of 6 December 1992, as the sun rose over the horizon, a huge throng of devotees descended upon the contested site.[378] With repeated chants and the rhythmic beat of drums, the karsevaks surged forward. And then, in a moment that would reverberate through the corridors of history, the first blows fell, shattering the fragile peace that had held sway over Ayodhya for centuries. The golden hues of the setting sun cast a mystical glow over the gathering, imbuing the moment with a sense of sacredness. Though some faced minor injuries in the tumult of the ensuing events, there was no loss of life. Unlike the adversarial stance of the police during previous encounters under Mulayam Yadav's administration, this time they found unexpected cooperation under the BJP government led by Kalyan Singh.[379]

As they ascended, the voices of prominent leaders, including L.K. Advani, urged caution and restraint, while figures like Uma Bharti and Sadhvi Rithambara rallied the masses with impassioned slogans, igniting a fervour to reclaim the sacred land in the name of Lord Ram.[380] As the atmosphere reverberated with 'Jai Shri Ram' chants, the domes of the Babri Masjid crumbled. In the aftermath of the devastation, a makeshift temple rose from the ashes. During an interview with another pracharak who was a part of the karseva, he closed his eyes and smiled, remembering it as the 'greatest day of my life'.[381]

---

[376]Ibid.

[377]Ibid.

[378]Ibid.

[379]Ibid.

[380]Ibid.

[381]Interview with Ranjan Debbarma (name changed).

Reviving the Roots: Indigenous Faith Movements

In the 1990s, alongside the Ram Mandir movement and efforts to galvanize support for it among the people in the Northeast, the RSS embarked on another ambitious project to revive and institutionalize indigenous and tribal faiths across the region. This initiative sought to formalize religious practices among non-Christian communities, many of whom had long maintained traditions that were not institutionalized in the same way as those of more dominant religions. The RSS worked to provide these faiths with symbols, establish places of worship, and develop written scriptures that could serve as guides for rituals. They introduced a structured framework for prayer, including *puja vidhi* (ritual procedures), hymns and traditional dances, which were designed to infuse the region's diverse tribal cultures with a sense of religious cohesion, while also promoting an overarching sense of unity within the broader Hindu nationalist philosophy.

Rangfrah Movement

One day, the God Rang decided to descend upon earth and test the human race. The word *frah* means form, with Rangfrah denoting the form of the God.[382] Rangfrah took a human form, holding a spear in one hand and the Wushu bird on the other, with matted hair, a fashionable goatee, and his left and right ears adorned with paddy and an earthworm, respectively. Rangfrah went from one house to another, begging for food and shelter, only to be shooed away by the entire village.

At last he appeared at the entrance of a platformed hut where two orphaned children lived—a boy and a girl. They welcomed Rangfrah into their home and gave him water and whatever little

[382]Interview with Rajesh Deshkar.

food was left, asking forgiveness for not having enough. Pleased, Rang appeared in his divine godly form, blessing them with abundance of food. He then instructed them to go to a cave and shut it close, and only come out when the Wushu bird called, for he intended to teach the human race a lesson. For days Rang unleashed *pralaya* (apocalypse). When the Wushu bird finally called, the young boy and girl stepped out into a new world. The progeny of the couple became followers of the god Rang and composed the early hymns. This was the first coming of Rangfrah, a legend that has lived on among the local residents for centuries in the form of stories, ritual sacrifices and other practices. However, its codification and institutionalization is a later development.

Rajesh Deshkar of the RSS first traversed the hills of Arunachal Pradesh in the early 1990s.[383] He found himself in the middle of the Changlang forests where the local population had very little direct contact with the outside world. Unable to find friends, he stayed in a crematorium for the first 13 months. His first contact with the local Tangsa people is an interesting tale. Deshkar first came in sampark with people through the act of bathing young children with soap in 1992.[384] Locals found it both amusing and relaxing. Soon, this evolved into a community tradition where women bathed their children with soap.

People from one village walked to another, taking this newfound phenomenon with them. Wives of village leaders and social workers also joined Deshkar and his newfound comrades on this mission to start a community-wide bathing and cleanliness campaign. 'This,' Deshkar claims, 'marked the inception of the Sangh's efforts in Changlang,' culminating in the establishment of the first Sangh shakha in Coffee Garden.[385]

---

[383]Ibid.

[384]Ibid.

[385]Ibid.

Deshkar recounts an intriguing incident. One day, after the evening shakha, he stepped out to find that it had been shut down by a local youth named Jongsom Kunkho, a tall and muscular Tutsa man, who was casually sipping tea at a nearby stall. Deshkar approached him and embraced him warmly. They later visited Jongsom's home, where he was offered *laopani* (local alcohol) and food, and they engaged in a lengthy conversation. Deshkar finally enquired, 'Why did you shut down the shakha?' Jongsom replied, 'Is it yours? Restart it tomorrow; I will join you.'[386]

The following day, Jongsom arrived at the shakha carrying an enormous bamboo pole taller than him. In accordance with tradition, everyone offered him greetings and namaskar, deeply moving him. He ultimately became a crucial ally for the Sangh.

Another major problem with this area was the rampant spread of malaria. Many people would die and the healthcare centre in Changlang would become overcrowded with patients. Deshkar, who had basic knowledge of medicine, both allopathic and Ayurvedic, would provide medical assistance, imported medicines and nursing services to the people of the village. Around 1996–97, the district commissioner noted that the healthcare centre had recorded zero patients. Upon enquiry, they realized that Rajesh Deshkar had started basic healthcare and nursing facilities in the village. He was summoned by the DC and Tinghap Taiju, the education minister and local MLA, who praised him for his efforts.[387] Around this time, the local administration sanctioned a school in New Changlang. Many suggested that the school be named after Indira Gandhi or Rajiv Gandhi. While pondering upon potential names, Deshkar asked people about their local traditions. He had seen the phrase 'Rangfrah *Ajong*' written on Taiju's jeep and other community places. He also observed

---

[386]Ibid.

[387]Ibid.

another jeep which had 'Rang *kothak* Rang' written on top. An elder mentioned their faith in their local deity, Rangfrah. Thus the Rangfrah Vidya Niketan was born.[388]

Prominent social workers of Changlang, such as Tinghap Taiju, Wangsam Jongsam, Phosom Khimhun, N. Changmi, C. Tekhil, Khommo Khomrang, Raisom Zongsom, Nokcham Kitnya, Yonbey Kitnya and L. Khimun, sat together and spearheaded a revivalist movement in the name of their deity Rangfrah. A painting competition was organized where several young Tangsa students visualized their imagination of Rangfrah as per descriptions given by the elders.

Finally, the image of Rangfrah described before—his ears adorned with paddy and earthworm, and a spear gripped in one hand—was chosen from 172 entries. About 5,000 pictures of the deity were printed and brought from Kolkata, while a 300 kg marble statue was imported from Jaipur through the RSS. On 4 November 1997, the people of New Changlang brought pieces of roof, wood and tin from their homes, built the first Rangfrah temple and installed the statue as chants of 'Jai Rangfrah' reverberated throughout the horizon.[389] This was the second coming of Rangfrah, in the form of the image/idol.

We asked Rajesh Deshkar, 'What was the RSS's role in the Rangfrah movement?' He replied, 'None. Everything was done by the community.[390] Our only involvement was that Sah Sarkaryavah Madan Das Devi was present at the foundation stone-laying ceremony. Whatever was done, was done by the community and their members. It was the first time an indigenous community had stood up as one to defend their identity and development. Sangh has and will always support indigenous faiths.'[391] In fact,

---

[388]Ibid.

[389]Ibid.

[390]Ibid.

[391]Ibid.

Mohan Bhagwat, the present sarsanghchalak, had once said during his visit to Arunachal Pradesh that indigenous faith was the mother of Hindutva.

Critics asked L. Khimun, the spiritual leader behind the Rangfrah movement, 'You never had idol worship before. Isn't this the RSS's attempt to Hinduize your people?'[392] Khimun, known for his wit and oratory skills, promptly replied, 'For ages, we used to cook rice in bamboo *chunga* (hallow). Now we use pressure cookers. But the rice remains the same. People need to adapt to changing times and take up new technologies to go forward while maintaining the core.'[393]

Khimun wrote several holy books to codify Rangfrahism, incorporating ideas and moral lessons from various sources while affirming its place within the Indic fold, along with regularizing puja (worship) and detailing the *paddhati* (method). This served as the third coming of Rangrah, in the form of the book.

Regarding the role of the RSS and its sister organizations, Khimun remarked, 'They are always with us to guide and help.' Kampa Taisam, the Miao block president of the Arunachal Vikas Parishad, reflected proudly on their contributions to the movement. 'We made a key contribution to the movement,' he stated confidently.[394] Their efforts encompassed distributing medicines, organizing medical camps and supporting the construction of temples. Taisam also cherished his meeting with RSS head Mohan Bhagwat in Nagpur, a significant milestone in his journey.

For the RSS, the Northeast—specifically Arunachal Pradesh—had long been a promising field for their mission to reconnect

---

[392]Ibid.

[393]Ibid.

[394]Sethi, Nitin, 'RSS turns Arunachal tribals towards Hinduism', *Business Standard*, 1 May 2014, https://tinyurl.com/3xphwkyt. Accessed on 09 May 2025.

tribals with their Sanatan roots. The state, with its approximately twenty main tribes and hundreds of sub-tribes, was scattered over challenging and rugged terrain. In the towns, those relatively better-off maintained traditional family structures while aspiring to a modern identity that aligned with the broader Indian cultural narrative. This aspiration for a unique identity that resonated with the rest of India fuelled the movement further.

The burgeoning Rangfrah religion resonated strongly in this landscape. Khimun articulated this sentiment openly. 'As per our definition, all those who are willing to die and live for Hindustan are Hindu. Those who are anti-Hindu or anti-national, they criticize Rangfrahites,' he declared.[395] Khimun authored several holy books that advocated for the reconversion of Christians, emphasizing the need to reclaim those who had been proselytized.

The Rangfrah faith today has grown to include several thousand members from the Tangsa, Tutsa and Nocte communities. These members are spread across Tirap, Changlang and Longding, representing just two to three per cent of the total population of these tribes. Despite the modest numbers, the impact is visible. Many villages now boast Rangfrah temples and appoint village-level convenors to guide the faithful.

Donyi-Polo Movement

The Donyi-Polo movement in Arunachal Pradesh was one of the many new faiths and reformist movements that emerged in the latter half of the twentieth century, aiming to protect and preserve indigenous religious beliefs and practices. It was spearheaded by the Tani group of tribes, primarily the Adi, Nyishi, Apatani, Tagin and Galo communities. The terms *donyi* and *polo* mean sun and moon, respectively. These celestial bodies are revered as symbols of prosperity and fertility, and serve as

[395] Ibid.

talismans of protection from calamities. The movement began on 28 August 1968, when Adi intellectuals convened in Along, West Siang district, to discuss forming a larger entity by combining the Adi and Galo tribes. The meeting marked the formal birth of Donyi-Poloism as an organized religious and cultural movement.

The late Talom Rukbo, a founding member of the Donyi-Polo movement, was a pivotal figure in this transformation. He articulated the need for institutionalizing the Adi religion, emphasising that tradition encompassed all aspects of social life inherited from time immemorial. Rukbo believed that the erosion of traditional rituals, prayers and hymns could only be countered through formal organization and institutionalization.[396] His vision gave rise to cultural societies such as the Tani Jagriti Foundation, the Donyi-Polo Youth Federation and the Donyi-Polo Yelam Kebang, all of which sought to revive and preserve the spiritual and ritualistic heritage of the Tani tribes.

Rukbo explained that Donyi-Poloism had multiple connotations. It represented the Almighty God, symbolized the sun and the moon, and embodied the traditional belief systems of the Tani tribes.[397] He differentiated between the material and spiritual aspects of Donyi-Polo: the former referred to the physical sun and moon, while the latter signified an absolute power governing the universe. This belief system, he argued, was akin to the scientific understanding that life on earth depended on light, heat, air and water. A myth among the Adi tribe narrated how there used to be two suns. In order to bring balance, one was turned into the moon. This myth, according to Rukbo, symbolized the balance of light and dark necessary

---

[396]Misra, Kamal K., 'Donyi-Polo As An "Indigenous Religion" in Arunachal Pradesh: A Facile Analysis', *Indian Journal of Anthropological Research*, Vol. 2, No. 1, 2023, pp. 1–11. https://tinyurl.com/35k6h5fx. Accessed on 13 February 2025.

[397]Ibid.

for life, reflecting the scientific basis of Donyi-Poloism.

The movement's emergence was also a response to the growing influence of Christianity among the tribes of Arunachal Pradesh. The Adi, like many other tribes, faced an identity crisis as Christian missionaries made inroads into their communities. Despite early attempts by the Indian state to promote indigenous religions and restrict missionary activities, Christianity gained significant ground. This led to substantial conversions, which were seen as a threat to the traditional cultural mosaic of the tribes.

In the face of these changes, Rukbo and other Adi intellectuals sought to reaffirm their cultural identity through Donyi-Poloism. They aimed to provide a structured and organized religious framework that could stand against the tide of external religious influences. The movement involved the building of temples, the invention of images of gods and goddesses, and the textualization of religious chants and oral traditions. These efforts mirrored the institutional practices of Hinduism, providing a robust and enduring foundation for the indigenous religion.

Donyi-Poloism thus became a channel for human aspirations, embodying the values of truth, purity, enlightenment, wisdom, justice, peace and non-violence. It was seen as a means to connect with the supreme deity, Sedi, who was believed to have sent various gods, goddesses, deities and spirits to look after humanity. The movement fostered a sense of unity and cultural pride among the Tani tribes, allowing them to preserve their heritage while adapting to the modern world.

The movement gained momentum in the 1990s as it touched the lives of many within the tribal communities of Arunachal Pradesh, offering a sense of belonging and a reaffirmation of their unique identity. It was not just about preserving religious practices but also about reclaiming a cultural and social identity that had been under threat from external influences, particularly Christianity.

One of the primary methods of institutionalizing Donyi-Poloism by the Vanavasi Kalyan Ashram was the construction of dedicated temples and *ganggings* (prayer halls). These places of worship became central to the community's spiritual life, offering a physical space for the practice and preservation of rituals and ceremonies. The architecture of these temples often incorporated traditional designs and motifs, further embedding them within the cultural landscape of the region. These temples were not merely religious centres but also hubs of cultural activity, where festivals, dances and communal gatherings were held, reinforcing social bonds and communal identity.

The movement also saw the formalization of religious texts. Traditional prayers and hymns, previously passed down orally, were transcribed and compiled into written texts. This not only helped in preserving these traditions but also made them accessible to younger generations who might have been losing touch with their cultural roots. The written form provided a sense of permanence and legitimacy to the beliefs and practices of the Donyi-Polo faith. These texts often included mythological stories, moral teachings and philosophical discourses that conveyed the values and principles of the faith.

Education played a crucial role in the Donyi-Polo movement. The establishment of schools that taught both modern subjects and traditional knowledge became a cornerstone of the movement. These schools aimed to provide a balanced education that would prepare the youth for the modern world while keeping them grounded in their cultural heritage. Subjects like the history of the Tani tribes, traditional folklore and the Donyi-Polo religion were integrated into the curriculum. This approach ensured that students developed a strong sense of identity and pride in their heritage while acquiring the skills needed to thrive in contemporary society.

One notable example of such educational efforts was the establishment of the Donyi-Polo Vidya Niketan schools with help from Kalyan Ashram.[398] These institutions aimed to provide holistic education, blending modern academic curricula with traditional teachings. The schools also encouraged the practice of traditional arts, crafts and music, thereby facilitating well-rounded development of the students. They became a model for other educational initiatives within the state, showcasing the possibility of integrating traditional knowledge with modern education.

The Donyi-Polo movement was also marked by its emphasis on cultural festivals and community events. Festivals like Solung, Etor and Aran, which were deeply rooted in the agrarian lifestyle of the tribes, were celebrated with renewed vigour.[399] These festivals, which involved rituals, music, dance and feasting, became occasions for communal bonding and cultural expression. The movement's leaders understood that these festivals were not just religious events but also integral to the social fabric of the community. By promoting these festivals, they ensured that the cultural heritage of the tribes was celebrated and preserved in its full vibrancy.

The movement's success can be attributed to its inclusive approach. While it sought to revive and preserve traditional beliefs, it also embraced modernity and change. The leaders of the movement were often educated individuals who understood the importance of adapting to the changing times. They advocated for a balanced approach that respected tradition while welcoming progress. This pragmatic approach helped the movement gain widespread acceptance among the tribes, who saw it as a way to navigate the challenges of modernity without losing their cultural identity.

---

[398]Interview with Sandip Kavishwar.

[399]Ibid.

The impact of the Donyi-Polo movement extended beyond religious and cultural revival. It also had socio-political implications. The movement instilled a sense of unity and collective identity among the Tani tribes, which was crucial in a region marked by ethnic diversity and external pressures. This unity became a source of strength, enabling the tribes to assert their rights and interests more effectively. The movement also fostered a sense of pride and self-respect, countering the marginalization and cultural erosion that many tribes had experienced.

Zeliangrong Heraka

The Zeliangrong Heraka movement represents a significant chapter in the socio-political and religious history of the Northeast.[400] This movement, centred around the Zeliangrong community, was not merely a struggle for political autonomy but also a profound quest for religious and cultural rejuvenation. It unfolded in the early twentieth century amid the broader context of British colonial rule and inter-tribal conflicts, primarily involving the Nagas and the Kukis.[401]

The seeds of the Heraka movement were sown in a period of immense turmoil and oppression for the Zeliangrong people. British colonial policies and the aggressive territorial expansions by the Kukis had severely destabilized the region. The Kukis, driven by a quest for resources, conducted brutal raids against the Nagas, including the Zeliangrong, leading to the slaughter of men, women and children, and the forceful annexation of their lands. These acts of violence, compounded by the imposition of heavy tributes and taxes, exacerbated the suffering and marginalization of the Zeliangrong people.

---

[400]Samson, K., 'The Zeliangrong Movement in North-East India: An Exegetical Study', *Sociological Bulletin*, Vol. 61, No. 2, 2017, pp. 64–78.
[401]Ibid.

In this climate of oppression and cultural disintegration, a young boy named Jadonang Malangmei from the Rongmei tribe emerged as a beacon of hope.[402] Born in the village of Puiluan in Manipur, Jadonang began his spiritual journey after experiencing a divine revelation in the Bhuvan cave. He started to preach against superstitions and animal sacrifices, advocating for a return to a purer form of their traditional belief system. Jadonang's vision extended beyond religious reform; he envisioned a unified Naga kingdom, free from British domination and internal strife.[403]

Jadonang's movement gained momentum as he mobilized the Nagas across Manipur, Nagaland and Assam, encouraging them to resist British taxation and control. This defiance led to his arrest and eventual execution by the British in 1931.[404] His death, however, did not mark the end of the movement. Leadership was passed to his cousin, Gaidinliu, who continued the struggle with renewed vigour.

Gaidinliu—later honoured with the title 'Rani' by Jawaharlal Nehru—played a pivotal role in sustaining and expanding the movement.[405] Under her leadership, the Heraka movement—meaning 'pure' or 'holy'—gained prominence.[406] Gaidinliu emphasized the preservation of Zeliangrong culture and identity, which she believed were under threat from both British colonialism and the spread of Christianity. The missionaries, while bringing education and other benefits, were seen as agents of

---

[402]Mazumder, Partha Pratim, 'The untold Story of Haipou Jadonang Malangmei, freedom fighter and protector of Hindus in the Northeast', *Organiser*, 07 September 2022, https://tinyurl.com/5bnz4xj4. Accessed on 13 February 2025.

[403]Ibid.

[404]Ibid.

[405]Longkumer, Arkotong, 'Religious and economic reform: The Gaidinliu movement and the Heraka in the North Cachar Hills', *South Asia: Journal of South Asian Studies*, Vol. 30, No. 3, 2007, pp. 499–515.

[406]Ibid.

cultural erosion, often dismissing traditional practices as immoral.

Under Gaidinliu's leadership, the Heraka movement saw significant religious reforms. Initially called 'Haraka' by Jadonang, this religion was later refined and solidified under Gaidinliu's guidance.[407] This new religious identity aimed to restore the spiritual and cultural fabric of the Zeliangrong people, fostering a sense of unity and purpose. The movement also aimed at social reforms, including the abolition of practices like head-hunting and promoting the welfare of the community. Under her guidance, the Heraka movement continued to advocate for the abandonment of superstitious practices and a return to a more authentic form of their traditional religion. This purification was intrinsically linked to their political struggle, as it fostered a strong sense of identity and unity among the Zeliangrong.

The later phase of the Heraka movement marked a significant shift in its objectives, transitioning from a broader emphasis on Naga nationalism to a more focused demand for a Zeliangrong homeland within the Indian Union. The mainstream Naga nationalist movement, primarily led by the Naga National Council (NNC) and later the National Socialist Council of Nagaland (NSCN), began to increasingly align itself with a Christian identity, diverging from Gaidinliu's vision of cultural and religious preservation based on indigenous traditions.

Gaidinliu observed that the Christianization of the Naga movement was creating a cultural rift, marginalizing those who adhered to traditional beliefs.[408] Consequently, she redirected her efforts towards securing a distinct Zeliangrong homeland. This shift was rooted in her commitment to protecting and preserving the unique cultural and religious heritage of the Zeliangrong people—comprising the Zeme, Liangmai and

---

[407]Ibid.

[408]Ibid.

Rongmei tribes—which she felt was being overshadowed in the broader Naga nationalist discourse.

The demand for a Zeliangrong homeland within the Indian Union represented a pragmatic approach to achieving self-determination. Gaidinliu and her followers recognized the importance of aligning with the Indian state, which promised the protection of minority rights and cultural autonomy under its federal structure. This approach aimed to ensure that the Zeliangrong people's distinct identity would be safeguarded within the larger Indian framework, free from the homogenizing tendencies of the dominant Naga nationalist narrative.[409] In the later stages, the Heraka Association found a critical ally in the RSS, who championed the cause of an indigenous Zeliangrong homeland that remained rooted to its Indic roots and within India's sacred geography.

Seng Khasi

We have mentioned H. Onderson Mawrie and the Seng Khasi movement in the previous chapters. The Seng Khasi, which literally translates to 'Khasi Sangh', has worked in tandem with the RSS and Vanavasi Kalyan Ashram to protect the indigenous faith of Khasi and Jaintia people. In 1989, under the guidance of K.S. Sudarshan, Sunil Deodhar arrived in the mountainous state of Meghalaya.[410] His mission was clear: to foster unity and preserve the rich cultural heritage of the indigenous communities. As he began his work, he noticed the deep divisions and the rich yet fragmented traditions of the Khasis, Garos and Jaintias.[411]

Inspired by the idea of communal harmony, Deodhar—along with the Sangh—introduced the concept of an annual village festival. This festival was designed to celebrate and honour the

---

[409]Ibid.

[410]Interview with Pravin Shewale.

[411]Ibid.

centuries-old rituals of the indigenous tribes, aiming to bring them closer together. The idea was simple yet profound—a cultural celebration that would serve as a bridge, connecting the diverse ethnic groups of Meghalaya through their shared heritage.[412] The initiative began modestly, but the response from the local communities was overwhelming. The Sangh's support and Sunil Deodhar's dedication turned the annual village festival into a much-anticipated event. It became a space where the Khasis, Garos and Jaintias could come together, celebrate their unique traditions, and find common ground in their shared cultural roots.[413]

Among the many festivals, the Wangala festival of the Garos and the Lungpung festival of the Khasis and Jaintias stood out.[414] These festivals became the beating hearts of the cultural revival. The Wangala festival, with its rhythmic drum beats and vibrant dances, celebrated the harvest season, invoking the deity Saljong for blessings. The Lungpung festival, on the other hand, was a grand spectacle of traditional music, dance and rituals, reflecting the deep spiritual and cultural values of the Khasis and Jaintias. In addition, the Sangh also celebrated Raksha Bandhan in villages throughout the Garo, Khasi and Jaintia Hills.[415]

Year after year, these festivals grew in scale and significance. What started as a modest initiative soon blossomed into a grand celebration, attracting lakhs of people. The festivals not only rejuvenated traditional practices but also fostered a sense of unity among the tribes. People from all walks of life, regardless of their ethnic backgrounds, came together in a spirit of joy and camaraderie. K.S. Sudarshan's vision, backed by Sunil Deodhar's efforts, had succeeded in weaving a tradition of unity and cultural

---

[412]Ibid.

[413]Ibid.

[414]Ibid.

[415]Ibid.

pride.[416] The festivals today stand as a testament to the enduring legacy of Seng Khasi's work, bringing the indigenous people of Meghalaya closer to each other and to the Sangh, celebrating their rich heritage with pride and unity.

Surge in Militancy

As a result of the growing influence of Hindu sentiments as well as the rise of indigenous faith movements that stood against conversions in tribal areas, the 1990s witnessed an escalation of violence against the Sangh. There was an increase in tensions and confrontations as the Sangh began to solidify its political influence through the BJP. The growing work of the Sangh and the Kalyan Ashram—which awakened the spark of patriotism in the tribal areas—became an obstacle in the path of the communist regime, separatist forces and the Church. In Tripura, the repressive and tyrannical rule of the communists started suppressing the work of the Sangh and the Kalyan Ashram.[417] The cycle of harassing swayamsevaks working in government services, frequent transfers and threats continued, alongside extortion of money and actions by the armed separatist organization National Liberation Front of Tripura (NLFT).[418] Assaulting people, attacking nationalist and Hindu religious organizations, and carrying out religious conversions at gunpoint in tribal areas had become common practice.[419] Even the government court didn't heed any complaints.

Shanti Kali Maharaj, a well-known Hindu saint working among the tribals in Tripura, was one of its victims. Known as

---

[416]Ibid.

[417]Kavishwar, Sandip, *Mrityunjay Veer*, Rouhin Deb and Nabaarun Barooah, Prachi Prakashan, Guwahati, 2022.

[418]Ibid.

[419]Ibid.

Shanti Tripura before his spiritual transformation, this humble saint dedicated his life to the service of the tribal communities in Tripura.[420] His story is one of profound devotion, tireless effort, and an unwavering commitment to the upliftment of the underprivileged.

Shanti Kali's journey began in the small, remote village of Fulchari, nestled in the southern district of Sabroom. Born as the thirteenth child to Dhananjay Tripura and Khanjan Devi, his early life was steeped in simplicity and the rich traditions of his tribal heritage.[421] The large family, though modest in means, was a cradle of warmth and cultural richness. From an early age, Shanti Kali showed a remarkable inclination towards spirituality and a deep empathy for the suffering of others. As a young man, Shanti Kali felt a calling that pulled him beyond the boundaries of his native village. Driven by a desire to seek deeper spiritual truths, he embarked on a pilgrimage that took him across the vast and diverse expanse of India. This journey was not just a physical traversal of the land but an internal voyage that transformed his soul. It was during this pilgrimage that he experienced a profound revelation and a sense of mission that would shape the rest of his life. He became determined to return to his homeland and dedicate his life to the service of Goddess Tripura Sundari and the welfare of the local tribal communities.

Upon his return to Tripura, Shanti Kali Maharaj set his vision into motion. He chose to establish a temple in honour of Tripura Sundari and an ashram that would serve as a sanctuary of spiritual solace and a hub of social service. His determination bore fruit on the auspicious day of Shiv Chaturdashi in 1979 when he consecrated the Shanti Kali Ashram at Manu in Sabroom.[422] This marked the beginning of a transformative chapter in the

[420]Ibid.
[421]Ibid.
[422]Ibid.

region's history. The Shanti Kali Ashram, though humble in its beginnings, quickly became a beacon of hope and a centre of community life. Shanti Kali's magnetic personality and boundless compassion drew people from far and wide. The ashram was not just a place of worship; it was a dynamic centre for social service. Recognizing the dire needs of the local population, Shanti Kali expanded the ashram's activities to include a wide range of humanitarian efforts.

Education was one of the cornerstones of Shanti Kali's mission. He understood that true empowerment could only come through education. The mission began establishing primary schools to provide free education to poor children. These schools became a lifeline for many tribal families who otherwise had no access to formal education. Over time, the network of schools grew—reaching remote corners of Tripura—and changed the lives of countless children. Health services were another critical area of focus for Shanti Kali.[423] The tribal communities of Tripura—neglected by the authorities and living in impoverished conditions—suffered from a lack of basic healthcare facilities. Shanti Kali helped set up health camps, provided medical aid, and worked tirelessly to improve the overall health and well-being of the community. These efforts saved lives and improved the quality of life for many.

The Shanti Kali Ashram also took on the task of running orphanages which sheltered the unfortunate children in a nurturing environment. Under his guidance, these children received education, care and the love they needed to grow into confident and capable individuals. As the years passed, the impact of Shanti Kali's work became increasingly evident. What began as a single ashram in 1979 grew into the Shanti Kali Mission, with 18 branches spread across Tripura. Each branch carried forward his legacy of compassion, service and

[423]Ibid.

spiritual guidance. The Mission's activities expanded, touching numerous lives and addressing critical needs. The work did not go unnoticed and Shanti Kali became a revered figure, not just among the tribals but among people from all walks of life. His life and work inspired many to join his Mission, and together they created a lasting legacy of service and devotion.[424]

The night of 27 August 2000 cast a shadow over the Shanti Kali Ashram near Khumulwng, shrouding it in a darkness that would be felt for years to come.[425] Shanti Kali had spent the day as he usually did, guiding his followers and attending to the needs of the local tribal community. The ashram was a sanctuary of peace and spiritual solace, but on that fateful night, it became the scene of a tragedy that shook the very foundations of the Mission. As twilight gave way to night, the gathering of local devotees lingered, enjoying the serene environment and the comforting presence of Shanti Kali. Unbeknownst to those inside, a group of NLFT insurgents was advancing towards them, their intentions shrouded in violence and hatred.[426]

The armed insurgents broke into the ashram under the cover of darkness. The tranquillity of the night was shattered by the sound of their forceful entry, and the air grew thick with fear and confusion. Shanti Kali, known for his unwavering courage and peaceful demeanour, stood his ground even in the face of such imminent danger. The militants demanded that he and his followers convert to Christianity, a demand rooted in their violent campaign against Hindu leaders and their communities.[427] Shanti Kali's refusal was resolute; his faith and commitment to his principles were unshakeable. In a brutal act of retaliation for

[424]Ibid.
[425]Ibid.
[426]Ibid.
[427]Ibid.

his refusal, the militants murdered Shanti Kali in cold blood.[428] The ashram, once a beacon of hope and spiritual guidance, was now stained with the blood of its revered leader. The militants' merciless actions left the local devotees in a state of shock and despair, their sanctuary desecrated and their leader lost.

The assassination of Shanti Kali sent ripples of grief and outrage throughout Tripura and beyond. His murder was not an isolated incident but part of a broader pattern of violence against Hindu leaders in the region. In the same month, Jaulushmoni Jamatia, a prominent Hindu leader of the Jamatia community, was also brutally murdered by the same group.[429] These targeted killings were a stark reminder of the volatile and dangerous environment in which these leaders worked, striving to uplift and support their communities against growing odds.

Nearly three months after Shanti Kali's death, on 4 December 2000, the violence escalated further. An ashram established by Shanti Kali at Chachu Bazar near the Sidhai Police Station was raided by the NLFT.[430] This attack was part of a systematic campaign to dismantle the infrastructure of support and spiritual guidance that Shanti Kali had painstakingly built over the years. The insurgents, driven by their extremist ideology, sought to erase the legacy of a man who had dedicated his life to serving the needy and uplifting the downtrodden. In the months following his assassination, the NLFT continued their ruthless campaign. Eleven of Shanti Kali's ashrams, schools and orphanages scattered across Tripura were forcibly shut down.[431] These institutions had been pillars of support for many marginalized communities, providing education, healthcare and shelter to those in need. Their closure was a devastating blow, leaving many without

---

[428]Ibid.

[429]Ibid.

[430]Ibid.

[431]Ibid.

the resources they had come to rely on. The fear instilled by the insurgents' actions created an environment of terror and uncertainty, undermining the very fabric of the community that Shanti Kali had worked so hard to strengthen.

This wasn't the only such incident in Tripura. The next one is perhaps the darkest chapter in the Sangh's history in the Northeast. It is the story of four swayamsevaks from Tripura who were kidnapped and killed during the height of the NLFT's exploits.

Shyamal Kanti Sengupta—who was the kshetra karyavah at the time of his death—was born in September 1932 in the serene village of Supatala in Sylhet district, now part of Bangladesh. From a young age, he was drawn to the ideals of the Sangh.[432] The partition of India in 1947 was a turning point for Sengupta and his family. Like many others, they were forced to leave their ancestral home and move to Dibrugarh, Assam, seeking refuge and a fresh start.

In Sibsagar, Assam, Sengupta took up a position with the Life Insurance Corporation of India (LIC). Here, he settled with his wife and four children—three sons and a daughter. Despite his professional commitments, his heart remained with the Sangh.[433] His home in Sibsagar became a makeshift karyalaya, a meeting place and a sanctuary for Sangh workers and various organizations. The spirit of service and community was palpable in his household, influencing not just his immediate family but also the broader network of Sangh volunteers.

His role in the Sangh extended far beyond administrative tasks. As the kshetra karyavah, he travelled extensively, covering a vast expanse, including Odisha, the Andaman Islands, West Bengal, Sikkim and the entire north-eastern region of India.[434]

[432]Ibid.
[433]Ibid.
[434]Ibid.

During a significant period, he was entrusted with managing the Uttar Purvanchal, a role that required not just administrative acumen but also deep empathy and a strategic vision.[435]

Another worker—Dinendranath De, after completing his BSc—decided to dedicate his life to the Sangh's work and left home to become a *vistarak*, a full-time worker for the organization.[436] His journey led him to Kanthi tehsil in the district of Midnapore. Upon his arrival at the Sangh karyalaya, he was welcomed by Shaktipad Thakur, a prominent figure who would later hold important positions within the Sangh, including the post of the state organizing secretary of Kalyan Ashram and the Akhil Bharatiya Sharirik Pramukh.[437]

No sooner had De settled in than he expressed a desire to explore his new surroundings. Thakur, concerned about Dinendra's unfamiliarity with the area, advised him to stay put. However, God had other plans. He had heard about the beautiful beach of Digha, 32 kilometres away, and was eager to see it.[438] Ignoring the advice, he hopped on a bus to Digha. Along the way, he spotted some students from Srirampur and decided to get off the bus to talk to them.

This spontaneous encounter led him to Hirapur, the village of one of the students. With his innate charm and enthusiasm, he quickly gathered a group of local youths and started a branch of the Sangh. That evening, he enjoyed a meal at a student's house, building a connection that would last a lifetime. Meanwhile, back in Kanthi, Thakur and the other workers grew increasingly worried about Dinendra's whereabouts. He had left for a 'short walk' and hadn't returned.[439] Their anxiety was finally alleviated

---

[435]Ibid.

[436]Ibid.

[437]Ibid.

[438]Ibid.

[439]Ibid.

when De arrived at the office the next morning, full of stories about his adventure and the new Sangh branch he had established. Such was the nature of Dinendranath De—bold, sociable and virtuous.[440] His ability to connect with people and his fearless spirit were truly remarkable.

Later, he was assigned to Dakshin Assam prant, which included the Barak Valley, Mizoram, Tripura and Manipur at the time.[441] As the sharirik pramukh of the prant, he travelled extensively across these regions, promoting the Sangh's mission and values. His journeys took him to some of the most remote and challenging areas, but his determination and commitment never wavered. His work in South Assam was marked by the same courage and friendliness that had defined his earlier days. He tirelessly visited villages, organized shakhas and inspired countless individuals with his dedication and spirit. His efforts helped to strengthen the Sangh's presence and foster a sense of unity and purpose among its members.

Similarly, Sudhamoy Dutta's journey into the Sangh began during his college years, where he was introduced to Anantlal Soni, a revered senior pracharak.[442] The hostel where Dutta lived had a vibrant Sangh shakha, which became a nurturing ground for many future leaders. It was from this environment that notable volunteers like Dr Sachindranath Singh, Shankar Bagh, Shaktipad Thakur and Sudhamoy Dutta himself emerged as full-time workers and pracharaks.[443]

In 1974, Dutta decided to dedicate his life to the Sangh as a pracharak.[444] His initial role was that of a *nagar pracharak*, but his capabilities quickly saw him being entrusted with more

---

[440]Ibid.
[441]Ibid.
[442]Ibid.
[443]Ibid.
[444]Ibid.

responsibilities. As he moved from the city to the district, he built close relationships with the families in the areas he served. His genuine care and commitment left a lasting impression on those he worked with. Later, he took on the responsibility of managing the Sangh's magazine, *Swastika*.[445] His keen editorial skills and deep understanding of the Sangh's mission ensured that the magazine thrived under his stewardship. For years, he skilfully managed the publication, making it a powerful tool for spreading the Sangh's message.

In July 1999, during a campaign meeting, it was announced that Dutta would take on a new role in Agartala.[446] This was a significant responsibility and it marked a new chapter in his dedicated service. It was decided that he would move to Tripura in August 1999. In Tripura, he continued to work with the same zeal and dedication that had characterized his previous roles.[447] His work in Agartala was marked by his ability to connect with people and build strong community ties. His empathetic approach and genuine concern for the well-being of others made him a beloved figure in the community.[448]

Shubhankar Chakraborty, affectionately known as Kanchan, was a resident of Bhatar village in the Bardhaman district of West Bengal.[449] He was a skilled pracharak, well-versed in the sharirik vertical of the Sangh. He was also a talented singer and trumpeter, known for his ability to connect effortlessly with people of all ages.

In 1994, Kanchan was sent to Tripura, where he was entrusted with the role of North Tripura Zila Pracharak.[450] His days were filled with travelling from village to village,

[445]Ibid.

[446]Ibid.

[447]Ibid.

[448]Ibid.

[449]Ibid.

[450]Ibid.

running shakhas with children and youth, and organizing various programmes. His magnetic personality drew children, teenagers and young adults towards him, making him a beloved figure in the community.

On the fateful day of 6 August 1999, Shyamlal Sengupta, Dinendranath De, Sudhamoy Dutta and Shubhankar Chakraborty reached the boys' hostel of Kalyan Ashram in the Birasi Mile area of North Tripura district. They were there for a programme organized by Digvijay Dev, a worker at the hostel, and Dalmohan Tripura, the hostel head. After their morning bath, the group sat together, enjoying refreshments and engaging in light-hearted conversations.[451]

However, trouble had been brewing elsewhere. The previous day, some hostel children had gone to the market and were approached by individuals associated with the separatist movement. These men asked the children, 'When is State Organizing Secretary Balram Das Roy coming?'[452] The children innocently replied that some guests from outside would be arriving the next day. The separatists had long had their eyes on Balram Das Roy, who they believed was responsible for spreading patriotic and unifying messages in the tribal areas. They thought he was a significant threat, and thus, he became their target.

On the morning of 6 August, gunmen from the separatist organization NLFT arrived at the hostel.[453] They enquired about Balram Das Roy from the children playing outside, who, unaware of the situation, directed them inside. The gunmen confronted Sanjeet Pal, who told them Das Roy was in Agartala and not present at the hostel. The gunmen, not convinced, took Shyamlal Sengupta, Dinendranath De, Sudhamoy Dutta and

[451]Ibid.
[452]Ibid.
[453]Ibid.

Shubhankar Chakraborty at gunpoint, believing one of them to be the man they wanted.[454]

The Sangh workers immediately informed key members in Agartala and Guwahati, sparking a widespread alert. The police were also notified, but despite numerous efforts, no information on the whereabouts of the four abducted swayamsevaks surfaced. As days turned into weeks, it became evident that the kidnappers had mistaken the identities of their captives. Realizing their mistake, the separatists demanded ransom for their release. However, conceding to this demand would set a dangerous precedent, potentially encouraging more kidnappings of Sangh workers across the Northeast and the country.

During this period, the NDA government was in power in New Delhi, while Tripura was under a communist regime. The lack of coordination between the two governments further complicated rescue efforts. Even the national leaders of the RSS wrote letters to the home minister, pleading for the safe return of the four workers. Rallies were organized and the issue garnered considerable public attention.

Meanwhile, the families of the abducted workers were in a state of constant anguish. The Sangh deployed experienced workers, including All India Sah-Sharirik Pramukh Ramchandra Sahastrabhojani, to manage the rescue operations.[455] Some searched the forests along the borders, while others coordinated with the governments in Agartala and Delhi. There were occasional glimmers of hope, but they were quickly extinguished, leaving the workers disheartened yet undeterred in their efforts.

A year and a half passed with little progress. Eventually, it was discovered that the four workers were being held in a forest in Bangladesh. Despite renewed efforts, the grim news arrived that the insurgents had killed Shyamlal Sengupta, Dinendranath

[454]Ibid.

[455]Ibid.

De, Sudhamoy Dutta and Shubhankar Chakraborty. The Sangh, along with patriotic citizens across the country, was plunged into mourning.

This tragic incident sent shockwaves through the Sangh, instilling a sense of fear and urgency. Yet, despite the loss, the local activists did not waver in their commitment to their cause. Their relentless efforts, spurred by the sacrifice of their comrades, ensured that the spirit of patriotism and unity continued to resonate throughout Tripura. Today, the province echoes with the cries of 'Bharat Mata Ki Jai', a testament to the unwavering dedication of these brave souls. Sanjeet Pal, an eyewitness to the incident, now serves in an important capacity within Kalyan Ashram, continuing the mission with unyielding resolve.[456]

Another sufferer of such attacks was Ba Rejoising Khongsha. From the outset, Ba Rejoy, as he was affectionately called, exhibited a deep reverence for his Khasi tribal roots and a profound love for his homeland, Meghalaya. Despite the challenges that life presented, his spirit remained unyielding.[457] Ba Rejoy's journey through life was marked by both personal triumphs and profound losses. The early years of his childhood were scarred by the sorrow of losing four brothers, a weight that would have broken many lesser spirits.[458] Yet, Ba Rejoy's resilience only seemed to grow stronger with each trial he faced. Rather than succumbing to despair, he drew strength from his community, his culture, and the enduring values instilled in him by his family.

Ba Rejoy found solace and purpose in the teachings and ideals of Mahatma Gandhi. The great leader's message of

---

[456]Interview with Sanjeet Pal.

[457]Kavishwar, Sandip, *Mrityunjay Veer*, Rouhin Deb and Nabaarun Barooah, Prachi Prakashan, Guwahati, 2022.

[458]Ibid.

non-violence and service to others resonated deeply with him, shaping his worldview and guiding his actions.[459] As he matured, he became increasingly involved in community affairs, emerging as a respected leader within his village. In recognition of his leadership qualities and his unwavering commitment to the welfare of his community, Ba Rejoy was bestowed with the title of *sardar shnong*, or village head. This position came with great responsibility, but Ba Rejoy embraced it wholeheartedly, viewing it as an opportunity to serve his people and preserve the rich cultural heritage of his village. One of Ba Rejoy's most enduring legacies was his dedication to education and rural development. Recognizing the transformative power of knowledge, he took it upon himself to establish the Mahatma Gandhi Smriti School in his village.[460] This institution was not just a place of learning but also a symbol of hope and opportunity for generations to come. Ba Rejoy understood that education was key to unlocking the full potential of his community, empowering them to shape their own destinies and break free from the shackles of poverty and ignorance.

But Ba Rejoy's vision extended far beyond the walls of the classroom. He was acutely aware of the social evils that plagued his village and was determined to combat them head-on. With characteristic determination and resolve, he launched various initiatives aimed at eradicating social ills such as alcoholism, substance abuse and gender discrimination. Through community outreach programmes, awareness campaigns and grassroots activism, Ba Rejoy sought to create a more just and equitable society for all. Despite the formidable challenges he faced, Ba Rejoy remained steadfast in his commitment to his people and principles. He led by example, inspiring others to join his quest for positive change and social justice.

---

[459]Ibid.

[460]Ibid.

As the first president of Seng Khasi Riwar Mihngi, an organization that brought together 170 villages along the eastern border, Ba Rejoy played a pivotal role in uniting communities and advocating for their rights.[461] The organization became a powerful force for change, challenging injustice and inequality wherever it was found. But Ba Rejoy's path was not without obstacles. Throughout his tenure, he faced numerous challenges from various quarters, including the Church. But the attempts to undermine his efforts, through persuasion, pressure and even threats, only served to strengthen his resolve. Ba Rejoy remained steadfast in his commitment to justice and fairness, refusing to be swayed by intimidation or coercion.

One of Ba Rejoy's most significant achievements was his campaign for the codification of customary law.[462] Recognizing the importance of preserving traditional practices and customs, he tirelessly advocated for the formal recognition of indigenous laws and institutions. His efforts garnered support from the District Council and posed a direct challenge to land encroachment by the Church and illegal constructions. However, Ba Rejoy's unwavering stance drew the ire of the Hynniewtrep National Liberation Council (HNLC), a separatist terrorist organization with ties to the Church.[463] In a brazen act of violence, Ba Rejoy was abducted from his residence in Shillong on 3 March 2000.[464]

Days and months went by, but there was no sign of Ba Rejoy. His family, friends and supporters clung to hope, praying for his safe return. But their worst fears were realized when his body was discovered buried in a forest, a victim of senseless brutality and cowardice. The news of Ba Rejoy's tragic demise reverberated across Meghalaya and especially among the Seng

---

[461]Ibid.

[462]Ibid.

[463]Ibid.

[464]Ibid.

Khasi.[465] The loss was felt deeply by all who knew him, but his spirit lived on in the hearts and minds of those who shared his vision for a better, more just society.[466] His legacy continued to inspire a generation to uphold the values of justice, integrity and devotion to their cultural heritage and homeland.

In 1966, Madhumangal Sharma arrived in Manipur with a mission to strengthen the presence of the Sangh in the state.[467] By 1970 Manipur had become a full-fledged *vibhag* (division) of the organization. Sharma was appointed as the karyavah, dedicating himself to the cause of uniting Hindus amidst the rising tensions in the region.

At the time, Manipur was experiencing a unique conflict—Hindus were pitted against other native Hindus by extremists. Militant organizations masquerading as Sanamahis—adherents of the indigenous faith of the Meitei community—held that their beliefs diverged from traditional Hindu practices. Their rise and the subsequent tensions created a deep rift, with occasional violence flaring up between the groups. One of the most shocking incidents occurred in the 1980s when a copy of the revered Srimad Bhagavat Gita was desecrated. They placed the sacred text in a coffin and burned it at Kangla, a site of immense cultural and spiritual significance for the people of Manipur.[468] This act shook the Hindu community to its core, leaving many disheartened and outraged.

Around this time, Sharma, a key figure in the Vishwa Hindu Parishad (VHP) and serving as its *mahamantri*, took notice of these troubling developments. Determined to rally the Hindus and restore their confidence, he initiated the plan for a massive

---

[465]Ibid.

[466]Interview with Premanand Sharma.

[467]Ibid.

[468]Ibid.

Hindu Sammelan in Manipur.[469] The groundwork for this event began in earnest, with dedicated workers going from village to village, spreading the message of unity and Hindu pride. However, this noble effort came at a severe cost.

One fateful day, Madhumangal and Brijmohan, the joint secretary of VHP, were traveling on a scooter. Unbeknownst to them, they had become targets for those opposed to their cause. A mini-bus, intentionally aiming to harm them, collided with their scooter. Though they survived, the injuries they sustained were severe. Madhumangal suffered a broken spine, while Brijmohan's legs were crushed. Their resolve, however, remained unshaken.[470]

Even after this attack, threats to Sharma's life continued. Posters warning him to cease his work for the Hindus were plastered around his home. Despite these ominous warnings, his resolve never faltered. In 1984 he joined the BJP, even taking charge of the state. Despite garnering 30 per cent of the votes, he ultimately lost the election. His political aspirations, however, continued unabated.[471]

By 1995, Sharma had been forced underground due to escalating threats. The calls to his house were relentless, warning him to leave the BJP or face certain death.[472] Once, a group of attackers managed to make their way to his home, determined to kill him. But in a remarkable turn of events, Madhumangal Sharma's ability to reason with them saved his life. His words convinced the would-be killers that he was not a man to be taken lightly.

However, the reprieve was short-lived. The orders were clear—Madhumangal Sharma had to be eliminated. On the

[469]Ibid.

[470]Ibid.

[471]Ibid.

[472]Ibid.

evening of 11 February 1995, two armed men approached his house. Without hesitation they opened fire, unleashing 12 rounds in quick succession. Eleven bullets struck him in the chest, leaving him bleeding and gravely wounded.[473]

But even in this darkest moment, fate seemed to offer a sliver of comfort. Sharma always carried a copy of the Srimad Bhagavat Gita. As the bullets rained down on him, the holy book soaked in his blood, now as red as the ink of the texts themselves.

Sharma's life was a story of unwavering courage and conviction. Even in the face of mortal danger, he remained true to his beliefs, defending his cause with dignity and strength. His sacrifice and heroism in the defence of Hindu values left an indelible mark on the history of Manipur and the hearts of those who knew him.

Acts of Defiance

In the late 1990s, the Upper Assam region was a hotbed of insurgency as tensions simmered between different ethnic groups, creating deep divides. It was in this complex landscape that Jogen Gogoi (name changed), a senior RSS pracharak, who had served in Sibsagar between 1996 and 2001, began his quiet but significant mission. He worked with the tribes and communities in ULFA's backyard, weaving them into the fabric of the RSS's vision of cultural and national unity.[474]

At the time, the tea gardens of Assam were a place not just of economic production but also of social stratification. There were 120 gardens scattered across the region and they were a microcosm of inequality, with owners and managers living in affluence while the workers lived in deprivation. Gogoi quickly

[473]Ibid.

[474]Interview with Jogen Gogoi (name changed).

recognized the class divide but saw it as an opportunity rather than a hurdle. While he maintained good relations with the managerial class, it was the workers he chose to live among, staying in the Lines, where their modest houses stood.[475] His choice was a powerful statement, and it became the foundation for the Sangh's outreach to the tea tribes—a demographic that today is among the BJP's most loyal supporters.

In the workers' homes, the pracharak focused on the youth. He spoke of dharma, taught them mantras, and slowly established *kirtans*, prayer gatherings that evolved into shakhas over time. He was aware of the issues plaguing the community, particularly the rampant alcoholism among the young. Initially, many came to kirtans and shakhas drunk. His more conservative colleagues objected, suggesting that it was improper to allow intoxicated youth into religious gatherings. But Gogoi took a different view. 'Something is better than nothing,' he would say, welcoming them no matter their state.[476] Gradually, as they immersed themselves in kirtans, deities and the discipline of the shakhas, many gave up alcohol. At the peak of this outreach, 74 shakhas were thriving in the tea gardens, a testament to his patient and pragmatic approach.[477]

While this work was progressing in the tea gardens, the Sangh simultaneously extended its outreach to the janajati communities. They formed alliances with tribal leaders and sent swayamsevaks to join the local unions and student organizations, such as the All Assam Tea Tribes Students Association. These efforts culminated in the creation of a parent body called the Jati Mahasabha, through which influential tribal leaders like Sanjay Kishan joined the RSS.[478] The Mahasabha also promoted

---

[475]Ibid.

[476]Ibid.

[477]Ibid.

[478]Ibid.

indigenous festivals like Karam Puja, organizing workshops in the tea gardens to celebrate local dance, music and rituals. Matri Sammelans (Conference of Mothers) were organized, building a deep-rooted connection with the local culture.

The RSS's outreach didn't stop with the tea tribes. They extended a hand to the Ahom community as well, reaching out to groups like the Ahom Karate Club. Members, including figures like Seemanta and Ratul Gogoi, began attending RSS camps. Small, intimate gatherings were organized where Ahom and tea adivasi communities were brought together.[479] They shared meals, slept side by side, and slowly, the inter-community tensions began to dissolve. These baithaks were often funded by Marwari businessmen who contributed food and resources. This act of generosity also helped to bridge the divide between the Hindi-speaking communities and the tribes.

However, this outreach was not without resistance. The Sangh's growing influence in the region soon led to clashes with the All Tai Ahom Students' Union (ATASU) and ULFA, both of whom opposed the RSS's presence. ULFA, in particular, demanded that the camps be stopped. But Gogoi, undeterred, held his ground. In a memorable exchange, he responded to ULFA's demands with a quiet conviction: 'I'm also an Assamese. I love Assam as much as you do. I respect your love for Assam but believe that we can only save Assam if it remains united with India. That's our only difference.'[480]

In time, the RSS's efforts bore fruit. What began as a humble outreach to disconnected communities had turned into a movement that bridged cultural divides and fostered unity. The pracharak's vision of integration, patience and cultural respect proved that even in the most volatile regions the Sangh could adapt and thrive.

---

[479] Ibid

[480] Ibid

In the remote Mishing belt, nestled along the banks of Assam's rivers, the RSS had little to no presence. Locals were wary of outsiders, and outreach seemed difficult. When Gogoi organized a camp there, the turnout was disheartening. For the first two days, the fields where he had set up camp remained mostly empty. Then, on the third day, a glimmer of hope arrived.

Two boys from the village appeared unexpectedly, saying they wanted to join the shakha, especially drawn by the games they had heard about. But there were rules in place: attendees were required to participate in the entire camp from the start, wear the proper uniform, and pay a small fee of ₹150.[481] While the pracharak relaxed the rule about the uniform, he held firm on the camp fee, hoping it would instil a sense of commitment. The boys, unable to pay, left, and the pracharak felt a wave of dejection, convinced that they would not return.

However, later that night, well past midnight, the boys returned, knocking on the door of his makeshift quarters. In their hands was the camp fee that they had somehow scraped together. Moved by their determination, Gogoi welcomed them warmly, and from that night on, the connection with the Mishing community began to take root. Both boys went on to become vistaraks, full-time volunteers, and through their efforts, the RSS's influence among the Mishing people blossomed.[482] Over time, the Sangh's presence grew, and the Mishing Sammelan was organized, bringing together students and their parents, many of whom were already involved with the Sankardev Vidya Niketan schools.

Gogoi recounts another story from his time in a Mishing village. During a visit, the villagers, following their customs, offered him ritualistic alcohol as part of a welcoming ceremony. He didn't drink alcohol, but rather than offend them by refusing

---

[481]Ibid

[482]Ibid.

outright, he carefully took a spoon and sipped a small amount, honouring their tradition without compromising his values. Similarly, when offered pork—a dish considered taboo by many orthodox Hindus—he took a small piece to show respect for the local customs.[483]

These gestures, though small, carried enormous weight. They broke the caste and cultural barriers that had long separated the plains-dwelling Hindus from the Mishing tribe. The villagers were so moved by his understanding and respect that the next time he visited, they made separate arrangements, ensuring he had food that aligned with his practices. The mutual respect forged between them solidified the Sangh's standing in the region.

Thanks to this groundwork, in 2001, a historic moment unfolded. The first-ever Bharat Mata Pujan was organized in Sibsagar, the same place where ULFA had once asserted its dominance. For Gogoi, this was more than just an event.[484] It marked the completion of a personal *sankalp*—a vow to raise the RSS flag in the very place where ULFA began, as an act of defiance for killing Murli Manohar in his hometown of Nalbari. The Bharat Mata Pujan was not just a spiritual gathering; it was a statement of unity, a reclamation of space once controlled by fear and separatism. Where once insurgency and division had thrived, Jogen Gogoi and his team of swayamsevaks had brought a new narrative—one of inclusivity, respect for local culture, and a deep, abiding commitment to Assam's unity within India.

Sangh at 50—Mass Recruitment in the Northeast

In 1996, the Rashtriya Swayamsevak Sangh celebrated a significant milestone: fifty years of dedicated work in the Northeast. The journey had begun with Dadarao Parmarth—the first pracharak

---

[483]Ibid.

[484]Ibid.

who arrived in 1946—setting the foundation for the Sangh's activities in this diverse and strategically important region. To commemorate this half-century of progress and to strengthen their mission, the Sangh launched an ambitious drive to induct fifty local pracharaks.

The story of this drive is both inspiring and intriguing, beginning with an unexpected protagonist—Manik Chandra Das. Das was a grihastha, a householder, and it was almost unheard of for a grihastha to become a pracharak.[485] Traditionally, pracharaks are full-time volunteers who dedicate their lives to the Sangh's cause, foregoing family responsibilities. However, Das was determined. Despite having no children to carry on his familial duties, he devised a plan to support his wife. He took voluntary retirement from his job, ensuring that his pension would provide for her needs. With this act of selflessness and foresight, he declared himself the first pracharak of the new drive.[486]

Manik Chandra Das's dedication did not stop there. His commitment and passion for the cause saw him rise to the position of prant pracharak, a significant role within the organization. His story set a powerful example and ignited a wave of enthusiasm across the region. Inspired by his sacrifice and leadership, more volunteers came forward to join the cause.

While the drive fell slightly short of its goal, inducting 46 local pracharaks instead of the targeted 50, it was nonetheless a remarkable achievement.[487] More importantly, it established a new tradition of mass recruitment in the Northeast, marking a turning point in the Sangh's efforts to integrate the region both physically and psychologically with the rest of India. The legacy of this drive continues to inspire, demonstrating how individual

---

[485] Interview with Shankar Das.
[486] Ibid.
[487] Ibid.

commitment can spark a broader movement, fostering unity and strengthening the bonds within the nation.

After five decades marked by enmity, opposition, incarceration and even violence, the tide in the Northeast began to turn. The local people, who had long viewed the RSS with suspicion and resistance, started to embrace the organization mainly due to the Ram Mandir movement as well as the efforts to preserve indigenous faiths. This shift was evident not only in the growing number of local pracharaks but also in the increasing acceptance and participation of the community in the Sangh's initiatives. This new-found acceptance laid a robust foundation for the new millennium. As the 2000s dawned, the RSS was poised to conquer new horizons, expanding its influence and uniting diverse regions under its vision of national integration. But that is a story we will tell in the next chapter.

6

The New Millennium

The acceptance that the Sangh Parivar had begun to attain in the previous decade, after years of struggle, laid a robust foundation for the new millennium. The turn of the century brought about new challenges for the RSS, and as a result, new opportunities for growth. The RSS developed into a vast network of over 45,000 shakhas by the year 2000.[488] The dawn of the new millennium marked a transformative era for the Sangh, as it endeavoured to shape the future of India with a renewed focus on infrastructure and social development. The 2000s saw the Sangh spearheading initiatives that combined the robust growth of physical infrastructure with a deep commitment to preserving tribal identities and uplifting marginalized communities through education and healthcare.

As India stepped into the twenty-first century, the RSS recognized that true progress could not merely be measured by economic indicators or technological advancements. They understood that for India to thrive, it needed to address the foundational issues that had long been neglected. This meant building roads, bridges and public facilities that would connect the remotest corners of the country to its burgeoning urban centres. However, their vision extended beyond concrete and

---

[488]Noorani, Abdul Gafoor Abdul Majeed, *The RSS and the BJP: A Division of Labour*, LeftWord Books, New Delhi, 2000.

steel; it was equally about fostering a sense of identity and pride among the country's diverse tribal populations.

One of the critical pillars of the Sangh's mission was the preservation of tribal identities. India is home to a multitude of tribes, each with its unique culture, language and traditions. The Sangh saw these communities not as relics of the past but as vibrant, integral parts of India's social fabric. To this end, they initiated various programmes aimed at preserving and promoting indigenous faiths, languages, arts and customs. They worked closely with the leaders and elders of these indigenous faiths, ensuring that modernization did not come at the expense of cultural erosion.

The RSS's efforts in tribal areas were multifaceted. On the one hand, they worked to protect and promote traditional practices and knowledge. On the other hand, they sought to integrate these communities into the broader Indian society in a manner that respected their uniqueness. Educational initiatives played a crucial role in this balancing act. The Sangh, through Vidya Bharati, established schools in remote tribal regions, providing children with access to modern education while incorporating elements of their indigenous cultures into the curriculum.[489] This approach not only improved literacy rates but also instilled a sense of pride and identity among the younger generations.

Healthcare was another area where the Sangh made significant strides. In many tribal regions, access to medical facilities was either severely limited or non-existent. The RSS, through Seva Bharati, addressed this gap by setting up hospitals and clinics, staffed by dedicated healthcare professionals who often travelled great distances to serve these communities.[490] These facilities provided essential medical services, maternal and child healthcare,

[489]Interview with Brahmaji Rao.

[490]Ibid.

and preventive care programmes, drastically improving the overall health and well-being of the tribal populations.

The infrastructural advancements spearheaded by the Sangh were not limited to tribal areas. Across the country, they championed the construction of roads, schools and hospitals, recognizing that infrastructure was the backbone of a thriving society. By improving connectivity, they enabled economic opportunities to reach previously inaccessible regions, fostering inclusive growth. The schools and hospitals built by the Sangh were often seen as beacons of hope in underserved areas, providing essential services and creating a foundation for sustainable development.

In the 2000s, the RSS's efforts were a testament to their holistic approach to nation-building. They understood that infrastructure was not just about physical development but also about creating an environment where every citizen, regardless of their background, could thrive. Their work during this period showcased a vision of progress that was as much about honouring the past as it was about building a brighter future. We will go through these different facets of nation-building one after another, starting with borderlands.

Defending Our Borders

On 13 April 2008, the Sangh Parivar welcomed a new organization within its ambit in the Northeast, Seemanta Chetana Mancha (Purvottar), to work on the nation-building process in the international borders surrounding Northeast India[491]. When we interviewed Pradeepan, the national secretary of the Mancha, he described to us the Mancha's role in fostering people-to-people contact in the bordering areas shared with China, Myanmar and Bangladesh.

---

[491]Interview with Pradeepan.

Seemanta Chetana Mancha actively engages with the bordering villages along the frontiers of China, Myanmar and Bangladesh, ensuring that the voices of the local people are heard and their concerns addressed. By lobbying with both state and Central governments, they play a pivotal role in solving the myriad problems faced by those living in these sensitive areas. Their efforts aim to mitigate friction between the local populations and the Border Security Forces (BSF) and the Indian Army, who are tasked with guarding these volatile borders.

On significant occasions like Independence Day and Republic Day, they arrange special events where local residents tie rakhis on soldiers, symbolizing a bond of protection and brotherhood.[492] These heartfelt interactions help build a bridge of trust and camaraderie between the soldiers and the local populace, fostering a sense of unity and mutual respect. This also helps create a first line of defence during combat.

In addition to these cultural endeavours, Seemanta Chetana Mancha is deeply committed to raising awareness about critical border issues that impact national security and local stability. They highlight the dangers of drug smuggling from Myanmar, a significant concern that threatens the safety and well-being of the communities in these regions.[493] The organization also sheds light on the issue of illegal infiltration from Bangladesh, which poses demographic and security challenges for India.[494] They bring attention to the aggressive posturing and territorial incursions by China in Arunachal Pradesh. By educating the local populations about these threats and encouraging a vigilant and informed community, the organization helps to strengthen India's border security from within.

---

[492]Ibid.

[493]Ibid.

[494]Ibid.

Through these multifaceted efforts, Seemanta Chetana Mancha not only works towards solving immediate problems but also aims to create a lasting impact on the social and cultural fabric of the border regions. Their dedication to fostering harmony, raising awareness and building bridges between the military and the local communities makes them a vital force in maintaining peace and stability along India's borders. More importantly, they contribute to the nation-making process by integrating the local frontier populations into the national fold.

Preserving Tribal Identities

In the heart of Diphu, a town nestled in the hills of Karbi Anglong, a quiet revolution was brewing. Bharat Agarwal, a committed researcher and thinker associated with the Sangh Parivar, had embarked on an ambitious endeavour—a large-scale survey aimed at understanding the spiritual landscape of the region's indigenous people.[495] This was no ordinary survey; it sought to explore the deepest recesses of their faith, examining the beliefs, rites and rituals that had guided their communities for generations.

The survey was meticulously designed, with a comprehensive questionnaire that delved into both the metaphysical and epidemiological aspects of their traditions. The questions ranged widely, touching on profound topics such as the mysteries of birth and rebirth, the role of karma in shaping destiny, the significance of ritual practices and the contentious issue of conversions.[496] Each query was crafted to uncover the core principles that underpinned these diverse faiths, revealing the tapestry of spiritual wisdom that had been woven over centuries.

---

[495]Interview with Krishna Gopal Sharma.

[496]Ibid.

For weeks, Bharat and his team went from village to village, meeting with indigenous leaders and spiritual elders, sitting cross-legged in community gatherings and listening intently to the stories and beliefs that had shaped their worldviews. The process was slow, deliberate and deeply respectful, allowing the indigenous people to voice their perspectives in their own words. They spoke of life and death, of the cycles of rebirth that governed existence, of karma as a cosmic law that linked actions to consequences, and of enlightenment as the ultimate goal of the soul's journey.

As the survey reached its conclusion, a pattern began to emerge from the multitude of responses. Despite the variety of tribes and the diversity of customs, there was a surprising alignment in their fundamental beliefs. Almost unanimously, the indigenous faiths echoed the same views on key metaphysical concepts: the law of karma, the cycle of rebirth and the pursuit of enlightenment were central to their spiritual philosophies. This realization was a moment of profound insight—a common thread ran through their different traditions, connecting them in ways that had not been fully recognized before.

When the findings were presented, they sparked a wave of reflection and dialogue among the indigenous leaders. They gathered once more, but this time with a new understanding. The similarities were too striking to ignore. Dr Krishna Gopal Sharma, the sah sarkaryavah, who had been closely involved with the process, noted the remarkable shift that began to take place.

Upon recognizing these shared beliefs, the indigenous leaders stood up and, with a sense of clarity and conviction, proclaimed themselves as branches of the Sanatan faith.[497] It was a powerful moment—a declaration that acknowledged their unique traditions while embracing a broader spiritual kinship.[498]

[497]Ibid.

[498]Ibid.

They saw themselves not as separate entities but as diverse expressions of a common spiritual heritage.[499]

This realization marked a turning point. What had begun as a quest to understand the beliefs of the indigenous people had become a profound affirmation of unity. It revealed that beneath the surface diversity of India's spiritual landscape, there lay a deep, underlying connection—a shared commitment to principles like karma, rebirth and the ultimate quest for enlightenment. And in this revelation, a new chapter was written in the story of India's spiritual mosaic, one that celebrated both the unity and the diversity of its rich heritage.

In April 2002, the Sangh organized the Janajati Faith and Cultural Protection Forum, an initiative aimed at preserving and promoting indigenous faiths and cultures.[500] This forum brought together leaders from various indigenous faiths, offering them a common platform for the first time. The event, held at the Vivekananda Kendra Institute of Culture (VKIC), Guwahati, and facilitated by Kalyan Ashram, featured in-depth discussions on preserving indigenous traditions.[501] Leaders explored ways to save their faiths through the establishment of weekly prayer halls and the revival of ancient practices.

In a similar vein, 2006 saw the organization of the Indigenous Youth Conference, an ambitious event that drew 5,000 youth leaders from 120 communities.[502] Remarkably, these young leaders covered their own expenses to attend. Despite the initial scepticism surrounding the event—many believed it would be risky and fraught with conflicts, given the diverse egos and issues of the communities involved—the conference was a resounding success. Contrary to fears of fighting and alcoholism, not a single

---

[499]Ibid.

[500]Interview with Sandip Kavishwar.

[501]Ibid.

[502]Ibid.

altercation occurred over the five days. The youths displayed remarkable discipline and unity.

The conference included a grand procession through Guwahati that lasted four hours, culminating in a collective dance at Nehru Stadium.[503] This powerful display of solidarity and shared culture instilled a new-found belief in the possibility of working together towards common goals. The event demonstrated that, despite their differences, the communities could collaborate harmoniously. This success laid the foundation for ongoing collaborations. Now, a youth festival is held in Arunachal Pradesh every three years, organized entirely by the local communities. This recurring event stands as a testament to the lasting impact of the 2006 conference, continuing to foster unity and cultural pride among the indigenous youth.

The Sangh embraced a philosophy of not indoctrinating its members, instead focusing on localization and respect for ancestral traditions. The pracharaks, deeply embedded in the communities they served, paid homage to local heroes and ancestors like Birsa Munda and Kalicharan Brahma. This approach fostered a sense of pride and continuity within the indigenous cultures. Around this time onwards, Pradeepan looked after the establishment of several janajati-focused Sanskriti Suraksha Parishads such as that for Bodo, Santhal, Rabha, Mishing, Karbi, Tiwa and other communities, using their local nomenclature.[504] This also helped generate awareness among local communities regarding the need to protect their indigenous faiths and customs.

In 2007, the Vanavasi Kalyan Ashram embarked on a mission known as sampark abhiyans, addressing a unique challenge faced by indigenous communities.[505] While Christian homes were adorned with stars and cross lockets, symbolizing their faith, the

---

[503]Ibid.

[504]Interview with Krishna Gopal Sharma.

[505]Interview with Sandip Kavishwar.

indigenous people lacked similar symbols to represent their own beliefs and traditions. From 1 to 31 December, a dedicated effort was made to visit every single household across 1,000 villages in the Donyi-Polo and Rangfrah belt.[506] Volunteers distributed symbolic items such as lockets, flags and photos of indigenous deities to these homes. The initiative aimed to instil a sense of identity and pride within the indigenous communities.

This endeavour was a massive success. Today, 50,000 houses in 2,000 villages proudly display these symbols.[507] The items were crafted by Kalyan Ashram and distributed by local organizations, ensuring that the cultural heritage was both preserved and celebrated. The distribution process was a communal effort. Regardless of whether one was a doctor, a professor, or in any other occupation, every evening saw people from all walks of life coming together to distribute these symbols. This collective effort not only strengthened the cultural fabric of the communities but also reinforced a shared sense of purpose and unity among the people. Through the sampark abhiyan, the Sangh reinforced the importance of visible symbols in fostering cultural pride and solidarity among indigenous populations.

Around 2007–08, within the Bajo circle in Tirap district, the dedicated efforts of the Kalyan Ashram Secretary and the Rangfrah Secretary bore fruit in the construction of a Rangfrah temple. This was a bold endeavour in an area where 70 per cent of the population was Christian.[508] Their peaceful initiative soon faced severe resistance. The NSCN issued a notice demanding the temple be shut down within eight days. Defiantly, one of the karyakartas reopened the temple, only to be brutally beaten and abandoned in the forests. His home was torched, forcing his parents to flee for their lives.

---

[506]Ibid.

[507]Ibid.

[508]Ibid.

Undeterred, a group of sixty *pujaris* from Changlang rallied to rebuild the temple.[509] In a twist of fate, an NSCN area commander named Chapte was killed by a misfire from his own gun. Initially, the NSCN denied that he was one of their cadres, but following his death, they accused the Sangh of having killed one of their men. The challenges did not end there. In 2009, in a different location, Kalyan Ashram and Rangfrah karyakartas faced an agonizing ordeal.[510] Forced at gunpoint, they had to set fire to their own temple, tears streaming down their faces as they watched it burn. Sandip Kavishwar mentioned that this incident prompted the then President of India, Smt. Pratibha Patil, to order an inquiry. However, the resilience and determination of the community shone through. By 2010, they had rebuilt their temple, standing once more as a symbol of their faith and spirit.[511]

Educating the Next Generation, Reforming Society

The Sangh's commitment to education is evident in the establishment of 50 schools across various regions, each carrying a unique name that reflects the local culture and heritage.[512] For instance, the Donyi-Polo Vidya Niketan in Arunachal Pradesh, named after the revered sun and moon deities of the region, was much more than a place of education. The school offered a sanctuary where the cultural and spiritual essence of the land was nurtured alongside academic pursuits.[513]

Further west, in the hills of Nagaland, the Zeliangrong Heraka School emerged as a tribute to the indigenous faith and traditions of the Zeliangrong people.[514] Here, education was

[509] Ibid.
[510] Ibid.
[511] Ibid.
[512] Ibid.
[513] Ibid.
[514] Ibid.

not a detached, bureaucratic endeavour but a living, breathing process that honoured the students' ancestral heritage. Each lesson was interwoven with stories, practices and values that had been passed down through generations, ensuring that the flame of their unique identity burned brightly.

What set these schools apart was their independence from government involvement. The Sangh's initiative to establish and run these institutions underscored their dedication to providing quality education while fiercely preserving and promoting local traditions and values. The RSS's efforts were not merely about filling classrooms but about cultivating environments where children grew up with a strong sense of identity and a profound respect for their cultural heritage.

In the remote villages of Arunachal Pradesh, the challenges were formidable. The residents—often the poorest of the poor—struggled with abysmal infrastructure and lived in a state of near disconnect from the outside world. This isolation fostered a deep sense of alienation, though it rarely culminated in secessionist desires. The villagers—resilient and proud—yearned for opportunities that would bridge the gap between their isolated lives and the larger world.

Amidst these challenges, many young people found a pathway to education and a broader cultural identity through the Vivekananda Kendra schools. These institutions not only provided formal education but also instilled the basic tenets of Hinduism, teaching Hindi along with Assamese, which became a lingua franca among the diverse tribal communities. The introduction of a common language helped to foster unity and a shared sense of purpose among the tribes. Among the Nyishi people, who saw the maximum number of conversions to Christianity, the Sangh started operating gurukuls.

A young Tangsa leader, reflecting on his journey, highlighted the pivotal role played by organizations like the RSS in filling the void left by the state. 'They provided basic health facilities and education. The missionaries did the same. The state was all but absent when it came to providing the basics. They came and filled the void,'[515] he explained, underlining the critical support the Sangh offered in the absence of adequate government services.

The RSS's schools were not just institutions of learning but lifelines for communities left behind in the march of progress. The curriculum, meticulously designed, included local folklore, traditional crafts and indigenous knowledge systems alongside modern subjects. This holistic approach ensured that students did not just learn, but thrived, becoming well-rounded individuals grounded in their heritage yet prepared for the future.

In these schools, the classrooms were alive with vibrant discussions about local legends, the sounds of traditional music, and the colours of indigenous art.[516] Festivals were celebrated with fervour, rituals were respected, and every child learned to take pride in their heritage. This integration of education and culture created a generation of confident, informed and culturally rooted individuals.

In Meghalaya in the late 1990s and early 2000s, the RSS, recognizing the potential of education as a tool for empowerment and integration, initiated a project to help Khasi students pursue quality higher education outside the Northeast.[517] In 1996, Seva Bharati's Surendra Talkhedkar spearheaded the establishment of a school in Belbari, which started in a humble thatched hut. Recognizing the importance of education, he also initiated the creation of the Tikrikila hostel.[518] By 1997, he began sending students to study outside Meghalaya, particularly to Maharashtra. Over 500 students from Meghalaya have benefited from this initiative, including notable alumni like Delina Khongdu, a

---

[515]Interview with K. Tangsa (name changed).

[516]Interview with Sandip Kavishwar.

[517]Interview with Surendra Talkhedkar.

[518]Ibid.

member of the National Women's Commission, and 25 doctors who are now serving as medical officers at Yognilayam.[519] In 1999, Talkhedkar sent the first batch of nine Garo students to study outside their home state, setting a precedent for many more to follow. The first batch of Khasi students also included two girls.[520] These pioneering students were trailblazers, leaving behind their familiar surroundings to embrace new horizons in a distant part of the country.

The experience of these students was transformative, not just for them but also for their families and communities back home. As they returned to Meghalaya—armed with new knowledge, skills and a broader perspective on the world—they became ambassadors of change. Their success stories began to circulate, inspiring other parents to consider similar opportunities for their children. Pravin Shewale of the RSS noted that the real fruits of this project were reaped in the 2000s, when the positive impact on these students led to widespread support for the Sangh's initiatives.[521]

This growing support was not confined to individual families. Entire neighbourhoods and communities began to see the value of RSS's educational outreach. Word spread like wildfire, and soon the Sangh's influence started to extend beyond its initial strongholds. Prior to this initiative, RSS shakhas in Meghalaya were limited to favourable places like Nartiang, Jowai, Shillong and Ri-Bhoi, where the Sangh had managed to establish a foothold. Today, Sangh shakhas are spread all over Khasi, Jaintia and Garo Hills.

As the educational project gained momentum, the Sangh's network began to expand. The success stories of the Khasi students created a ripple effect, breaking down barriers of

[519]Ibid.

[520]Ibid.

[521]Interview with Pravin Shewale.

scepticism and resistance. The RSS started to establish shakhas in previously unreached areas, spreading its message of unity, discipline and national integration. These regions, with their diverse ethnic and cultural backgrounds, began to see the RSS as a positive force for change and development.

The grassroots efforts of the RSS in Meghalaya were not just about spreading ideological influence; it provided local youth with opportunities that were previously beyond their reach, helping them to aspire for and achieve greater heights. This, in turn, fostered a sense of loyalty and gratitude towards the Sangh, creating a robust support base.

By the mid-2000s, the RSS had firmly established itself in the social and cultural fabric of Meghalaya.[522] Today, the RSS in Meghalaya operates independently of the Guwahati Kendra, the regional headquarters that once provided guidance and support. The transformation is evident in the widespread acceptance and participation of local communities in RSS activities. The Sangh's focus on education, cultural integration and community service has paid off, creating a network of dedicated karyakartas who continue to work towards the goal of national unity. Looking back at these struggles and how the times had changed, one senior pracharak commented, 'Money can't buy everything. Trust building is important. The reason we survived in Meghalaya is because our workers stayed for 10 years.' In an obvious jibe at BJP, he added, 'Those who come for two to three months in five years cannot change the politics of the state.'[523]

During the tenure of Ulhas Kulkarni, there was only one school in the serene town of Nagaon named Sankardev Sishu Niketan.[524] It was a humble institution, quietly nurturing young minds. However, a significant shift occurred when a student

---

[522]Interview with Surendra Talkhedkar.

[523]Interview with Thaneswar Sangma (name changed).

[524]Interview with Ulhas Kulkarni.

from this very school made it to the merit list. This remarkable achievement acted as a catalyst, drawing attention from far and wide. The school's reputation soared, and it wasn't long before the echoes of its success reached neighbouring villages and towns.

Ulhas Kulkarni found himself inundated with applications from people eager to replicate the success of Sankardev Sishu Niketan. Parents and community leaders from Jagiroad, Morigaon, and even the quaint village of Pathori approached him, each with a shared vision of providing quality education.[525] Their fervour and determination were palpable, and Kulkarni, with his characteristic dedication, responded to their pleas.

New Sankardev schools began to sprout across the region, each one a beacon of hope and learning.[526] These schools were remarkable not only for their academic prowess but also for their inclusivity. They welcomed students from diverse backgrounds, including Assamese, Bengali and tribal communities. The schools quickly transformed into a powerful movement, driven by the collective will of the people.

One of the unique aspects of these institutions was their emphasis on skills. Unlike conventional schools, where degrees often outweighed practical abilities, these schools valued skill above all. Consequently, about 50 per cent of the teaching staff were 12th-pass individuals. Yet, they were incredibly adept and resourceful, their skills honed through experience and practical knowledge. Their competence shone through, and many of them rose to the position of principal.

The results were nothing short of extraordinary. The failure rate of the students in these schools was zero per cent, a testament to the effectiveness of their unique approach to education. During Ulhas Kulkarni's time at Nagaon, the network of Sankardev schools expanded rapidly. By the time he left, there

---

[525]Ibid.

[526]Ibid.

were about eighteen schools, each one a pillar of strength and enlightenment in its community.[527]

Similar efforts were undertaken in all the different states. In 2003, the Rashtra Sevika Samiti led by Sunita Haldekar started the first hostel for girls in Haflong.[528] Today the hostel houses forty-five *balikas* (girls) who receive education as well as training to serve society.[529] They also expanded to Mizoram in 2012 through the Swadharmi Mizo Sangathan and worked with Chakma and Reang communities through the Sanghamitra Charitable Trust in Lunglei.[530] The key initiatives included education and awareness to promote indigenous identity in the face of evangelical activity.

Another story in the transformative journey of education in the region was marked by the establishment of Ekal Vidyalayas. The genesis of this initiative began with a meticulous survey conducted in the remote tea garden areas, the picturesque landscapes of Meghalaya, the challenging terrains of Bodoland near the Bhutan border, and the rugged hills of Karbi Anglong. The survey revealed a stark reality—a severe lack of basic educational facilities that left many children without access to even the most rudimentary forms of learning.

In response to these findings, a ground-breaking decision was made in 2001: to establish single-teacher schools called Ekal Vidyalayas.[531] These 90 pioneering schools were unlike any traditional educational institutions. Instead of focusing solely on theoretical knowledge, they prioritized imparting life skills essential for survival. Practical knowledge and hands-on skills became the core of the curriculum, empowering students

---

[527]Ibid.

[528]Interview with Sunita Haldekar.

[529]Ibid.

[530]Ibid.

[531]Interview with Brahmaji Rao.

to navigate their everyday challenges with confidence and competence.

The acceptance of these schools by the local communities was overwhelming. Parents saw the tangible benefits of such an education for their children, and the positive impact on the students was undeniable. Buoyed by this success, the Sangh decided to expand this initiative further. The responsibility of this monumental task was entrusted to Narayan Sharma, a dedicated pracharak of Vidya Bharati.

Narayan Sharma embraced this challenge with unwavering commitment. His efforts were relentless, travelling across difficult terrains, reaching out to the most isolated communities, and ensuring that the seeds of education were sown in the most barren of lands. Under his guidance, the number of Ekal Vidyalayas grew exponentially. By the end of his tireless campaign, about 350 such schools had been established, each one a beacon of hope and opportunity.[532]

The impact of these schools was profound. They played a crucial role in connecting the untouched and often forgotten areas of society. The children, who once had no access to education, were now learning skills that not only educated them but also equipped them to better their lives and communities. The Ekal Vidyalayas became more than just schools; they became the bridge linking remote communities to the broader currents of progress and development.

Through the establishment of Ekal Vidyalayas, a significant stride was made in the mission to provide education for all. More importantly, it helped establish connections with the last man of society, truly penetrating the grassroots of Northeast India which were hitherto considered untouched.

The Sangh's educational endeavours in the 2000s were a testament to their vision of a unified yet diverse India. They

---

[532]Ibid.

understood that true progress did not come from erasing the past but from embracing it. By investing in the restoration of education, they built bridges between tradition and modernity, ensuring that the march towards progress was inclusive and respectful of India's rich cultural tapestry.

In the remote villages and tribal hamlets scattered across the Northeast, a unique challenge existed that had long been overlooked. Marriage, an institution that was formalized and recognized everywhere else, often lacked any legal or societal structure in these regions. The absence of an institutionalized marital structure gave rise to troubling social practices. Bride capturing and groom capturing were disturbingly common, and in the absence of any legal framework, there was no avenue for redress when these unions turned abusive or violent. Partners had no recourse to legal protection or support, trapped in relationships that were never officially acknowledged by law.

Pradeepan saw this situation and felt compelled to act. He knew that this was not just a problem of administrative oversight but a grave social evil that needed urgent intervention. With a determination to bring about change, Pradeepan conceived a unique campaign called Burha Vivah, or old-age marriage.[533] The idea was bold, imaginative, and grounded in the realities of the community he sought to serve. If formal marriages were rare, why not start by solemnizing them for everyone, regardless of age?

The vision was simple yet revolutionary: to institutionalize marriage by formalizing unions that had existed for years, even decades, without any legal recognition. The plan was to host weddings for elderly couples who had been living together without any formal marriage rites, alongside younger couples, in grand community events that celebrated their unions with proper rituals, ceremonies and the presence of family and friends.

---

[533]Interview with Krishna Gopal Sharma.

The first step in bringing this vision to life required funding. Pradeepan approached Dr Krishna Gopal Sharma, the kshetra pracharak, with a request for financial support.[534] He explained his plan passionately, detailing how he intended to conduct a mass-wedding ceremony to set an example and show the community the value of a formal marriage and the stability it could bring. Dr Sharma, recognizing the importance of this mission, arranged for a sum of ₹1 lakh to fund the first round of marriages.[535]

With the funds in hand, Pradeepan set to work, organizing the first Burha Vivah with meticulous care. Invitations were sent out, and elders who had never had the chance to marry formally were encouraged to participate. On the day of the event, 100 couples were wed in a grand ceremony that followed all the traditional rituals, complete with priests, blessings and family gatherings.[536] Relatives were invited and a community feast was prepared, filling the air with the aroma of freshly cooked food and the sounds of joyous celebration.

The spectacle of the event was unlike anything the community had seen before. There was a profound sense of celebration as three generations of the same family—grandparents, parents and grandchildren—stood side by side, all participating in formal wedding ceremonies. It was a powerful moment that underscored the purpose of Pradeepan's campaign. The community watched in awe as couples who had spent decades together finally exchanged vows, their unions blessed in the presence of their loved ones. It was a celebration of commitment, a public declaration of love and partnership, and a resounding affirmation of the importance of marriage as an institution.

---

[534]Ibid.
[535]Ibid.
[536]Ibid.

Word spread quickly throughout the region. The success of the first Burha Vivah inspired more communities to take part. The campaign grew rapidly, and soon, more ceremonies were being organized across various states in the Northeast. In a few short years, Burha Vivah became a movement, and over 20,000 weddings were conducted in tribal areas.[537]

The impact was profound. By formalizing marriages, the campaign provided legal protection and social legitimacy to countless couples who had been living together without any formal recognition. It offered them dignity and respect in the eyes of the community and the law. For many, it also meant access to legal rights and protections they had previously been denied. Social evils like bride capturing and groom capturing began to diminish as the community embraced the idea of formalized unions.

This initiative was a shining example of how the RSS sought to address social evils and reform society. It demonstrated that change could be achieved not by force or imposition, but by understanding local customs, respecting traditions, and gently guiding communities towards more progressive and just practices. The RSS showed that even the most deep-rooted social practices could be reformed with compassion, creativity and a genuine commitment to the well-being of the people.

Building Healthcare Infrastructure

One of the most remarkable milestones achieved by the RSS in the Northeast was the training of village health workers through an initiative known as Aarogya Mitra. This visionary programme was conceived by Bhaskar Kulkarni, who was the seva pramukh then.

Ulhas Kulkarni faced a daunting challenge when he was transferred to Guwahati. Fear of militants was pervasive, and

---

[537]Ibid.

as a result, rural areas were severely lacking in essential staff for schools, colleges and banks.[538] The situation demanded an innovative solution to address the health needs of these vulnerable communities. It was in this context that Aarogya Mitra was born.

Two branches of Seva Bharati were established: one in Guwahati and the other in Purvanchal in 2006. Bhaskar Kulkarni and his team knew that empowering local villagers with health training was the key to improving the dire situation. Young villagers were meticulously trained and equipped with medical kits containing both allopathic and homoeopathic supplies. These newly minted health workers, christened as the eponymous *aarogya mitras*, would gather once a month to replenish their supplies and receive further training.[539]

The impact of this initiative was transformative. Over time, approximately 15,000 health workers were trained, each one becoming a lifeline in their respective communities. They provided crucial health services, bridging the gap created by the absence of professional medical staff. The success of Aarogya Mitra was so profound that Bhaskar Kulkarni was given the responsibility to supervise its implementation at the national level.

Around the same time, an initiative known as the Dhanvantari Seva Yatra was launched with a simple yet powerful idea. Dr Krishna Gopal Sharma, the kshetra pracharak, recognized the urgent need for medical services in the remote areas of Assam and reached out to the doctors in Banaras Hindu University (BHU).[540] He urged them to devote a portion of their time each year to serve the people of Assam. The response was immediate and heartening.

In 2005, the first batch of nine doctors from BHU embarked on this noble journey. Travelling at their own expense, these

[538]Interview with Ulhas Kulkarni.

[539]Interview with Bhaskar Kulkarni.

[540]Interview with Surendra Talkhedkar

doctors brought with them not only their medical expertise but also a deep sense of compassion and commitment. Thus the Dhanvantari Seva Yatra was born, and has continued uninterrupted since that first expedition.[541]

What started as a modest effort quickly gained momentum. By 2010–11, the initiative had grown significantly, with 8–10 teams being sent to Assam annually.[542] These teams consisted of doctors and medical students who willingly dedicated their time and resources to the cause. The scale of the project expanded even further in 2012, when the scope of the Yatra extended beyond Assam to encompass every state in the Northeast.[543] Each district in Assam received a dedicated team, ensuring that medical aid reached even the most remote and inaccessible areas.

Under Ulhas Kulkarni, the Sangh extended the Dhanvantri Seva Yatra to the remotest corners of Mizoram, Nagaland and Meghalaya, even during the heights of militancy. This ambitious expansion was made possible with the support of the Border Security Force (BSF) and the Central Reserve Police Force (CRPF), whose camps served as training grounds.[544] Doctors sent by the Sangh conducted the training sessions, ensuring that even the most isolated communities received the care they needed.

The impact of the Dhanvantari Seva Yatra has been profound. Over 2,000 doctors and medical students have participated in the Yatra, often funding their own travel and expenses.[545] This selfless dedication has not only provided much-needed medical care to under served populations but also built strong bonds between the visiting doctors and local communities. These teams do not stay in hotels or lodges; instead, they live and eat with the locals,

---

[541]Ibid.

[542]Ibid.

[543]Ibid.

[544]Ibid.

[545]Ibid.

sharing their lives and cultures. This people-to-people contact has significantly strengthened the doctor fraternity and fostered a deeper understanding and respect between different cultures.

The Yatra has also demonstrated remarkable resilience in the face of natural disasters. During the annual monsoon floods that wreak havoc in Assam, the doctors of the Dhanvantari Seva Yatra are on the front lines, providing critical medical care and relief to those affected. Their dedication was particularly evident during the COVID-19 pandemic when they continued with their mission, bringing hope and healing to communities in dire need.

Recognizing the importance of preparedness and disaster management, Seva Bharati, the organization behind the Dhanvantari Seva Yatra, has expanded its efforts into other critical areas. They started a post-graduate diploma course in fire safety and disaster management, a first for Assam. This course has filled a significant gap in the region's disaster preparedness and has empowered many individuals with the knowledge and skills needed to respond effectively during emergencies.

The commitment to education and empowerment extends beyond disaster management. As per Surendra Talkhedkar, Seva Bharati has trained over 1,500 yoga teachers since 2000, spreading the benefits of yoga across the region.[546] These teachers play a vital role in promoting physical and mental well-being in their communities, furthering Seva Bharati's mission of holistic development.

New Challenges

On a humid July day in 1996, Surendra Talkhedkar arrived in Guwahati for the first time.[547] The journey was prompted by his commitment to the Rashtriya Swayamsevak Sangh (RSS),

[546]Interview with Surendra Talkhedkar.

[547]Ibid.

where he had dedicated himself as a pracharak. Guwahati, with its vibrant mix of cultures and political tensions, presented a new challenge for him. Upon arrival, he was welcomed by Shashikant Chauthaiwale, the prant pracharak, and Sunil Kulkarni, the mahanagar pracharak. They introduced him to the intricate dynamics of the region, preparing him for the work ahead. He visited the Barkona Ashram, located about 40 kilometres from Tura and 12–23 kilometres from Mancachar in Assam.[548] The Ashram stood on the Assam side of a road, with Meghalaya on the opposite side. Here, the brahmachari of the ashram had generously allotted a room to the Sangh, which became a base for Talkhedkar's operations.

Life in the Northeast was far from easy. Talkhedkar endured multiple bouts of *falciparum* malaria, contracting the disease ten times. Yet, his spirit remained unbroken. This persistent illness accompanied him to the Sangh Shiksha Varg (OTC) every year, where the physical exertion would inevitably trigger another relapse.[549] However, in the OTC of 2004–05, a turning point came during a baithak led by Dr Krishna Gopal Sharma. In this meeting, Dr Sharma encouraged everyone to take a sankalp. Late Dayal Krishna Bora, a respected figure, vowed to abstain from areca nuts for 20 days. Inspired by this, Talkhedkar stood up and made a bold declaration: he vowed not to fall sick during that OTC.[550] Laughing about it now, he says that from that moment onward, he never experienced another bout of malaria.

Mukundrao Palshikar, a senior RSS functionary, played a pivotal role in shaping Talkhedkar's path. Palshikar urged him to go to the Northeast, a region often overlooked and fraught with challenges.[551] Reluctant at first, Talkhedkar was persuaded

[548]Ibid.

[549]Ibid.

[550]Ibid.

[551]Ibid.

after three days of persistent encouragement. 'Go there,' Palshikar had told him. 'If you think it's impossible, come back. But go first.'[552] This challenge resonated with Talkhedkar, who embraced the mantra that 'impossible was not in his dictionary'.[553] Thus, what began as a one-year commitment extended far beyond his initial intention.

When questioned about his motivations, his response was profound. It wasn't solely about Hindutva or religious nationalism. His mission transcended religious boundaries. Having served in predominantly Christian regions, he formed deep friendships with Christians, staying in their homes and celebrating Christmas with them. His opposition was not against any religion per se, but against the practice of forceful conversion. He believed in amicable coexistence, stressing that *ghar wapsi* (the reconversion of people back to Hinduism) should be a last resort.[554] Acceptance and mutual respect were his guiding principles.

During his fourteen years in the Garo Hills (1996–2010), he immersed himself in the local culture. He became fluent in Garo, Koch and Hajong languages, showcasing his commitment to understanding and integrating with the communities he served.[555] His previous tenure in Goa had already seen him master Konkani. This linguistic proficiency was more than just a communication tool; it was a bridge to foster trust and solidarity.

His commitment to uplifting the indigenous Garo people led to the formation of the Rishizilma Organization in 2001–02, aimed at preserving and promoting Garo heritage and identity.[556] He also played a crucial role in honouring Garo freedom fighter

---

[552]Ibid.

[553]Ibid.

[554]Ibid.

[555]Ibid.

[556]Ibid.

Thogan Sangma. Despite having no statue or photograph to commemorate him, Talkhedkar ensured Sangma received due recognition by taking his photo from the Tura Museum and celebrating his legacy.

One of Talkhedkar's most impactful contributions was his grassroots work. He engaged in extensive sampark, going from village to village, living in people's houses, and building trust within the community. During his tenure, there were forty shakhas in the Garo Hills.[557] His efforts often brought him face to face with extremists, yet he remained undeterred.

In 2005, when the government introduced the National Rural Employment Guarantee Act (NREGA), Talkhedkar's Seva Bharati was entrusted with the social audit work for fifty villages.[558] Their efficiency and transparency in spreading awareness about the scheme were so impressive that the government expanded their responsibility to 350 villages.[559] This initiative showcased Seva Bharati's commitment to community welfare and governance.

Seva Bharati's influence extended beyond economic development. They formed women's self-help groups across all communities, Hindu and Christian alike, fostering a sense of unity and empowerment. They also established a mobile medical dispensary that operated for four years, conducting camps in remote areas. This initiative significantly bolstered Seva Bharati and the Sangh's presence and impact in the region.

Under Talkhedkar's leadership, Seva Bharati grew into a formidable force for social change. In the Brahmaputra Valley alone, they have seventy full-time workers, with ninety full-timers across the Northeast.[560] Their annual turnover of

---

[557]Ibid.

[558]Ibid.

[559]Ibid.

[560]Ibid.

₹5 crore is a testament to the scale and effectiveness of their operations.[561]

Talkhedkar talks about many challenges and interesting stories. One day in July 2006, at around 9.30 p.m., he was returning home from the house of a karyakarta named Kamleshwar.[562] As he approached the Central School of Tura, his phone rang. He stopped his motorcycle to take the call, unaware of the danger lurking nearby.[563] Suddenly, three drunk Garo boys surrounded him. One of them climbed onto the back of his motorcycle, another positioned himself at the front, and the third stood firmly in his path. Mistaking him for a wealthy businessman because he was speaking Hindi, they demanded money.

He quickly assessed the situation. Knowing that Holy Cross Hospital was just 1.5 km away, he decided to use his knowledge of the Garo language to his advantage. Calmly, he said, 'I am the Father of the Garo Church; I came from Holy Cross Hospital.'[564] The boy behind him immediately dismounted, followed by the one on the bonnet. They apologized profusely, saying, 'Forgive me, Father.'[565] Seizing the moment, Talkhedkar confidently added, 'The Bible says never cheat anyone. Jesus won't feel bad.'[566] Relieved, they let him go without further incident.

This encounter highlighted the delicate balance the Sangh maintained in the Garo Hills. To avoid resistance, they adopted a strategic approach. They never openly declared their affiliation with the RSS. Instead, they introduced themselves as teachers from Belbari School. This non-aggressive stance minimized pushback and helped them blend in with the community. Talkhedkar's own background was a testament to such adaptation. Coming from

[561]Ibid.

[562]Ibid.

[563]Ibid.

[564]Ibid.

[565]Ibid.

[566]Ibid.

a strictly vegetarian family, he had never touched an egg before becoming a pracharak. Yet, in Goa and Meghalaya, he adapted to the local diet, even eating pork before 2003. He never faced any difficulty because sharing meals in people's homes helped build deep connections.

He had earlier moved to Thakranbari near Mancachar to learn the Garo language. He stayed with a teacher named Madison Sangma and another friend named Bibhisan Marak. For 15 days, he lived at Marak's house, having lunch there, and dinner at Sangma's house. One evening, as he was about to head to Sangma's for dinner, Bibhisan's wife insisted he stay and eat with them.[567] Talkhedkar didn't understand why. He later discovered that beef was being cooked at Madison's house that night, and she didn't want him to feel uncomfortable. This small act of consideration highlighted the simplicity and warmth of the people.

Sonsak, known as a hub of extremists, was another challenging area. The Sangh started two Ekal Vidyalayas there to provide education and foster goodwill.[568] In Barkona Ashram, two teachers, Ijah and Sarom, were invited to teach. During a ceremony, someone applied a *tika* on Ijah's forehead, causing him to cry because he was a Christian. The Sangh immediately apologized and ensured he never felt discriminated against again. Ijah later joined their efforts, promoting their work in the village.

One memorable incident involved a visit to Sonsak with a fellow pracharak named Marak. They had told Ijah they would have dinner at his place at around 5.30–6.00 p.m.[569] He was surprised and sceptical that they wanted to dine at his home. At 3.00 p.m., they met at the Sonsak market, and Ijah asked

[567]Ibid.

[568]Ibid.

[569]Ibid.

them again if they were sure they would come.[570] When they arrived at his house by 6.00 p.m., he was still unsure and asked once more if they would really eat there.[571] They reassured him, and he became emotional, saying, 'I have been a Christian for so many years, yet our Father (pastor) never visited our house to eat food. But despite being a Hindu Father, you came to have food at my house.'[572] This deeply moved Talkhedkar and reinforced the power of personal connections.

Overcoming Challenges and Bridging Gap between Communities

The late 1990s and early 2000s were a period marked by severe ethnic conflicts and violence in Northeast India. The Sangh argues that the turbulence was largely fuelled by decades of divisive politics, particularly the vote-bank strategies employed by the Congress party, which often involved pitting one community against another to consolidate electoral gains. The result was a volatile region plagued by inter-community clashes, riots and secessionist movements that left deep scars on the social and political fabric of the Northeast.

The Bru-Reang conflict in Mizoram saw significant violence in 1997, when tensions between the Bru and the majority Mizos flared up.[573] The Bru community faced persecution and violence, leading to the mass displacement of nearly 40,000 Brus who fled to neighbouring Tripura.[574] The conflict created a protracted refugee crisis, with the displaced Bru population living in camps

[570]Ibid.

[571]Ibid.

[572]Ibid.

[573]EPW Engage, 'Examining the Bru–Mizo Conflict in India's North East', *Ethnicity and Belonging* series, https://tinyurl.com/bddtbkvm. Accessed on 17 February 2025.

[574]Ibid.

under harsh conditions for years. Recognizing the severity of the situation, the RSS took up the cause of their rehabilitation and resettlement. Throughout the 2000s, the Sangh conducted tremendous relief work among Bru refugees and became their voice, vociferously taking up the cause of their resettlement in the governmental corridors of Delhi.[575] It took them twenty years and a BJP-led government at the Centre to work towards a resettlement plan, spearheaded by the RSS. This long-term commitment highlighted the Sangh's dedication to addressing the plight of displaced communities and finding lasting solutions to ethnic conflicts.

At that time, the cultural and religious landscape of Mizoram had dramatically shifted, with about 98 per cent of Mizos having converted to Christianity. Only a small remnant of around 3,000 individuals still adhered to their indigenous beliefs. It was within this context that Professor Sanjay Ranade began his extensive work with the remaining indigenous Mizos, striving to keep their ancestral traditions alive. In 2009, the Mizo Sakhua initiative was launched, aiming to revive and protect the traditional Mizo faith and practices. This cultural renaissance was bolstered by the establishment of the Friends of People in 2012, an organization dedicated to supporting the indigenous communities.

A considerable number of Mizo students found refuge and education in Kalyan Ashram and Vidya Bharati hostels. Additionally, the Sevika Samiti operated a hostel in Kamalanagar, providing a supportive environment for young learners. These educational institutions did more than offer academic instruction; they became centres of cultural preservation and community support. By providing a safe space for students, they fostered a sense of belonging and continuity for the indigenous traditions. These endeavours ensured that even in the face of overwhelming adversity, the cultural identity and traditional practices of the

[575]Ibid.

Mizos were not only protected but also revitalized for future generations.

In the early 2000s, the Hmar and Dimasa tribes in Mizoram and Assam were embroiled in violent clashes—primarily driven by territorial disputes and ethnic tensions—in the North Cachar Hills district, now known as Dima Hasao. The conflict reached its peak in 2003, resulting in several deaths, numerous injuries, and the displacement of many families.[576] In Karimganj, a small town in Assam, the situation took a particularly dark turn. Here, the communal violence manifested in the form of heinous crimes against women, with Hindu girls, as young as 12, becoming the victims of brutal assaults by grooming gangs. The town was gripped by fear, and the women, bearing the trauma of their horrific experiences, found themselves voiceless and powerless.

In the midst of this chaos and suffering, a figure of hope and justice emerged—Nirmala Sitharaman.[577] At that time, she was a dedicated and fiery advocate for women's rights in the National Commission for Women. Upon hearing about the atrocities in Karimganj as per reports and complaints filed by the Sevika Samiti—then led by Sunita Haldekar—Sitharaman decided to take action. She understood the urgency of the situation and the importance of standing up for the victims who had been left defenceless in the face of such barbarity.[578]

Her presence brought a semblance of hope to the shattered community of Karimganj. She met with the victims, listened to their harrowing tales, and assured them that their voices would not be silenced. Understanding the complexities of the situation, Sevika Samiti activists knew that securing justice in such a charged environment would not be easy.[579] The local

---

[576]Interview with Sunita Haldekar.

[577]Ibid.

[578]Ibid.

[579]Ibid.

authorities were hesitant to act and communal tensions were at an all-time high. Despite these challenges, the team continued to put pressure on the system. The RSS rallied support from various women's rights organizations and human rights activists, creating a coalition that was determined to see justice served.

Their approach was multifaceted. They not only worked tirelessly to gather evidence and testimonies but also made sure to garner media attention to highlight the plight of the victims. They believed that public awareness and pressure were crucial in a case where the local authorities seemed reluctant to act. Their efforts paid off when national and international media began covering the story, bringing much-needed attention to the atrocities committed in Karimganj.

With the spotlight on the case, the authorities could no longer afford to be complacent. Under immense pressure, investigations were launched and the police began making arrests. Sitharaman and her team were relentless, ensuring that the legal process was followed meticulously and the victims were provided with the necessary support to testify against their assailants.[580] Her dedication to the cause was unwavering, and she spent countless hours working with the legal team, preparing for what would be a long and arduous fight for justice.

The courtroom battles were intense. The RSS faced numerous obstacles, including threats and attempts to intimidate key figures such as Sitharaman and Haldekar, as well as the victims. One by one, the guilty were brought to justice. Throughout this ordeal, Nirmala Sitharaman was more than just an advocate; she became a symbol of hope and resilience for the women of Karimganj.[581] Her efforts not only brought justice to the victims but also sparked a broader movement for women's rights and safety in the region.

---

[580]Ibid.

[581]Ibid.

Similarly, the Karbi-Kuki and Karbi-Dimasa clashes in Assam's Karbi Anglong district erupted in 2003, fuelled by competition over land and political power.[582] Violent confrontations between the two communities resulted in the deaths of several people and the displacement of hundreds. The clashes highlighted the complex and often volatile nature of ethnic relations in the region, demonstrating how deep-seated grievances and political manoeuvring could lead to devastating consequences. These riots not only saw widespread violence but also left many women widowed and destitute. These women, draped in white and devoid of *sindoor*, became the living symbols of the region's turmoil and suffering. The Sangh, recognizing the plight of these women and the urgent need for rehabilitation, took proactive measures to restore their dignity and build self-sufficiency. They established the Mahila Sangharsh Manch, a dedicated wing focused on the empowerment and rehabilitation of women affected by the ethnic violence. This initiative aimed to provide these women with the means to rebuild their lives and regain their lost sense of purpose.

In Mizoram, the Rashtra Sevika Samiti spearheaded numerous efforts to uplift these women. They provided sewing machines and handloom training, enabling women to produce traditional garments and handicrafts. The Sevika Samiti also helped set up tea stalls and small shops, creating opportunities for these women to engage in commerce and trade.[583] These initiatives were not merely acts of charity but well-thought-out strategies to foster independence and self-reliance. The Sevika Samiti adopted a unique approach to ensure that the aid given did not turn the recipients into dependents. They presented the support as loans that needed to be repaid, instilling a sense of responsibility and ownership among the women. However, in

---

[582]Ibid.

[583]Ibid.

practice, when the women offered to repay these loans, the Sevika Samiti graciously declined. They explained that the notion of repayment was a psychological tool to prevent the women from becoming freeloaders and to encourage them to earn their livelihood with dignity.

One such example is of Mapuii (name changed), a widow from a small village in Mizoram.[584] Left alone with three children after her husband was killed in the riots, Mapuii found herself struggling to make ends meet. The Rashtra Sevika Samiti provided her with a sewing machine and trained her in tailoring. With these new skills, Mapuii started her own small tailoring business. Over time, she began to earn enough to support her family and even employed other local women, extending the empowerment she had benefited from. In another instance, Kimpi (name changed), whose husband was killed during the Dimasa-Karbi clashes, was given a small loan to set up a tea stall.[585] Initially hesitant and sceptical, she gradually built a thriving business, serving tea and snacks to locals and travellers alike. The pride and confidence she gained through this venture transformed her life, and she became a beacon of hope for other widows in her community.

The stories of Mapuii and Kimpi are not isolated. Across Mizoram and other affected regions, countless women benefited from the Sangh's initiatives. The Mahila Sangharsh Manch and the Rashtra Sevika Samiti's efforts to provide vocational training and support were instrumental in turning victims of violence into empowered individuals. These initiatives fostered a sense of community and solidarity among the women, who found strength in each other's company and support. The Sangh's approach to rehabilitation was more than just a response to immediate needs; it was a long-term strategy aimed at social transformation. By enabling these women to become financially

[584]Ibid.

[585]Ibid.

independent and socially active, the Sangh helped integrate them back into the mainstream, ensuring they could live with dignity and self-respect. This empowerment had a ripple effect, gradually transforming the communities and contributing to a more resilient and cohesive society.

In the broader context of the Northeast's turbulent history, the initiatives by Mahila Sangharsh Manch and Rashtra Sevika Samiti stand out as significant efforts toward healing and reconstruction.[586] They exemplify how targeted, compassionate interventions can make a profound difference in the lives of individuals and communities. Through these efforts, the Sangh not only addressed the immediate aftermath of ethnic violence but also laid the groundwork for lasting peace and integration in the region. The following years also saw continued expansion of the Rashtra Sevika Samiti, with hostels opening in Gossaingaon in 2007 and Guwahati in 2008.[587] We visited the Guwahati hostel and saw young girls from tribal communities residing there and receiving quality education.

In the early 2000s, Assam was in turmoil. The Bodoland movement had turned violent, with the Bodoland Liberation Tigers Force (BLTF) and its members such as Hagrama Mohilary and Chandan Brahma leading the charge for an autonomous Bodo region. The atmosphere in Kokrajhar, the heart of the movement, was tense and fraught with conflict. As the Bodo demand for a separate state intensified, the adivasis, many of whom were tea garden labourers, found themselves at odds with the Bodos. Violent clashes broke out in Kokrajhar and Bongaigaon districts, leading to the deaths of hundreds and the displacement of thousands.

Amidst this, Advik Pillai (name changed), a pracharak from Kerala who was stationed in Kokrajhar as the RSS Vibhag

---

[586]Ibid.

[587]Ibid.

Pracharak, sought a way to ease the unrest.[588] He adopted a unique strategy, leveraging the Vidya Bharati programme, which aimed to send students from the Northeast to study in schools across India. He focused on the children and relatives of Bodo elites, particularly those affiliated with the BLTF.[589] By ensuring that these students received their higher education in Kannauj, far from the epicentre of conflict, he initiated a subtle yet powerful intervention. This educational opportunity not only broadened their horizons but also introduced them to a different way of thinking. Over time, as these young men experienced life outside the conflict zone, their perspectives began to shift. More importantly, his efforts did not go unnoticed.

The Bodo people, who had initially viewed the RSS with suspicion, began to see the organization in a new light. Pillai's genuine concern for the well-being of their youth and his innovative approach to conflict resolution earned him their trust. It also brought them closer to the Bodo elite, particularly those who were spearheading the Bodoland secessionist movement.

When the BJP, led by Prime Minister Atal Bihari Vajpayee, came to power in New Delhi, the stage was set for a significant breakthrough. Recognizing Pillai's influence and the changed mindset of the Bodo leaders, the Bodo community approached him for help in settling the ongoing conflict.

In 2003, the Sangh played a crucial role in brokering the Bodoland Territorial Council (BTC) Accord. RSS facilitated the negotiations between Home Minister Lal Krishna Advani and the BLTF leaders.[590] The accord was a historic achievement, leading to the surrender of 2,641 militants.[591] This peace agreement paved the way for the forming of the Bodoland Territorial Council,

[588]Interview with Advik Pillai (name changed).

[589]Ibid.

[590]Ibid.

[591]Ibid.

granting a degree of autonomy to the Bodo people.[592]

The success of the accord had far-reaching implications. Hagrama Mohilary, who had once been a militant leader, emerged as a political leader. His party, the Bodoland People's Front (BPF), later aligned with the BJP, marking a significant shift in the region's political landscape.[593] This story is a testament to the power of education, trust-building and the importance of thinking outside the box in the pursuit of peace.

However, one faction of Bodo leaders rejected the accord and formed the National Democratic Front of Bodoland (NDFB) and continued their armed struggle, culminating in the dreaded 2008 Assam serial blasts.[594] While there was a severe crackdown, bringing the movement to a halt, Bodoland continued to be plagued by ethnic conflicts.

In 2012, Bodo-Muslim riots rocked Kokrajhar. Many indigenous Bodos were killed and women were mass-raped.[595] A local pracharika from the Sevika Samiti tells us about how grooming gangs kidnapped girls and forced them to eat beef. Later, many of them were mass-raped.[596] The Rashtra Sevika Samiti ran a nation-wide campaign, generating awareness through *Organiser*. These girls were eventually rescued, though Sunita Haldekar faced harassment from CPIM-affiliated journalist Neha Dixit for her efforts.[597] Other ethnic strife such as the one with adivasis or the many conflicts in Karbi Anglong and Dima Hasao were doused by the Vanavasi Kalyan Ashram.[598] Sandip Kavishwar revealed to us the strategy behind mitigating conflicts—the Kalyan Ashram, through its networks, brought the community leaders

---

[592]Ibid.

[593]Ibid.

[594]Ibid.

[595]Interview with Aditi Kalita (name changed).

[596]Ibid.

[597]Interview with Sunita Haldekar.

[598]Interview with Sandip Kavishwar.

together in face-to-face, closed-door meetings and explained to them that their communities had co-existed for centuries without conflict. He urged them to identify the 'third element' that was creating these fissures between the communities.[599]

As the violence raged, the Bodo community was painted as the aggressors, fuelling tensions and deepening divides. But the RSS saw the situation differently. They believed the real issue was not between Bodos and Muslims, but rather between indigenous communities and illegal infiltrators, primarily from Bangladesh.[600] To counter the narrative of division, the RSS decided to act.

Their plan was bold: take Assamese artists and intellectuals to Kokrajhar to show solidarity between the Bodo and Assamese communities.[601] However, this was easier said than done. Many artists and thinkers declined the invitation, hesitant to get involved in what had become a highly charged situation. Some suggested that if they were to go, they should visit Muslim areas as well, in an attempt to maintain a balance and avoid controversy. Despite these setbacks, a few prominent figures agreed to join the RSS on their mission. Among them were Janardan Prabhu, the renowned Assamese scholar Rabin Deb Choudhury, and the esteemed intellectual Rohini Barua.

Together, they travelled to the Bodo areas, meeting with local leaders and communities, engaging in dialogue and listening to their grievances. This outreach had a profound impact. The tribal leaders, who had felt isolated and misrepresented, saw that they were not alone in their struggle. Shortly after, many of these leaders came to the Vivekananda Kendra Institute of Culture (VKIC) in Guwahati, where they passed a significant

[599]Ibid.

[600]Interview with Ratul Chandra Barua (name changed).

[601]Ibid.

resolution.[602] It was no longer framed as a conflict between Bodos and Muslims, but rather as a larger battle between indigenous communities and infiltrators threatening the region's demographic balance.[603]

This outreach effort set the stage for a political turning point in Assam. Later that year, the Bangladeshi Mukto Sangrami Manch was launched, which would become a watershed moment in Assam's political landscape. A massive public meeting and rally took place at Sonaram Field, drawing a crowd of 35,000 tribal leaders, Assamese intellectuals, religious figures, and local communities. The event was presided over by Ranoj Pegu, an influential figure in Assam's tribal politics.[604]

The Sangrami Manch crystallized the anxieties of Assam's indigenous communities about illegal immigration from Bangladesh, uniting various ethnic and tribal groups under a common cause. Many of these tribal leaders, once independent or allied with smaller regional parties, soon found themselves gravitating toward the Bharatiya Janata Party, which had begun making inroads in the Northeast. By the 2014 general elections, leaders such as Ranoj Pegu, Bhubon Pegu, Sanjay Kishan, and others who had been part of the Mahasabha and the Sangrami Manch joined the BJP. Their entry into national politics helped the BJP secure a foothold in Assam, and many went on to become MLAs and MPs, further strengthening the party's presence in the region.

When Dr Krishna Gopal Sharma arrived in Assam as the kshetra pracharak in 2003, he was met with a landscape that was as complex as it was beautiful. As he began his work, Dr Sharma quickly realized that the local population harboured a certain

---

[602]Ibid.
[603]Ibid.
[604]Ibid.

distance from national symbols and celebrations.[605] Independence Day and Republic Day, which stirred pride and patriotism in many corners of India, did not evoke the same fervour here. For many Assamese, these occasions felt imposed, disconnected from their local history, culture and identity.

This was not a challenge to be ignored. Dr Sharma knew that for the Rashtriya Swayamsevak Sangh to establish a meaningful presence in Assam, they would have to bridge this gap, to find a way to connect the regional sentiments with the national spirit.[606] He pondered this conundrum carefully, understanding that the solution lay not in imposing the mainstream but in embracing and celebrating the unique culture of Assam itself.

With time, an idea began to take shape. The Sangh decided to commemorate Lachit Diwas in 2005, a day dedicated to the memory of Lachit Borphukan, the revered Ahom general who had become a symbol of Assamese pride and resistance.[607] Lachit Borphukan was a name etched in the hearts of the people. He was the valiant warrior who had defended Assam against the mighty Mughal forces in the Battle of Saraighat in 1671, a man whose courage and tactical brilliance had preserved the sovereignty of his homeland.[608] To the Assamese, Lachit was more than a historical figure; he was a cultural icon, a symbol of their strength, resilience and identity.

By choosing to celebrate Lachit Diwas, the Sangh demonstrated a deep understanding of the local sentiments. They planned a grand commemoration on the birth anniversary of Lachit Borphukan, inviting people from all walks of life to honour the legacy of the beloved general. The event was to be held under the aegis of Lok Jagran Manch with Rohini Barua as the president. The decision

---

[605] Interview with Krishna Gopal Sharma.

[606] Ibid.

[607] Ibid.

[608] Ibid.

was met with curiosity and cautious optimism. ULFA released a statement in the local newspapers asking people to not attend the event.

As the day of the celebration approached, the atmosphere in Assam began to shift. Word spread quickly across towns and villages, reaching the ears of local communities, regionalist groups and ordinary citizens alike. The Sangh's plan was not just to host an event, but to create a moment of shared pride and unity. While the rally was stopped by the Congress government using police forces, there was no stopping the public meeting at Chandmari Field.

When the day finally arrived, it was met with overwhelming support. People turned out in large numbers—amounting to more than 25,000 by some counts—their hearts swelling with pride as they listened to stories of Lachit's bravery, his strategic genius, and his unwavering commitment to his land and people.[609] There were cultural performances, speeches by intellectuals such as Dayal Krishna Bora and Dhiren Chakraborty, and songs that celebrated Assamese heritage and valour. For many, it was the first time they had seen a national organization like the RSS align itself so closely with local culture and values.

The celebration resonated deeply with the Assamese people. It was not merely an event; it was a recognition of their history, their heroes and their identity. By commemorating Lachit Diwas, the Sangh struck a chord with the local populace, and won the hearts of many in the process. Regionalist groups, who had once viewed the Sangh with suspicion, began to see it in a new light. Assamese citizens from diverse backgrounds—farmers, teachers, students, business people—started to engage with the RSS, their initial reservations gradually giving way to curiosity and then to a genuine sense of participation.

Lachit Diwas became more than a celebration; it became

---

[609]Ibid.

a bridge—a way to connect the regional with the national, the local pride with the broader idea of a united India. Through this thoughtful gesture, the Sangh had shown that national integration did not require the erasure of local identities, but could be achieved by embracing and celebrating them.

And so, in the years that followed, Lachit Diwas became a symbol of new-found unity in Assam. The Sangh's approach had transformed a moment of commemoration into a movement of solidarity, one that brought Assamese and national pride together, side by side. Dr Krishna Gopal Sharma had found the key to Assam's heart by honouring the spirit of Lachit Borphukan, and in turn, the spirit of Assam itself.[610]

What began as a regional commemoration soon evolved into broader celebrations of national pride. Over time, it ignited the spirit of patriotism, eventually leading to the observance of national festivals like Independence Day in parts of the state where such events were once overshadowed by insurgency and separatist sentiments.

In 2009, the Hindu Jagran Manch, under the leadership of its president Pranjal Saikia, decided to take a bold step.[611] On 15 August, they organized Bharat Mata Pujan at Dighalipukhuri, a historic lake in Guwahati.[612] The event aimed to celebrate India's Independence in a uniquely cultural and devotional manner, placing the image of Bharat Mata at the heart of the celebration. Ram Madhav, a key figure in the RSS, was present to lend his support and guidance.[613]

However, the celebration was not without controversy. On the opposite side of Dighalipukhuri, AASU staged a protest, observing Independence Day as a black day. Despite the tension,

[610]Ibid.

[611]Interview with Basistha Bujarbaruah.

[612]Ibid.

[613]Ibid.

the Bharat Mata Pujan drew a crowd of 700 people, outnumbering the AASU gathering.[614] It was a significant moment, signalling that the tide was turning, and patriotism was once again gaining a foothold in Assam, even in areas where it had previously been met with scepticism or opposition.

By 2010, the Bharat Mata Pujan had gained momentum. The following year, attendance swelled to 2,000 people, and Indresh Kumar, another prominent leader from the RSS, attended the event, further solidifying its significance.[615] The atmosphere was one of fervent nationalism, with people from all walks of life coming together to honour India and its ideals. The event was no longer just a celebration—it was becoming a movement.

In 2011 and 2012, the Bharat Mata Pujan expanded further. Multiple locations across Assam began organizing similar events, each marked by the same spirit of devotion and national pride.[616] To amplify the message, the organizers introduced a new element—a bike rally.[617] The sight of hundreds of motorbikes—draped in the Indian tricolour—roaring through the streets created a palpable sense of unity and strength.[618] These rallies became a symbol of renewed energy in the region, a statement that the people were reclaiming their national identity with vigour and pride.

By 2013, the movement had grown so much that it no longer required formal organization by the Hindu Jagran Manch or the RSS. Public enthusiasm had taken over.[619] Local communities began organizing the Bharat Mata Pujan themselves, showing that the spirit of the event had deeply resonated with the

[614] Ibid.
[615] Ibid.
[616] Ibid.
[617] Ibid.
[618] Ibid.
[619] Ibid.

people.[620] What had started as an RSS initiative was now a public celebration, a testament to the power of grassroots nationalism.

In 2015, the impact of this movement extended beyond Assam.[621] For the first time, a bike rally was held on 15 August in Shillong, the capital of Meghalaya.[622] This was a remarkable achievement, as it showed that the spirit of the Bharat Mata Pujan had transcended borders, bringing together people from diverse communities in a unified display of patriotism. The rally in Shillong was a vibrant spectacle, with young men and women riding through the streets, the sound of revving engines mingling with the chants of 'Bharat Mata Ki Jai'.[623]

What began as a modest celebration in Dighalipukhuri had evolved into a widespread movement, blending devotion, national pride and community participation. It was a remarkable transformation—a reflection of how cultural and patriotic celebrations, once contested, had come to embody the hopes and aspirations of a new generation in the Northeast.

As a result of these various projects undertaken by the Sangh Parivar, be it to mitigate conflicts, promote indigenous faiths, or augment healthcare and education, the RSS had become the strongest social force in the Northeast. As the pages of the calendar flipped to 2013, this formidable social force was all set to bring about the biggest political change the region had ever seen.

---

[620]Ibid.

[621]Ibid.

[622]Ibid.

[623]Ibid.

7

A Rendezvous with Destiny

The Northeast is India's ashtalakshmi.

—Prime Minister Narendra Modi[624]
(At the inauguration of the Ashtalakshmi Mahotsav, 2024)

In the annals of Indian political history, the year 2014 will stand as a watershed moment—a pivotal juncture where the aspirations of a nation converged with the vision of a singular leader. Narendra Modi's resounding election victory was not merely the triumph of a political campaign, but the culmination of decades of meticulous groundwork laid by the RSS in some of the most remote and diverse corners of India—the Northeast.

Prime Minister Narendra Modi's journey from being a humble pracharak to becoming the leader of our nation is a testament to the indomitable spirit and strategic foresight of the Sangh Parivar. Born into modest means, his early years were shaped by his association with the RSS, where he imbibed the values of discipline, dedication and service to the nation.[625] His numerous

[624]Prime Minister's Office, 'Prime Minister Shri Narendra Modi inaugurates the Ashtalakshmi Mahotsav', *Press Bureau of India*, 06 December 2024, https://tinyurl.com/hptmes7s. Accessed on 17 February 2025.

[625]Singh, A., *The Architect of the New BJP: How Narendra Modi Transformed the Party*, Penguin, India, 2022.

visits to the Northeast during his tenure with the RSS were more than routine engagements; they were missions of integration, aimed at fostering a sense of unity and national identity in a region often perceived as distant from the heart of India.

The Northeast, with its intricate tapestry of ethnicities, languages and cultures, had long felt marginalized in the grand narrative of Indian polity. Yet, through the relentless efforts of the Sangh Parivar karyakartas, the RSS began to weave threads of common purpose and shared destiny. In the early 2000s, RSS pracharaks traversed the undulating hills and valleys of the Northeast, engaging with local communities, understanding their issues and slowly building trust. They established schools, organized health camps, and promoted cultural activities that resonated with the indigenous populations.

This grassroots engagement laid a robust foundation for the BJP's foray into the region. By the time the 2013 and 2014 elections approached, the groundwork was firmly in place. The Sangh Parivar's cadres, galvanized by the prospect of one of their own ascending to the highest office in the land, mobilized with unprecedented vigour. Karyakartas fanned out across the Northeast, leveraging the goodwill and networks built over years of consistent social work. They tapped into the latent desire for development and change, offering Modi's vision of *Sabka Saath, Sabka Vikas* (Collective Efforts, Inclusive Growth) and *Achche Din* (Good Days Ahead) as the beacon of hope.[626]

In states like Assam, Manipur and Arunachal Pradesh, the BJP's message of development and integration struck a deep chord. The RSS's sustained efforts to promote local leadership and address regional concerns had already created a conducive environment for political change. When Prime Minister Modi

---

[626]Goyal, Mukta, 'A New Empowering India Under Leadership of PM Modi: Promises and Reality', *Prosperity: Journal of Society and Empowerment*, Vol. 2, No.1, 2022, pp. 49–62.

campaigned in these states, he was not seen as an outsider but as a leader who understood and respected their unique identities and aspirations.

The Sangh Parivar's strategic focus on youth and education also paid rich dividends. The establishment of shakhas and schools in remote areas had nurtured a generation of young leaders who were committed to the idea of a unified India. These young men and women, inspired by the values of the RSS, emerged as key campaigners for the BJP, spreading the message of development and national integration.

The election results were nothing short of historic. The BJP, for the first time, made significant inroads into the Northeast, winning crucial seats and forming alliances that would reshape the political landscape. Narendra Modi's victory was a vindication of the RSS's decades-long mission to integrate the Northeast with the rest of India, not just politically but also culturally and emotionally.

In Assam, the BJP secured a significant number of seats, dislodging the long-dominant Congress and establishing itself as a major political force. The state had been a bastion of Congress power, but years of RSS outreach had slowly but surely built a new narrative. Modi's promise of development and job creation resonated with Assam's young voters in particular. The RSS's focus on the NRC, delimitation and immigration problem had also helped address local grievances, winning hearts and minds in regions long neglected by the Central government.

In Arunachal Pradesh, the BJP's rise was equally dramatic. The RSS had worked quietly but effectively in the state, promoting education and cultural initiatives that respected local traditions while fostering a sense of Indian unity. The groundwork laid by the Vanavasi Kalyan Ashram and the Vivekananda Kendra ensured that these messages were well received, leading to significant electoral gains.

In Manipur, the BJP capitalized on the RSS's extensive network to mobilize support. The state, with its complex ethnic composition and history of insurgency, posed unique challenges. However, the RSS's focus on youth engagement, community development projects such as protection of the Sanamahi indigenous faith, and mitigation of riots created a favourable environment for the BJP's message of peace and prosperity. Prime Minister Modi's emphasis on infrastructural development and connectivity struck a chord with voters eager for change.

In Tripura, the RSS's efforts over the years helped the BJP make a remarkable breakthrough in a state traditionally dominated by the Left Front. The establishment of schools and vocational training centres and launch of healthcare initiatives by the RSS played a crucial role in changing the socio-political landscape. The BJP's promise of good governance and ridding the people of the Left's *goonda raj* resonated with the masses, leading to a historic shift in the state's political alignment.

In the remaining states of Meghalaya, Mizoram and Nagaland, the BJP made alliances with the various regional parties to form an umbrella coalition called the North-East Democratic Alliance (NEDA).[627]

The Sangh Parivar's strategic engagement with indigenous communities across the Northeast was perhaps the most critical factor. The RSS respected and celebrated the diverse cultural heritage of the region, promoting local festivals and traditions while integrating them into the broader narrative of Indian unity. This approach helped dispel the notion of cultural imperialism and fostered a sense of belonging among the people.

The 2014 election win was a culmination of these multifaceted efforts. The BJP's victory was not just about numbers; it was

---

[627]Gogoi, Tarun, 'North East Democratic Alliance (NEDA) and Political Change in Northeast India', *Dialogue Quarterly,* Vol. 20, No. 4, 2019, pp. 114–124, https://tinyurl.com/58ja7n64. Accessed on 17 February 2025.

about the resonance of a vision that promised inclusive growth and national integration. Narendra Modi, a leader who had walked the rugged paths of the Northeast as a pracharak, now stood at the helm of the nation, embodying the hopes and aspirations of millions.

As the sun set on the historic day of 16 May 2014, it was clear that Narendra Modi's ascent to the Prime Minister's Office was not just a personal triumph, but a collective achievement of the Sangh Parivar. It was the fruition of a journey that had begun in the remote villages of the Northeast, where humble pracharaks had sown the seeds of unity and progress. The 2014 election win was a testament to the power of sustained grassroots work and the unwavering belief in the idea of a united India.

New Horizons

The electoral victory of the Bharatiya Janata Party and its allies in all the states of the Northeast marked a pivotal change for the Sangh Parivar. For the first time in the history of the region, it did not have the opposition of antagonistic Central and state governments. While social opposition still existed in the Christian-majority states, the time had come for the Sangh to make a lasting mark.

In a wave of administrative changes and structural reforms, the Assam Kshetra was created in 2012, breaking away from the Calcutta Kendra. Assam Kshetra currently has five parts—Uttar Assam, Dakshin Assam, Manipur, Tripura and Arunachal. Nagaland and Meghalaya are a part of the Uttar Assam Division, while Mizoram is a part of Dakshin Assam. In the Sangh's vision from 1950 to 2012, Nagaland was under Imphal Division as a district. Nagaland as a state got recognition in 1962. From 2012, Nagaland was recognized as a part of Assam's Diphu Division and was divided into two zones, North and South.

In the lush and complex landscape of Nagaland, the Sangh's early efforts were modest and supportive, providing back-end assistance to the Zeliangrong Heraka Association, a local organization dedicated to preserving the cultural heritage and traditions of the Zeliangrong people. This initial engagement, though limited in scope, laid the groundwork for a more direct and impactful presence of the Sangh in the region. It was a challenging endeavour, marked by resistance and suspicion, but the Sangh's persistence began to bear fruit from 2012 onwards as they gradually established good sampark, or connections, within the community. Today, the RSS has established a foothold in Dimapur and Dhansiripar, where it operates four to five shakhas among Naga janajatis and Dimasa communities. In addition, one or two Sammelans have been organized among the Nepali and Hindi-*bhashi* populations in Kohima.

A pivotal figure in this transformative journey was Shantanu Raghunath Shinde, a dedicated pracharak whose vision for Nagaland's educational landscape was both ambitious and rooted in the values of the Sangh.[628] As part of Vidya Bharati's Nagaland Committee, Shinde played a crucial role in bridging gaps and fostering trust among the local population.[629] His efforts were focused on expanding educational opportunities and creating pathways for higher education, particularly in states like Maharashtra where educational infrastructure was more robust.

Post-2014, Shinde's dream began to take shape in a more concrete manner. Vidya Bharati, the educational arm of the Sangh Parivar, intensified its efforts to build schools and educational programmes in Nagaland. These institutions were not just centres of learning but also hubs of cultural exchange and community building. They provided students with quality education and opportunities that were previously inaccessible, and the initiative

---

[628]Interview with Brahmaji Rao.

[629]Ibid.

quickly gained momentum.[630] The establishment of these schools marked a significant shift in the educational landscape of Nagaland, bringing new hope and aspirations to its youth.

This has been an innovative entry point for the RSS in Nagaland. Many students who stayed in hostels run by these organizations studied Hindi and have since become Hindi teachers in Nagaland schools, creating a strong link between the local population and the larger Indian cultural framework. This has proven particularly effective in rural Naga areas where the RSS's presence is still growing. The RSS has also introduced Sunday Schools led by women, catering to indigenous people who do not attend church. This initiative allows non-Christian children to feel a sense of belonging in a predominantly Christian environment, fostering a non-religious community experience while subtly reinforcing indigenous and Hindu traditions.

One of the most striking indicators of the Sangh's growing influence and acceptance in Nagaland was the recent Nagpur Sammelan of the Rashtra Sevika Samiti. This gathering, held in the cultural heartland of the Sangh in Nagpur, saw the participation of thirty-five Naga girls.[631] This diverse group included not only those from Hindu backgrounds but also Christian girls, a testament to the inclusive and integrative approach adopted by the Sangh. The presence of these girls at the Sammelan was a powerful symbol of the significant rise in support for the Sangh Parivar in regions that were once considered hostile or indifferent to its ideals.

Among these thirty-five girls was Liani (name changed), a bright young student from a remote village in Nagaland. Her journey to Nagpur was a reflection of the broader narrative of change sweeping through her homeland.[632] Encouraged

---

[630]Ibid.

[631]Interview with Sunita Haldekar.

[632]Ibid.

by Shinde's outreach programmes, Liani had excelled in her studies and earned a scholarship to continue her education in Maharashtra.[633] Her participation in the Sammelan was both a personal milestone and a representation of the new educational opportunities being embraced by Naga students.[634]

The Sangh's initiatives were not just about education in the traditional sense but also about fostering a sense of cultural identity and unity. The curriculum in Vidya Bharati schools included teachings on Indian culture, values and traditions, which helped students connect with their heritage while also preparing them for modern challenges. This holistic approach resonated with many families in Nagaland, who saw the benefits of an education that was both rooted and forward-looking.

The involvement of the Rashtra Sevika Samiti added another layer to this transformation. Their focus on women's empowerment and community service struck a chord in Nagaland, where many women and girls were eager for opportunities to contribute to their communities. The Sammelan in Nagpur provided a platform for these girls to share their experiences, learn from others, and return to their villages with renewed confidence and a sense of purpose.

This growing support for the Sangh Parivar in Nagaland was a remarkable development, considering the historical context of the region. The Northeast had long been a challenging terrain for the Sangh, with its unique cultural dynamics and history of insurgency and political instability. However, the persistent efforts of individuals like Shinde, coupled with the Sangh's focus on education and empowerment, began to change perceptions and build trust.

In essence, the Sangh's journey in Nagaland was a story of perseverance, adaptation and genuine engagement with the

[633]Ibid.

[634]Ibid.

local communities. The initial support to the Zeliangrong Heraka Association evolved into a comprehensive strategy that included education, cultural integration and community building. The transformation seen post-2014, particularly with the involvement of Vidya Bharati and the Rashtra Sevika Samiti, underscored the power of education and empowerment in bringing about lasting change. The participation of Naga girls, including those from Christian backgrounds, in the Nagpur Sammelan was a clear signal that the Sangh's efforts were making a meaningful impact, fostering unity and progress in a region once marred by division and conflict.

In 2021, a historic event unfolded in the Nagaland Legislative Assembly: for the first time in the state's sixty-year history, the Indian national anthem was played.[635] This momentous occasion symbolized a profound shift in Nagaland's political and cultural landscape, a state long plagued by insurgency and separatist movements. The playing of the national anthem in the assembly was not just a ceremonial act; it was a powerful testament to the growing sense of national unity and pride among the people of Nagaland.

The transformation was further highlighted during the Independence Day celebrations of the same year. Responding to Prime Minister Narendra Modi's call to hoist the Indian national flag in every household, the streets of Nagaland were adorned with the tricolour. This vibrant display of patriotism was unprecedented in a state that had historically seen the national flag and anthem as symbols of an external authority. The widespread participation in these celebrations reflected a deepening connection to the Indian nation, transcending decades of political and social strife.

---

[635]Das, Yudhajit Shankar, 'Nagaland assembly plays national anthem for first time in almost 60 years', *The Times of India,* 21 February 2021, https://tinyurl.com/5ajyb9ew. Accessed on 17 February 2025.

This change in Nagaland was not just political but also socio-cultural, marking a significant departure from its tumultuous past. The efforts to foster a sense of national identity and unity were deeply rooted in the initiatives of the RSS and its affiliates. The Sangh's nation-building project had been meticulously crafted and executed over the years, focusing on education, cultural integration and community empowerment. The transformation in Nagaland was a testament to the power of consistent grassroots-level engagement and the importance of education in nation-building.

The RSS's role in this socio-cultural shift cannot be overstated. Their initiatives in Nagaland were not merely about political alignment but about integrating the state into the larger national narrative. The playing of the national anthem in the Nagaland Legislative Assembly and the widespread display of the national flag were symbolic of a deeper, more enduring change. It was a change that signified not just acceptance but also a proud embrace of the Indian identity, fostering a sense of belonging and unity that had long been elusive in the region. This remarkable transformation highlighted the success of the RSS's vision and efforts in nation-building and their genuine commitment to the idea of a unified nation.

In the heart of Mizoram, amid the scenic hills and valleys, a young girl named Lalhlimpuii (name changed) nurtured a dream that seemed distant and unreachable: she wanted to become a fashion designer.[636] Growing up in a region marred by ethnic conflicts and economic struggles, her aspirations were unconventional and ambitious. Yet, Lalhlimpuii's determination set her apart, and when the Rashtra Sevika Samiti offered her a chance to study fashion designing in Nagpur, she seized the opportunity with both hands.[637]

---

[636]Interview with Lalhlimpuii (name changed).

[637]Ibid.

In Nagpur, Lalhlimpuii immersed herself in her studies, learning the intricacies of fashion design.[638] The experience was transformative. Not only did she acquire new skills and knowledge, but she also absorbed the ethos of the Sangh, which emphasised self-reliance, community service and national integration. Her time at the Rashtra Sevika Samiti broadened her horizons and instilled in her a deep sense of purpose.

Upon returning to Mizoram, Lalhlimpuii found herself at a crossroads. She was no longer just a girl with a dream; she was a trained fashion designer with the potential to make a difference. Settling back into her community, she began to integrate her new-found skills into the local fabric, slowly gaining recognition for her work.[639] Her journey took another turn when she met and married the son of a prominent Congress minister. Their union was a blend of tradition and modernity, much like Lalhlimpuii's approach to fashion.[640]

Curious about the journey that had transformed his daughter-in-law, the minister accompanied Lalhlimpuii to Nagpur. There, he witnessed first-hand the nurturing environment of the Rashtra Sevika Samiti, the dedication of its volunteers, and the profound impact it had on young women like Lalhlimpuii. This visit was an eye-opener for him. He saw beyond the political divides and recognized the Sangh's genuine efforts in empowering individuals and fostering community development.

Inspired by what he saw, the minister returned to Mizoram with a renewed perspective. He began to support the Sangh's initiatives and encouraged others in his political circle to do the same. His most significant gesture of support came in 2014, when he urged Lalhlimpuii to start a hostel for girls in Lunglei, a district in southern Mizoram known for its serene beauty and

---

[638] Ibid.

[639] Ibid.

[640] Ibid.

cultural richness.[641] Understanding the importance of education and safe accommodation for young girls pursuing their dreams, the minister offered significant funding and land for the project.[642]

With the minister's backing, Lalhlimpuii set out to establish the hostel. Drawing on her experience in Nagpur, she envisioned a place where young girls could be provided not just accommodation but also mentorship and vocational training.[643] The hostel was to be a sanctuary where girls from different parts of Mizoram could come together, learn and grow in a supportive environment.

Similarly, Brahmaji Rao played a crucial role in establishing a Vidya Bharati school in Mizoram, which was run by an ex-military man.[644] The school and the hostel quickly became a beacon of opportunity for young girls, offering them a chance to pursue their education and dreams without fear or hindrance.

Lalhlimpuii's story became a source of inspiration for many. Her journey from a small village in Mizoram to the fashion institutes of Nagpur and back, now as a community leader, resonated with countless young women who harboured dreams of their own. Today in the centre of her village, which was once a hotbed of Mizo nationalism and insurgency, the Indian tricolour proudly flies. The hostel in Lunglei flourished, and its success stories began to multiply, each girl finding her path and purpose.

This narrative of transformation is more than just a personal journey; it is a convergence of ideals and actions across political and social boundaries. It highlights how the Sangh's grassroots initiatives could bridge divides and create lasting impact even in the most unexpected places. Through the collective efforts of Lalhlimpuii, her father-in-law, and the Rashtra Sevika Samiti, the

[641]Ibid.

[642]Ibid.

[643]Ibid.

[644]Interview with Brahmaji Rao.

seeds of change were sown in the hills of Mizoram, promising a brighter and more unified future for its people.

Moving on to Arunachal Pradesh—a critical border state sharing its frontier with China—the Sangh took a different approach. In 2014, Sunil Mohanty, then the prant pracharak of Arunachal Pradesh and now a distinguished member of the Assam Kshetra Prachar Vibhag, along with his compatriots initiated a profound and heartfelt programme known as Sarhad Ko Swaranjali.[645] This initiative commemorated fifty years of Lata Mangeshkar's iconic 'Ae Mere Watan Ke Logon' and aimed to honour the families of martyrs and veterans of the 1962 Sino-Indian War, a conflict that had left an indelible mark on the history and psyche of Arunachal Pradesh.

The Sarhad Ko Swaranjali programme was a deeply emotional and significant event.[646] Many families of the martyrs and veterans gathered to participate in the ceremonies, which were marked by a deep sense of respect and gratitude. Sunil Mohanty, with his unwavering commitment to national service, ensured that the sacrifices of these brave souls were remembered and celebrated.[647] The programme not only paid homage to those who had laid down their lives for the country but also provided a sense of solace and recognition to their families, who had borne the weight of their loss with quiet dignity.

The impact of this initiative was profound. It brought together families from various parts of Arunachal Pradesh, fostering a sense of unity and shared purpose. The programme served as a reminder of the collective resilience and patriotism that had defined the people of Arunachal Pradesh during the tumultuous times of the 1962 War.

In addition to honouring the martyrs, Sunil Mohanty aimed

[645]Interview with Sunil Mohanty.

[646]Ibid.

[647]Ibid.

to advance the already ongoing Bharat Mera Ghar campaign with renewed zeal.[648] This programme was designed to promote cultural exchange and build national unity by organizing trips for groups of individuals from Arunachal Pradesh to different parts of India. These trips, lasting 10–15 days, allowed participants to experience the diverse cultural, historical and social fabric of the nation.[649]

The Bharat Mera Ghar programme provided a unique opportunity for the people of Arunachal Pradesh to connect with their fellow citizens from other states. Participants visited historical landmarks, cultural sites and important institutions across the country. They engaged in meaningful interactions with people from different backgrounds, fostering a deeper understanding and appreciation of India's rich diversity.

This cultural exchange initiative was instrumental in breaking down barriers and building bridges of understanding and unity. It allowed the participants to see themselves as part of a larger national identity, strengthening their sense of belonging to the Indian nation. The experiences and memories from these trips left a lasting impression on the participants, who returned to Arunachal Pradesh with a renewed sense of pride and commitment to their country.

Through these efforts, the RSS continued to reinforce its role as a unifying force in the Northeast, bridging cultural and regional divides and promoting a sense of national solidarity. The success of these programmes highlighted the power of remembrance, recognition and cultural exchange in strengthening the bonds that hold the nation together.

In Arunachal Pradesh, the RSS's work has grown significantly over the years. From once being marked by sporadic attendance, shakhas have become regular and well-attended, with around

---

[648] Ibid.

[649] Ibid.

35–40 of these now operational across the state. Previously, people would attend the morning shakhas and then leave to engage in daily activities like fishing. But, over time, discipline and regularity have been instilled in the swayamsevaks. Importantly, the RSS has also focused on creating teachers from within the local communities, furthering its cultural and educational outreach. Local pracharaks have been trained to carry forward the work, ensuring that the RSS message resonates at the grassroots level.

In Meghalaya, the Sangh and Seng Khasi's commitment to preserving and promoting indigenous culture led to the restoration and development of the ancient shrine at U Lum Sohpetbneng, a revered hillock near Umiam Lake. This sacred site, whose name translates to 'Navel of the Universe', holds profound significance for the Khasi people, who believe that seven families, known as U Hynñiewtrep, descended to Earth to propagate 'truth' and nurture Mother Earth through a bridge of golden vines known as Ka Jingkieng Ksiar.

Once a simple and unadorned hillock, U Lum Sohpetbneng has been transformed into a sacred sanctuary, thanks to the dedicated efforts of the Sangh and Seng Khasi. In 2013, a magnificent gateway was erected, welcoming devotees to the shrine. Archaeologists, working diligently post-2014, uncovered numerous monoliths that further underscored the site's historical and spiritual significance. These developments have not only revitalized the shrine but also strengthened the support for Seng Khasi among the local people. Every year, on the first Sunday of February, a sea of devotees ascends the sacred peak, believed to be the origin point of mankind on Earth. This pilgrimage has become a profound expression of faith and unity, drawing thousands to celebrate and honour their ancestral heritage.

In 2022, a significant milestone was reached when Sarsanghchalak Mohan Bhagwat, adorned in traditional Khasi-Jaintia attire, offered prayers at the sanctum sanctorum of the sacred peak. His prayers for the prosperity of *Ka Mei Ri*

India, or Bharat Mata, were a powerful gesture that cemented the RSS's role in promoting and protecting the indigenous faiths of the Northeast, particularly in Meghalaya. Through these efforts, the Sangh and Seng Khasi have not only restored a sacred site but also reignited a sense of pride and connection among the indigenous communities. The story of U Lum Sohpetbneng stands as a testament to the enduring power of cultural heritage and the profound impact of unity and faith. Due to such efforts, nearly 1.5 lakh people are now directly associated with Seng Khasi, as estimated by Ulhas Kulkarni.[650]

An intriguing postscript to this event was shared by Pravin Shewale, highlighting the resonance of indigenous sentiments in the region. In response to the revitalized interest and activity at U Lum Sohpetbneng, the Church undertook some construction on the hillock. However, shortly after, a lightning strike set the new structure ablaze. The incident was widely perceived as divine intervention, further affirming the sacredness of the hillock in the eyes of the Khasi and Jaintia people. News of this extraordinary event spread quickly, reinforcing the belief in the spiritual power of U Lum Sohpetbneng.

In Meghalaya, as of today, the RSS has focused on reconversion efforts among the indigenous Seng Khasi community, who practise their traditional Khasi faith. These efforts are gaining momentum, particularly in revitalizing local spiritual practices that had been overshadowed by external influences. The RSS has helped develop a pujari system to formalize religious rituals and a prayer system that aligns with Khasi traditions, offering a sense of continuity and cultural pride. This work aims to preserve the identity of the Seng Khasi community while offering them an alternative path from conversion to other faiths.

Similar works of religio-cultural significance have been implemented throughout the Northeast. At present there are

---

[650]Interview with Ulhas Kulkarni.

over 115 local units in Manipur, including shakhas, *milans* and *mondolis*.[651] Most recently, twelve new pracharaks have been inducted from Manipur, even at the height of violence. Nine of them are STEM graduates. The RSS has made significant strides in reaching out to both Meitei and Kuki communities.[652] They have worked to bridge communal divides and foster a sense of unity through cultural programmes and educational initiatives. However, this progress has been temporarily halted due to the ongoing ethnic violence and riots between these communities. Despite the current challenges, the groundwork laid by the RSS has created a framework for reconciliation and future cooperation.

In Tripura, twenty-two local pracharaks have been recently inducted. The state has seen remarkable progress in the RSS's outreach. Local pracharaks have been trained and nurtured, ensuring that the movement has deep roots in the local culture and traditions. The development of local leadership has enabled the RSS to grow steadily, with swayamsevaks taking ownership of various initiatives. The RSS has made a significant impact by integrating local customs within its core principles, allowing the movement to resonate with Tripura's diverse tribal population.

In a remarkable display of unity and strength, the RSS organized the massive Luitporiya Hindu Samavesh in Guwahati in 2017. This landmark event saw unprecedented participation from Sangh workers across the Brahmaputra Valley, Meghalaya and Nagaland—belonging to the Uttar Assam Prant—converging in the city to showcase their solidarity and commitment to the organization's ideals. The Samavesh was graced by the presence of Mohan Bhagwat, who addressed the gathering and underscored the significance of their collective efforts.

The Luitporiya Hindu Samavesh was a testament to the profound impact and reach of the RSS in the Northeast, a region

[651]Interview with M.M. Asokan.

[652]Ibid.

that had once been resistant to its influence. The sheer scale of the event, with thousands of Sangh workers participating, highlighted the deep-rooted presence the organization had established over the years. It was a moment of pride and affirmation for the RSS, demonstrating their ability to mobilize and inspire large numbers of people across diverse communities.

Two decades ago, such an event would have been unimaginable. The Northeast, with its unique cultural and ethnic landscape, had posed significant challenges to the RSS's mission. The region's history of insurgency, ethnic conflicts and political instability made it a difficult terrain for the Sangh's outreach. However, through persistent efforts, grassroots engagement, and a focus on social service and education, the RSS gradually built trust and acceptance among the local populations.

The presence of Mohan Bhagwat at the Samavesh was a significant moment, symbolizing the culmination of years of dedicated work by Sangh workers in the Northeast. His address to the gathering emphasised the importance of unity, cultural preservation and national integration. Bhagwat's words resonated deeply with the participants, reinforcing their commitment to the Sangh's mission and values.[653]

The Samavesh was a celebration of the journey the RSS had undertaken in the Northeast.[654] It highlighted the progress made in integrating the region into the broader national framework and the growing acceptance of the Sangh's ideology. The event was a powerful reminder of the transformative impact of sustained, grassroots-level efforts in nation-building.

As the participants dispersed, they carried with them a renewed sense of purpose and determination. The success of

---

[653]Staff Reporter, 'Over 50,000 people throng Luitporiya Hindu Samavesh', *The Assam Tribune*, 15 September 2010, https://tinyurl.com/5n78kth6. Accessed on 17 February 2025.

[654]Ibid.

the Samavesh was a clear indication of the RSS's evolving role in the Northeast, signalling a future of continued engagement and integration. The event stood as a milestone in the Sangh's journey, marking a new chapter of influence and acceptance in a region that had once seemed distant and challenging.

New Challenges, Renewed Vigour

In the sprawling and diverse state of Assam, the National Register of Citizens (NRC) exercise was conducted with the aim of identifying genuine Indian citizens and rooting out illegal immigrants.[655] The process, fraught with complexities and tensions, demanded meticulous data collection and verification. Amid this backdrop, the RSS played a significant role in ensuring that the local populace was informed and engaged. They meticulously gathered data and organized block-level meetings known as Nagorik Socheton Mancha.[656] These meetings, held from block to block, aimed to educate citizens about the NRC process, ensuring transparency and awareness.

As the NRC process unfolded, it became a focal point of both administrative and social activity in Assam. The Sangh's efforts in mobilizing and educating the community were critical in navigating the complexities of the exercise. However, as the NRC data collection neared completion, another storm was brewing on the horizon—the introduction of the Citizenship Amendment Act (CAA) in late 2019.[657]

The CAA, designed to provide a pathway to Indian citizenship for persecuted minorities from neighbouring

---

[655]Pisharoty, S.B., *Assam: The Accord, the Discord*, Penguin, India, 2019.

[656]Interview with Shankar Das.

[657]Deka, Balen Chandra, 'Contemporary Political Scenario of Assam and the Role of Youth Organisations', *Journal of Emerging Technologies and Innovative Research*, Vol. 7, Issue 10, 2020, pp. 3373–3379, https://tinyurl.com/359huhyx. Accessed on 17 February 2025.

countries, sparked widespread protests across the Northeast, including Assam.[658] The region, with its unique demographic concerns and historical sensitivities, saw the Act as a threat to its cultural and ethnic identity. The protests quickly escalated, becoming intense and violent in many areas. RSS offices were torched and workers were attacked in a wave of unrest that swept through the region.

In the midst of this chaos, Shankar Das, the current baudhik pramukh, took it upon himself to counter the misinformation and false allegations about the CAA.[659] Conducting meetings in Upper Assam, Das distributed leaflets and engaged with locals to explain the provisions and intentions of the Act. He worked tirelessly to reassure the community that the CAA was not a threat to their identity but a humanitarian gesture towards persecuted minorities.

Despite his efforts, the resistance from the All Assam Students Union (AASU) and other activist groups was fierce. AASU activists disrupted meetings, threw stones and physically attacked RSS workers, creating an atmosphere of fear and hostility.[660] The confrontations were reminiscent of the turbulent insurgent years of the 1980s and 1990s, marking this period as one of the lowest points for the RSS in Assam.

The Sangh's workers, though shaken, remained resilient. They continued to organize and spread their message amidst the violence and disruption. Shankar Das, in particular, became a symbol of perseverance, standing firm in his resolve to educate and inform the populace about the CAA.[661] His efforts, along with those of his fellow workers, were crucial in slowly turning the tide of public opinion.

---

[658]Ibid.

[659]Interview with Shankar Das.

[660]Ibid.

[661]Ibid.

The torched offices and injured workers were stark reminders of the challenges faced by the RSS in its mission of nation-building. The violent backlash against the CAA highlighted the deep-seated fears and insecurities within the local communities. Yet, the Sangh's response, characterized by dialogue and engagement rather than retaliation, showcased their commitment to their principles.

Through this period of turmoil, the RSS's approach remained steadfastly focused on communication and education. They believed that understanding and awareness were key to overcoming fear and misinformation. The block-level meetings, despite the interruptions and attacks, continued to serve as platforms for dialogue and discussion.

This chapter in the RSS's journey in Assam was marked by both conflict and resilience. The challenges they faced were formidable, echoing the insurgent struggles of the past. However, the Sangh's determination to foster unity and understanding, even in the face of violence, underscored their enduring commitment to their mission. The path to national integration was fraught with obstacles, but the efforts of individuals like Shankar Das exemplified the spirit of perseverance and dedication that defined the RSS's approach. Through their relentless work, the Sangh sought to bridge divides, dispel fears, and build a more cohesive and unified society in Assam and the broader Northeast.

As the world grappled with the unprecedented challenges posed by the COVID-19 pandemic, life in Assam, like everywhere else, came to a standstill. The streets, once bustling with activity, were now eerily quiet. Lockdowns, curfews and social distancing became the new norm, disrupting daily life and creating an atmosphere of uncertainty and fear. Amidst this global halt, the RSS found an opportunity to continue their mission of social service, stepping up to support communities in dire need.

With their extensive network of volunteers and a deep-rooted ethos of service, the RSS swiftly mobilized resources to respond to the crisis. They launched numerous initiatives to provide critical support to the affected populations. Free medical camps were set up across the Northeast, offering healthcare services to those who could not access hospitals. These camps provided much-needed relief, offering consultations, distributing medicines, and educating people about COVID-19 safety protocols.

The Dhanvantari Seva Yatra, a significant initiative by Seva Bharati, was launched to extend medical services to remote and under-served areas.[662] Mobile medical units travelled from village to village, ensuring that healthcare reached even the most isolated communities. This effort not only addressed immediate health concerns but also built a bridge of trust between the RSS and the local population.

In addition to medical camps, the RSS organized free COVID-19 testing facilities. These centres and their dedicated assistance with contact tracing played a crucial role in helping local administrations manage the spread of the virus. Their involvement in these efforts showcased their commitment to public health and safety.

As the pandemic caused widespread economic hardship, the RSS also focused on addressing food security. Volunteers distributed food packets, essential supplies and cooked meals to those in need. This relief work was especially critical for daily wage earners and marginalized communities who were severely impacted by the lockdowns. The RSS's food distribution drives ensured that no one whom they could reach went hungry during those trying times.

Moreover, RSS volunteers assisted in cleaning and sanitizing hospitals, a task that was vital for maintaining hygiene and preventing the spread of the virus. Their efforts in supporting healthcare infrastructure highlighted their dedication to public service and their ability to adapt to the needs of the community.

[662]Interview with Surendra Talkhedkar.

Many Sangh workers contracted the virus and some even perished. Yet, the large body of members remained committed to seva.

Through these comprehensive efforts, the RSS worked tirelessly to alleviate the suffering caused by the pandemic. Their proactive and compassionate response helped them regain the trust of the people, particularly in regions like Assam where their presence had been met with resistance and suspicion. The visible and tangible impact of their work during the pandemic fostered a renewed sense of respect and appreciation for the Sangh.

In the midst of a global crisis, the RSS's actions reaffirmed their role as a reliable and committed organization dedicated to the welfare of the nation. Their initiatives during the COVID-19 pandemic were not just acts of service but also powerful statements of solidarity and compassion. By standing with the people during one of the most challenging times in recent history, the RSS demonstrated the true essence of their mission: to serve and uplift society.

This period of intense social service helped the RSS rebuild and strengthen their relationship with the communities they served. The trust they regained was not merely a result of their immediate relief efforts but also a testament to their enduring commitment to the well-being of the nation. As the world began to slowly recover from the pandemic, the RSS's work during the crisis stood as a reminder of the power of selfless service and the impact of unwavering dedication to the greater good.

Amidst the calm that had finally settled over the Northeast, the recent riots between the Meiteis and the Kukis in Manipur have brought a resurgence of chaos and conflict to the region.[663] The violence has upended the fragile peace, igniting deep-seated ethnic tensions and resulting in widespread turmoil. In the midst

---

[663]Ranjan, Mukesh, 'Manipur violence needs urgent attention, decorum needs to be maintained: Mohan Bhagwat', *The New Indian Express*, 11 June 2024, https://tinyurl.com/yc46bz3z. Accessed on 17 February 2025.

of this upheaval, Sangh workers have been tirelessly travelling from place to place in the riot-hit zones, working to pacify the warring communities and restore a semblance of order.

These dedicated volunteers are on the ground, engaging in dialogue with local leaders, organizing peace marches, and providing relief to those affected by the violence. Their efforts are aimed at calming tempers and fostering reconciliation between the Meiteis and the Kukis, demonstrating the Sangh's commitment to maintaining harmony in the Northeast.

Senior Sangh leaders, including Sarsanghchalak Mohan Bhagwat, have not shied away from criticizing the government for its complacency in dealing with the situation.[664] They have openly expressed their disappointment with the authorities' failure to anticipate and mitigate the conflict, urging more proactive and effective measures to address the root causes of the violence.

The Manipur riots have underscored the persistent volatility that can disrupt the hard-won peace in the Northeast. Even as we were writing this book, our interviewees were constantly travelling to Manipur every week, working on the frontlines of this conflict. Their experiences and insights continue to shape our understanding of the region's complexities and the ongoing efforts to build lasting peace.

As the Sangh navigates these turbulent times, its ability to respond to such crises with compassion and resolve will be crucial in determining its future trajectory. Overcoming the challenge of maintaining peace and unity in the face of recurrent conflicts is a testament to the resilience and dedication of the Sangh's workers. Their relentless efforts to pacify the people and rebuild in riot-hit Manipur reflect the enduring spirit of the organization, committed to fostering harmony and integration in the diverse tapestry of the Northeast.

[664]Ibid.

A Fairytale?

As the chapter of the RSS's journey in the Northeast draws to a close, one might ponder: Is this a fairytale for the Sangh? Has it reached the peak of its success? Undoubtedly, the RSS has made remarkable strides in integrating the Northeast with the rest of India, building trust and acceptance through relentless efforts in social service, education and cultural engagement. However, as old challenges faded, new ones have emerged, threatening to undermine the very foundation of the Sangh's ideological purity. With the BJP's rise to power, many individuals have joined the Sangh, driven by aspirations of wealth and power rather than a genuine commitment to its core values. This influx of opportunists poses a significant threat to the ideological integrity that has been the bedrock of the RSS.

Many Sangh stalwarts have voiced their concerns over this trend, warning that the pursuit of personal gain over collective good could lead to ideological corruption. The fear is that the Sangh's noble mission of nation-building could be overshadowed by the ambitions of those who see it merely as a stepping stone to political or economic power. Ulhas Kulkarni, in his interview, joked about this, 'Yes, we have to digest everyone within our organization. But they are so strong and powerful, they can digest us, not vice versa.'[665]

'Sampark is essential,' another pracharak stressed, emphasising the importance of maintaining relationships with everyone, whether new or old. But he cautioned against being too trusting. 'Be aware of those with agendas,' he warned, acknowledging that some individuals may join with personal ambitions rather than a genuine commitment to the Sangh's ideology.[666] The balance, he said, was to 'not expect too much

[665]Interview with Ulhas Kulkarni.

[666]Interview with Naba Kumar Sharma (name changed).

from people, yet get as much work done as possible.' It was a fine line between managing expectations and maximizing contributions—a skill the pracharak had clearly honed over the years.

Reflecting on the differences between the old and new cadre, he was candid. 'The old cadre was sharper and smarter,' he said.[667] He attributed this sharpness to the obstacles that earlier volunteers faced when the RSS was operating without the backing of political power. 'Obstacles sharpen you,' he noted, pointing out that the struggles of the past had forged a resilient and committed cadre.[668] In contrast, he observed, the new wave of recruits, coming in after 2014 when the BJP rose to national prominence, seemed more drawn by fame and the prestige that now came with being associated with the RSS.

But he did not view the new challenges lightly. 'The challenge today is bigger than when the government was not in power,' he said, acknowledging the heightened expectations placed on the RSS now that it was seen as a driving force behind the government. 'Earlier, the challenge was external. Now, it is internal.'[669] Managing the internal dynamics of the organization—balancing the old guard with the new, and ensuring the Sangh's principles are upheld amidst rising influence—is a more delicate task than before.

One of the key challenges, he added, was keeping the old guard satisfied. 'You have to satisfy the old cadre to prevent factionalism,' he noted, hinting at the potential rifts that could form if the original members felt sidelined or undervalued.[670] For the pracharak, maintaining unity within the RSS, especially in this new era of increased visibility and influence, was paramount.

---

[667]Ibid.

[668]Ibid.

[669]Ibid.

[670]Ibid.

He knew that managing these dynamics was crucial to ensuring the organization's future success.

As the RSS stands at this critical juncture, the true test of its future success lies in how it addresses the challenge of opportunism. The organization's ability to preserve its ideological commitment and resist the lure of materialism will determine whether it can continue to build on its achievements or will succumb to the pitfalls of power and corruption.

The coming years will be pivotal for the Sangh. Its journey so far has been marked by resilience, dedication and an unwavering belief in its mission. To maintain its momentum and integrity, the RSS must remain vigilant and steadfast, ensuring that its ranks are filled with individuals who are truly committed to its cause. The legacy of the Sangh, and its future role in the Northeast and beyond, will depend on how effectively it navigates these new challenges and stays true to its foundational principles.

While discussing the potential dilution of RSS ideology in the face of new entrants, we sought insights from Pradeepan. His response was revealing: 'The secret of the RSS lies in its "door-to-door approach, man-to-man contact, and heart-to-heart talk".'[671] According to Pradeepan, this is the essence of the RSS—an organization driven not by the pursuit of power but by the mission to build human connections.

Pradeepan elaborated on how this approach had been the cornerstone of the RSS's resilience, especially during the dark days of the Emergency. He recounted how the RSS had managed to survive that period, not through clandestine strategies or sheer force, but because of the deep and genuine connections its members had forged with people across the country.[672] The individuals they had built relationships with—through sampark—became their protectors, sheltering them in their homes and

[671]Interview with Pradeepan.
[672]Ibid.

offering them safety. When the police came knocking, these hosts did not see the RSS members as mere political affiliates; they saw them as family, referring to them affectionately as *dada* (grandfather), *mama* or *chacha* (uncle), and *bhai* (brother). These terms of endearment provided a safe space and shielded them from the authorities.

'This is the real RSS,' Pradeepan emphasised. 'It is about becoming people's dada, mama, chacha and bhai.'[673] He underscored that this familial bond, this integration into the social fabric, was the true strength of the RSS. It was this commitment to personal relationships that had seen the organization through its toughest challenges.

Pradeepan's conviction was clear: the RSS's enduring legacy and strength lay in its ability to connect with people on a deeply personal level. 'The RSS will be finished the day it stops doing this,' he warned.[674] He stressed that the essence of the RSS was not in its organizational structure or its political influence, but in the simple, profound acts of building and nurturing human connections.

As we listened to Pradeepan, it became evident that the RSS's true power was its ability to transcend traditional notions of organization and power. It was an entity that thrived on the trust and love of the people, grounded in the values of kinship and community. The secret of the RSS, as Pradeepan articulated, was its heart-to-heart approach, its steadfast dedication to becoming a part of the lives and families of the people it served.

This insight painted a vivid picture of the RSS not merely as a political entity, but also as a movement rooted in the timeless values of human connection and mutual support. It was a reminder that true influence and resilience come from the bonds we forge and the hearts we touch, one person at a time.

---

[673]Ibid.

[674]Ibid.

Epilogue

As the sun rises over the tranquil landscapes, casting a golden glow on bustling towns and remote villages alike, the RSS sees a region poised for transformation. Where diversity thrives in a kaleidoscope of ethnicities and cultures, the Rashtriya Swayamsevak Sangh has quietly woven a tapestry of unity and resilience.

The journey of RSS in the Northeast has been fraught with obstacles. Geographically, the region is marked by difficult terrain, making communication and connectivity a perpetual challenge.[675] Culturally, it is a mosaic of tribes, each with its traditions and languages, often leading to localized identities overshadowing a broader sense of belonging to the Indian nation. As RSS volunteers ventured into the region with the mission to integrate and contribute to its development, they faced significant opposition. In some areas, their presence was met with suspicion and hostility. Local communities, entrenched in their histories and autonomy, viewed the RSS with scepticism, perceiving it as an outsider attempting to impose unfamiliar ideologies.[676]

Tensions escalated in certain instances, leading to confrontations that turned violent. Reports emerged of RSS volunteers being targeted and attacked. In some cases volunteers were killed, their lives tragically cut short in the pursuit of a

[675]Dikshit, K.R., and Jutta K. Dikshit, *North-East India: Land, People and Economy*, Springer, India, 2014.

[676]Ibid (as established by this book).

vision of national unity that clashed with local aspirations for autonomy and independence. The violence didn't just manifest in personal attacks; RSS offices became targets as well. In places like Manipur, Assam and Nagaland, where separatist movements simmered and ethnic identities held sway, the RSS faced an uphill battle to earn trust. Shakhas established by the RSS were vandalized and burned down, symbols of the friction between a centralized national identity and the diverse, localized identities that characterized the Northeast.[677]

Despite these challenges and the personal risks faced by its volunteers, the RSS persevered. The organization understood that earning trust and acceptance required more than ideological conviction; it demanded patient engagement, an understanding of local sensitivities, and a genuine commitment to contributing positively to the region's development. Over time, as the RSS moulded its approach and engaged in dialogue with local communities, perceptions began to evolve. Through its grassroots efforts, the RSS has promoted education, establishing schools and educational programmes that have brought literacy and knowledge to remote communities. Healthcare initiatives have addressed long-standing gaps in medical services, improving access to healthcare and raising public health awareness.[678] Roads, bridges and other critical infrastructure projects were initiated to improve connectivity and facilitate economic growth.[679] Culturally, the RSS played a pivotal role in celebrating and preserving the rich heritage of the Northeast, which not only bolstered local identities but also reinforced the idea of a unified India where every tradition and community has a valued place. Besides all of this, by promoting dialogue, understanding and mutual respect among different ethnic groups and communities,

[677]Ibid (as established by this book).
[678]Ibid (as established by this book).
[679]Ibid (as established by this book).

the RSS contributed to reducing tensions and fostering a more inclusive society where diversity is celebrated as a strength rather than seen as a source of division.

All of this comes down to one significant question: Why has the Rashtriya Swayamsevak Sangh worked so diligently for the Northeast? A layman's answer would be that it was to help the BJP win power in the region. No. The party's coming to power merely marks the commencement of the harmonious union of the Northeast with the rest of India. It is only the beginning that lays down the ground for their vision of 2047, *Amrit Kaal,* a 100 years since Independence; to unify the whole of India in patriotism—'From Kashmir to Kanyakumari and Gujarat to Nagaland.'

For the RSS, Northeast India represents not just a geographical region but a crucial frontier in realizing its vision of a united and culturally vibrant India. Rooted in the ideology of an *Akhand* Bharat (Undivided India), it envisions every corner of the country, including the Northeast, as integral to a cohesive national identity.[680]

In this vision, the RSS sees a Northeast where communities thrive in harmony, having transcended historical grievances and ethnic divides. The goal is to create a society where every individual, regardless of their background, feels a deep connection to the Indian nation.[681] This vision is not merely about political or administrative integration but about fostering a sense of belonging that transcends the Chicken's Neck—the narrow corridor that physically connects the Northeast to the rest of India.

The RSS's vision for 2047 is rooted in the rich cultural heritage and Indic values that have shaped India's civilizational ethos. The Sangh aspires to see the Northeast embrace and celebrate its diverse traditions while simultaneously integrating with the

---

[680]Interview with Basistha Bujarbaruah.

[681]Ibid.

broader tapestry of Indian culture. This cultural renaissance is envisioned as a revival of local arts, languages and traditions, enriched by the shared heritage of the Indian civilization.

The RSS's vision presents a strategic and ambitious roadmap aimed at empowering Hindus in India by focusing on self-reliance, cultural revival and demographic strength. A central aspect of this vision is to instil confidence among the Hindu youth. This perception of vulnerability must be removed. To address this, the RSS plans to organize youth baithaks that will focus on building physical, mental and cultural strength, promoting self-defence and the idea that Hindus should take responsibility for their own security rather than relying solely on the state.

Additionally, the RSS aims to build temples in Hindu-minority areas in Assam and Tripura, which will serve as centres of unity and strength, and organize large *mela*s (fairs) around these temples to foster solidarity. This will give Hindus from different regions the opportunity to visit these areas, show support and assure local Hindus that they are not alone, especially during times of conflict or riots.

Improving the Hindu demographic is also a major focus. The RSS seeks to encourage family values and the importance of nurturing future generations. Emphasis will be placed on the shared responsibilities of both men and women in building a strong and prosperous society. Role models—successful women who have balanced marriage, motherhood and careers—will be showcased to young girls in schools, alongside examples of supportive men, to demonstrate that family life and professional success can coexist through mutual support and shared responsibilities. Meetings with Hindu religious leaders, temple boards and satradhikars (monastic heads) will further push the agenda of demographic growth, with financial support from religious institutions being offered to Hindu families who choose to have more children. The RSS plans to mobilize resources for socio-religious efforts among Hindus.

In addition to demographic efforts, the RSS recognizes the importance of mobilizing indigenous and tribal leaders, working to eliminate caste barriers and bridge traditional fault lines such as tribal vs. non-tribal and anti-Hindi-bhashi sentiments. By engaging with these leaders, the RSS hopes to build a unified Hindu identity that transcends regional and caste divisions. Economic empowerment is another key part of the vision.

The RSS seeks to encourage Hindus to take control of professions traditionally seen as 'odd jobs' and bring pride to manual labour. Rickshaw pullers, fishermen and other labourers will be recognized and celebrated, with efforts made to include them in leadership positions in puja committees, thus integrating them into mainstream Hindu society. This shift in attitude toward manual labour is intended to break down class and caste barriers and create a more self-sufficient community.

It envisions a deeply transformed Hindu society—one that is confident, united and capable of defending itself. By fostering cultural revival, promoting demographic growth, breaking down internal divisions and enhancing economic participation, the RSS aims to ensure that Hindus not only preserve their identity but also thrive in a modern, pluralistic India.

Education is at the heart of this transformative vision. By 2047, the RSS aims to have established a network of educational institutions across the Northeast that not only impart academic knowledge but also instil values of patriotism, unity and social responsibility. These institutions will serve as nurseries of future leaders who are deeply rooted in their cultural identity and committed to the nation's progress.

Social change is another cornerstone of the RSS's vision. The organization envisions a Northeast where social disparities are minimized, and opportunities for growth and development are accessible to all. Through various initiatives in healthcare, vocational training and women's empowerment, the Sangh aims to uplift marginalized communities, ensuring that everyone can contribute to and benefit from the region's progress.

A key element of this vision is fostering national unity. The RSS aims to bridge the physical and psychological distances between the Northeast and the rest of India. Through cultural exchange programmes, inter-regional dialogues and collaborative projects, the Sangh seeks to cultivate mutual understanding and respect among diverse communities.[682] The goal is to create a seamless integration where the people of the Northeast feel as connected to Mumbai, Chennai or Delhi as they do to Guwahati or Imphal.

In this imagined 2047, the RSS sees the Northeast as a region that exemplifies the best of India's unity in diversity. It is a place where traditional values and modern aspirations coexist harmoniously, where every individual is proud of their heritage and equally proud to be Indian. The Sangh's efforts over the decades would culminate in a society that embodies the spirit of *Ek Bharat, Shreshtha Bharat*—One India, Great India.

The journey towards this vision involves not just grand strategies but countless small, meaningful actions as well. It is about building schools and hospitals, organizing cultural festivals, holding peace dialogues and providing disaster relief. It is about inspiring individuals to see beyond their immediate identities and embrace a broader national identity.

As the RSS looks towards 2047, it sees the Northeast not just as a part of India but as an integral and vibrant contributor to the nation's destiny. This vision is ambitious, yet grounded in the enduring values of the Sangh—service, unity and cultural pride. The RSS's commitment to this vision is unwavering, with every step taken today aimed at realizing a future where the Northeast stands as a testament to the power of unity, the richness of diversity, and the strength of a shared cultural heritage.

As the journey unfolds, the RSS's vision for Northeast India

---

[682]Interview with Basistha Bujarbaruah.

is not merely a dream but a commitment to action—a dedication to empowering communities, nurturing talent and fostering an environment where every individual can contribute to the region's progress and the nation's unity. With optimism and perseverance, the RSS looks ahead to a future where Northeast India stands as a beacon of resilience, cultural richness and shared prosperity within the diverse mosaic of India.

When we asked a senior RSS pracharak about the remarkable journey of bringing the frontier regions close to the heartland of India—a theme that forms the crux of this book—his response was both humble and profound.

'How did the RSS manage to bring the Northeast closer to Delhi?'[683] We enquired, expecting a detailed account of strategic initiatives and meticulous planning. However, his answer was far from what we anticipated. With a calm demeanour and a gentle smile, he began to unravel a narrative that was as enlightening as it was modest.

'The RSS did not bring the Northeast closer to Delhi,' he said. 'It always was. The connection was never severed; it was merely hidden, suppressed within the hearts of the people. What we see today is not the creation of a new bond but the revival of an ancient one, a bond that existed long before any of us.'[684]

He paused, allowing his words to sink in, before continuing, 'It is the people who brought this connection to light. It was their inherent desire to belong, to be part of a larger whole, that rekindled this relationship. The RSS merely facilitated this process to a small degree. We provided the platform—the support—but the true credit belongs to society.'[685]

His words were a testament to the organization's ethos of humility and self-effacement. The RSS pracharak emphasised

---

[683]Interview with anonymous.

[684]Ibid.

[685]Ibid.

that the organization's role was not to seek credit but to serve as enablers. They created opportunities, fostered understanding and bridged gaps, but the real transformation was driven by the people themselves.

'Our role,' he continued, 'was that of a gardener. We did not create the seeds of connection; they were always there, embedded deep within the soil. We merely nurtured them, providing the right conditions for them to grow. The blossoming of these connections—the strengthening of this bond between the Northeast and the rest of India—is a testament to the resilience and unity of our society.'[686]

The pracharak's words resonated deeply. The narrative was not about the RSS claiming triumphs but about acknowledging the intrinsic strength and unity of the people. It was a story of revival, of latent bonds being rediscovered and cherished.

As we reflected on his insights, it became clear that the true essence of our book lay not in the achievements of an organization but in the spirit of the people. It was their enduring connections, their shared history and their collective efforts that had brought the frontier closer to the heartland. The RSS had played its part, but the heart of the story belonged to the people—resilient, united and ever connected.

In capturing this narrative, we realized that the journey of bringing the frontier close to the heartland was not a new path forged, but an ancient one rediscovered. And in this rediscovery, the true credit indeed belonged to society. To understand the Sangh Parivar's role in this social experiment, we have to quote Dadarao Parmarth, the man who started this social experiment in the Northeast in 1946: 'RSS is the evolution of the life mission of the Hindu Nation.'

---

[686]Ibid.

We want to end our book just like we started it, with an anecdote—the story of Deepak Ranjan Sharma's interaction with veteran communist leader Baidyanath Majumdar.

Baidyanath Majumdar was one of the few communist leaders respected across party lines because of his dedication to his cause.[687] A communist leader of his repute leading the life that he preached to the cadres was worth imbibing. Sangh cadres from Tripura even loved his speeches and often went to listen to him.

One day, Deepak Ranjan Sharma went to meet him at his house and have a conversation with his idol.[688] Seeing RSS pracharaks at his doorstep, he asked them to leave immediately. Sharma replied, 'Dada, despite knowing that you are from a different ideology, we go to listen to your speeches because we respect your intellect beyond party lines. But what you are doing to us today is not what we expected from you.'[689] Hearing this, he let them in, though with some hesitation.

He pulled down the curtains as it would spark outrage if he was seen sitting with RSS pracharaks at his residence. Once they sat together, Majumdar started criticizing and even abusing the Sangh on a rant that went on for almost an hour.

Sharma and his friends neither countered him nor tried to stop him. But after he was done, Deepak Sharma just asked him one question. He asked, 'Dada, you have been an ardent communist throughout your life and are nearing your end now. But tell me, in your lifetime how many cadres could you produce with similarly high ethical values, who follow your ideology the way you do?'[690] He had no answers to that, given the lavish lifestyle his contemporary comrades were used to leading. Sharma continued, 'But here in our Sangh, based on

---

[687]Interview with Deepak Ranjan Sharma.

[688]Ibid.

[689]Ibid.

[690]Ibid.

the ideology of Doctorji and Guruji, thousands of pracharaks leave their homes and families, and dedicate themselves to the cause of the nation every year. This is why our systems and our ideology have worked and yours hasn't.'[691]

Majumdar had no answers but he nodded in affirmation. Before they left, the veteran Left leader stopped them and said, 'Work hard towards your cause, the future of the nation lies in the hands of people like you.'[692]

---

[691]Ibid.

[692]Ibid.

Afterword

The Northeast emerges as a captivating terrain, presenting a distinct challenge for nationalist organizations like the Sangh Parivar and mainstream political entities. Its tapestry is woven with a rich, ethnic diversity, fostering a profound sense of identity among its communities. Despite the intricate complexities, the Sangh Parivar has etched a remarkable presence within the region, gently extending its outreach and resonating with the hearts and minds of the people. Our book embarks on a journey to unravel the Sangh Parivar's endeavours and ethos, tracing its trajectory from the dawn of Independence in 1947.

Only Assam, Tripura, Manipur and Arunachal Pradesh boast thriving Hindu communities, along with various indigenous groups with diverse animist beliefs. The remaining states, which include Nagaland, Mizoram and Meghalaya, embraced Christianity during colonial rule, influenced by the Church. Additionally, states such as Assam and Tripura face challenges such as illegal immigration of Bengali-speaking Muslims, while Nagaland, Manipur, Mizoram and Assam have witnessed ethnic insurgencies, adding layers to the socio-political canvas. Hence, the success of the Sangh Parivar's social experiment in such an environment is worthy of being delved into academically.

The history of British rule in Northeast India (1757–1946) saw significant changes, including the spread of Christianity, the settlement of Muslims in Assam and Tripura, and the introduction of the Inner Line Permit system in the hill states. After India gained independence in 1947, the post-colonial landscape of

Northeast faced manifold challenges and ethnic movements. The Sangh's involvement in relief efforts, especially during the 1950 Assam earthquake, and its response to militancy in Nagaland and Mizoram are key points of discussion, as is its limited success in establishing a strong base in the region during the 1962 War and the Language Movement.

The 1970s were marked by the RSS being banned during the Emergency, forcing many members underground in the Northeast. In the 1980s, regionalism offered the Sangh Parivar new opportunities for mobilization, particularly during the Assam Agitation over illegal immigration from Bangladesh. This era also saw the rise of ethnic militancy, which occasionally targeted Sangh affiliates. The 1990s saw the Sangh Parivar mobilize on Hindutva lines, particularly following the 1992 Babri Masjid demolition. Around this time, the Sangh Parivar also helped indigenous communities assert their cultural identity through the formalization of their religious procedures and rituals. However, due to their growing influence, attacks on karyakartas and pracharaks were at a peak during this decade.

The 2000s brought new opportunities as the political landscape shifted. The Sangh Parivar focused on healthcare, education and mitigating ethnic conflicts to cement a base in northeastern society. This new-found acceptance highlights the strength of the Sangh Parivar's democratic efforts to build a strong social coalition even in a challenging physical and social geography such as the Northeast. As a result, since 2014, the Northeast has seen a shift towards nationalism under Prime Minister Modi's leadership, with the Sangh Parivar playing a key role in bridging the difference between the heartland and the frontier, by providing effective last-mile delivery of public goods like healthcare and education.

The Northeast captivates political scientists, beckoning them to probe beyond the conventional nationalist sentiments prevalent in other states. Here, the essence lies in the tapestry of regional, linguistic and tribal identities, urging the Sangh Parivar to embrace and harmonize with these rich variegations before fostering a sense of nationalistic fervour. Amidst mainstream academic narratives that often cast shadows of prejudice upon the Sangh Parivar's endeavours, our book attempts not only to bridge the void in existing literature but also to challenge prevailing biases. It seeks to present the Sangh Parivar's efforts as a testament to inclusivity and resilience, countering misperceptions rooted in centralizing Hindu proselytism.

Through vivid narratives and insightful interviews, the book unveils an insider's perspective on the Sangh Parivar's voyage across the Northeast, from the nascent days of Independence to the present juncture. It delves into their adaptive strategies amidst the region's dynamic political landscapes, narrating tales of courage, endurance and unwavering commitment. Within these pages lie the chronicles of pracharaks and karyakartas, whose steadfast dedication has not only shaped the Sangh Parivar's narrative but also paved the path for the BJP's historic triumph across all seven sister states. Their collective endeavours stand as a testament to the enduring influence and resonance of the Sangh Parivar within the verdant landscapes of the Northeast.

Maha Shivarathri
26 February 2025

A. Balakrishnan
President
Vivekananda Rock Memorial
and Vivekananda Kendra
Vivekanandapuram
Kanyakumari

Acknowledgements

This book is the result of a collective journey, and we are deeply grateful to those who have supported and guided us throughout the process.

First and foremost, we would like to thank our mothers for their unwavering love, encouragement and belief in us. Both of our mothers are single parents and their strength and wisdom have been constant sources of inspiration, and we dedicate this work to them.

We extend our heartfelt gratitude to Hon'ble Chief Minister of Assam, Dr Himanta Biswa Sarma, for being an invaluable guide during this endeavour. His deep insights into the political and cultural dynamics of the Northeast have enriched this book immeasurably. His leadership continues to shape the region and provide hope for its future.

We would also like to express our sincere appreciation to Shri Pramod Kalita, Secretary of Assam Prakashan Parishad, who offered valuable guidance throughout this project. His thoughtful reading and feedback on the manuscript were instrumental in shaping its final form.

Our sincere thanks go to the swayamsevaks and pracharaks of the RSS and karyakartas of various organizations such as Sevika Samiti, Vanavasi Kalyan Ashram, Seva Bharati, Vidya Bharati, Akhil Bharatiya Vidyarthi Parishad, Seemanta Chetana Mancha, Heritage Foundation, Niri Sansthan, Vivekananda Kendra, and others, whose generosity in sharing their time and experiences made this book possible. Their openness and willingness to allow us into their lives and work have provided us with an invaluable perspective, and their dedication to the people of the Northeast is both humbling and inspiring. Many of them also cross-checked our book, corrected errors, and provided their feedback on this journey.

We also wish to express our appreciation for Harsh Jha, an intern who contributed significantly to the translation work during our research. His attention to detail ensured the accuracy and accessibility of our narrative. We would like to sincerely thank Dr Himadri S. Barthakur for taking the time to read our manuscript and for offering valuable feedback, despite his demanding medical schedule.

To all those who participated in interviews, offering their insights and perspectives—thank you. Your voices have helped shape this book, providing depth and richness to our understanding of the region and its complexities.

We are grateful to our families, friends and colleagues for their support, encouragement and patience throughout this process. Their belief in the importance of this work kept us motivated and focused, even during the most challenging moments.

This book is the result of a collective effort and we are fortunate to have had the support of so many remarkable individuals along the way. We hope that through these pages, we can contribute to a deeper understanding of the Sangh Parivar's influence in the Northeast and the region's rich cultural tapestry.

Glossary

baudhik	intellectual
bhojan	food
grihasta	householder
karyakarini	executive council
karyakarta	organizer/worker
karyalaya	office
karyavah	secretary (de facto head of a division/unit)
kshetra	region (a group of prants put together)
mandal	circle (3–10 shakhas put together)
nagar	town (5–10 mandals put together)
prachar	public relations
pracharak/pracharika	promoter
pramukh	in-charge
prant	province (a group of vibhags put together)
pravas	tour
purnakalik	full-timer
sabha	assembly
sah sarkaryavah	assistant general secretary
sambhag	division (5–15 vibhags put together)
sampark	outreach
sanghchalak	chief (de jure head of a division/unit)
sankalp	vow
sarkaryavah	general secretary (de facto head of the organization)

sarsanghchalak	chief (de jure head of the organization)
seva	social service
shakha	branch
sharirik	physical
swayamsevak	volunteer
vibhag	sector (a group of zilas put together)
vistarak/vistarika	amplifier
vyavastha	logistics
zila	district (towns and villages put together)

Index

www.ingramcontent.com/pod-product-compliance
Lightning Source LLC
Chambersburg PA
CBHW020441100426
42812CB00036B/3410/J

* 9 7 8 9 3 7 0 0 3 4 9 5 2 *